EASY OIL PAINTING

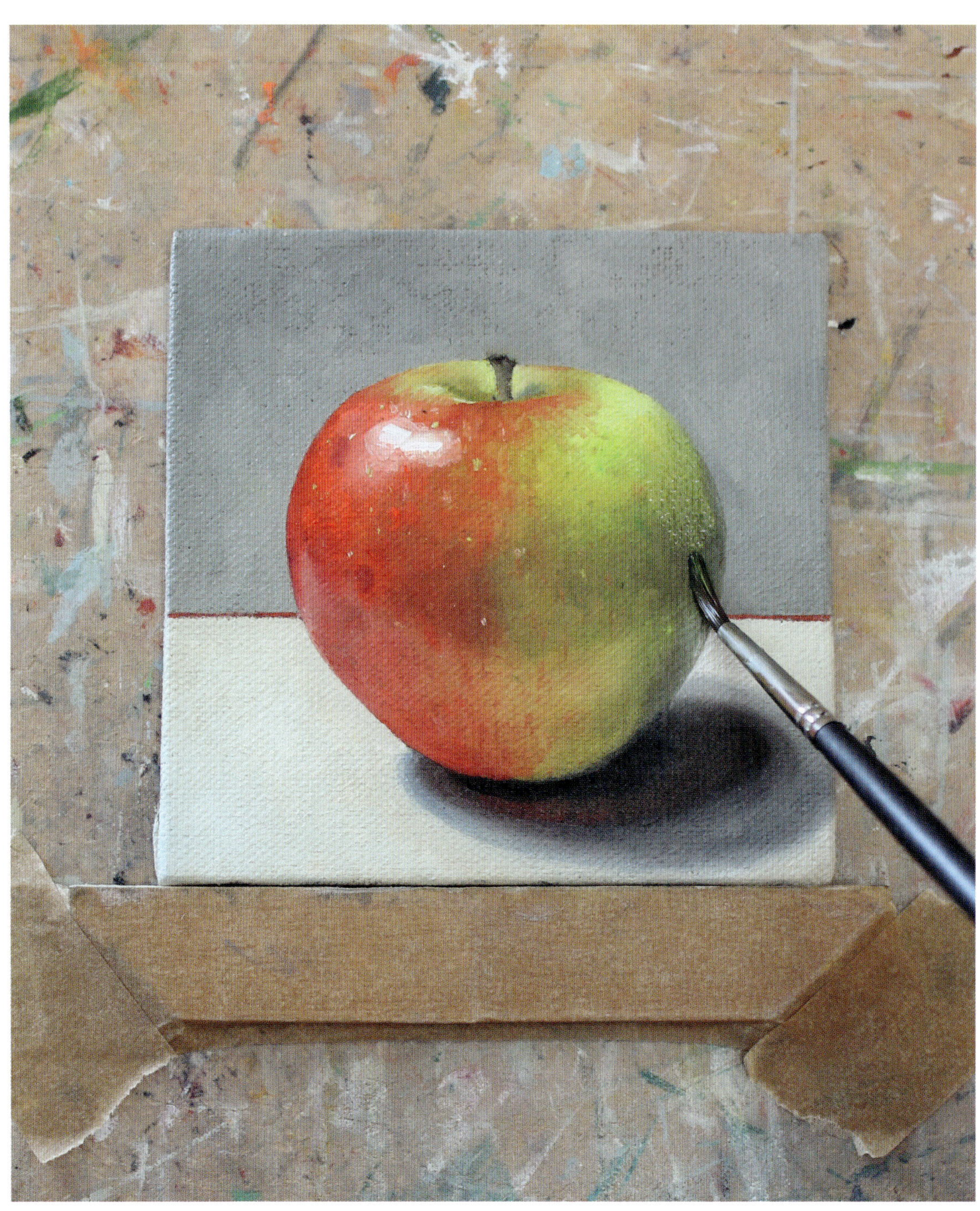

EASY OIL PAINTING

BEGINNER TUTORIALS FOR SMALL STILL LIFES

ESTELLE DAY

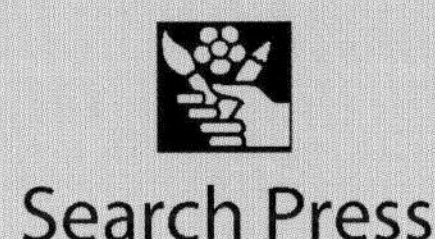

Search Press

To my daughters Scarlett & Mathilda xx

A QUARTO BOOK

Published in 2022 by
Search Press Ltd
Wellwood
North Farm Rd
Tunbridge Wells
Kent TN2 3DR

Reprinted 2023, 2024

Copyright © 2022 Quarto plc

ISBN: 978-1-80092-079-8
ebook ISBN: 978-1-80093-070-4

Conceived, designed and produced by
Quarto Publishing plc
1 Triptych Place,
London, SE1 9SH,
United Kingdom
www.quarto.com

QUAR.342332

Editor: Katie Hardwicke
Projects editor: Anna Galkina
Editorial assistant: Ella Whiting
Photographers: Nicki Dowey and Estelle Day
Designer: Rachel Cross
Illustrator: Kuo Kang Chen
Art director: Gemma Wilson
Publisher: Lorraine Dickey

Printed in China

10 9 8 7 6 5 4 3

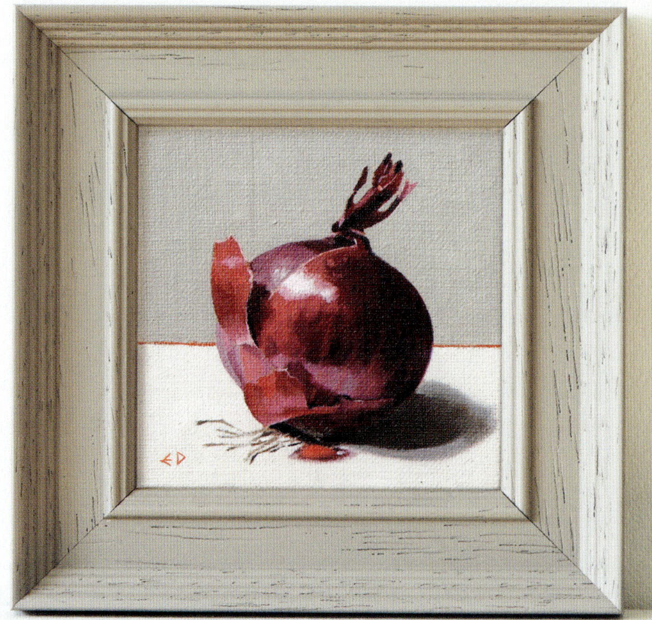

CONTENTS

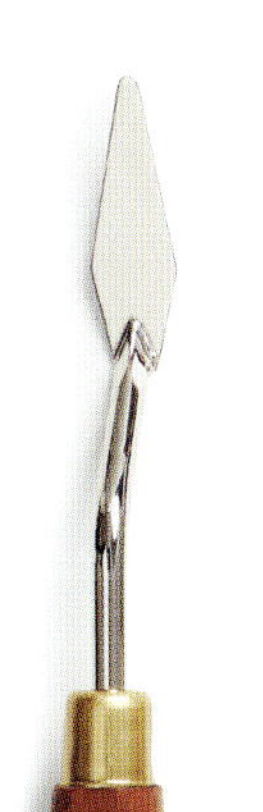
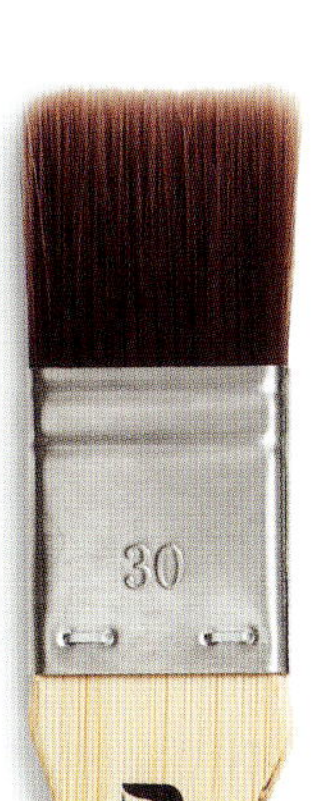
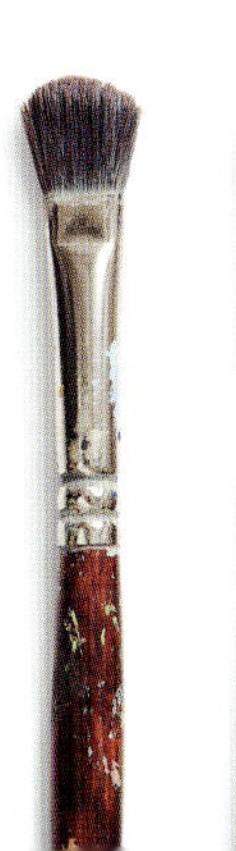
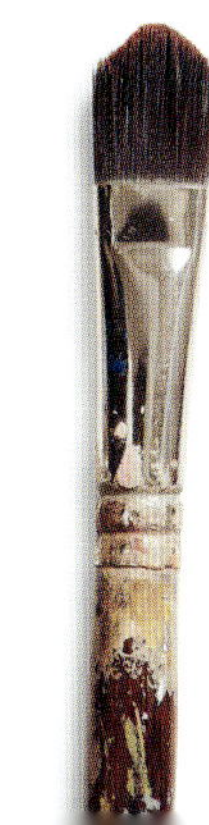

Meet Estelle

I was first introduced to oil painting by my parents when I was very young. I often watched them both paint in their spare time and I can remember being shown how to mix colours and clean brushes at the kitchen table. My parents would take me on regular visits to galleries and exhibitions, and I owe my love of art and painting to them.

During my years at art college and university, I enjoyed trying out different mediums – sculpture, woodworking and printmaking – and over the years, I have experimented with watercolour, acrylic paints and ink drawing. Oil painting, however, has always been (and probably always will be!) my favourite medium to work with. I love the vibrancy of oil paints, their smooth, buttery consistency, and the fact that you can build up layers (I even love the smell!). It is also a very forgiving medium, with a long drying time that allows you to make adjustments.

As a student, I worked for years in the National Gallery shop in London. I loved wandering around the galleries during my breaks, in awe of the great masterpieces, including those of the Dutch and Flemish still-life masters, whose work undoubtedly had an influence.

One painting that really caught my eye and made a lasting impression on me was a small still life by Spanish artist Francisco de Zurbarán called *A Cup of Water and a Rose*. The observer is not distracted by a busy or complicated composition but instead focuses entirely on a few simple, everyday objects, so beautifully rendered by the artist that they appear far from ordinary. I believe that any object can be beautiful and interesting to paint and, as Zurbarán's painting showed me, a still life doesn't need to be complicated in order to be captivating.

In this book we will focus our attention on one object at a time (thus eliminating the problem of composition) and I will offer guidance on how to paint various textures and materials, including glass, silver and natural forms.

The paintings in this book are ideal if you don't have a large area to work in – I speak from experience! We'll be working on small linen boards, so in terms of space, you'll require little more than a desk and somewhere to set up your still-life objects. The projects are achievable if you only have small pockets of time in a busy life, too – the paintings can be completed in one session or worked on over a period of days; it's completely up to you.

If you are new to oil painting, I suggest that you read the first part of the book (pages 8–51), as it is always a good idea to arm yourself with information about materials, techniques, colours and how to set up a workspace before beginning any real painting.

When starting anything new, it always takes time and practice, and there will inevitably be a few bumps along the way. I continue to learn so much through trial and error, so don't be afraid to make mistakes – they are a valuable part of the process. The best way to learn is to dive in, experiment and, most importantly, have fun!

Happy painting,

Estelle

About this book

Before you put brush to canvas, make sure you read through chapters 1–4 to familiarize yourself with the basics. Chapter 1: Paint, supplies, workspace (pages 8–17) covers paints, brushes and other tools you need to begin. Chapter 2: Techniques (pages 18–33) is where to look if you need more detail about any of the processes mentioned in the projects. Chapter 3: Understanding Colour (pages 34–43) contains an introduction to the fascinating world of colour and how to mix paints, and Chapter 4: Subjects (pages 44–51) has all the information you need for choosing what to paint and how to set up a still life properly.

Before starting to paint, it is a good idea to organize your palette and to premix your colours according to tonal value (see page 38) – this will save you a lot of time as you will have all the colours you need to hand.

While you can start with any project in the book, the projects are ordered so that you pick up new skills as you progress, so if you are a beginner, it is best to begin with the first two projects.

Here you will find details on the set-up used for each still life. All the projects in this book have a consistent light source coming from the top left, and there are ideas for experimenting with lighting and set-ups on page 48.

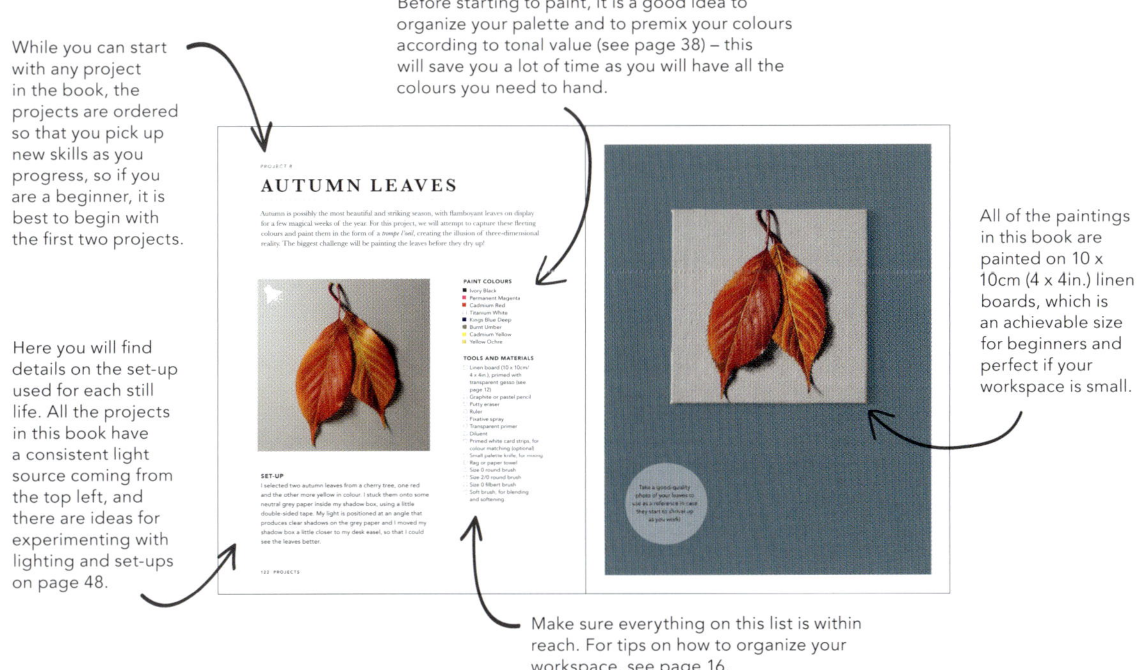

All of the paintings in this book are painted on 10 x 10cm (4 x 4in.) linen boards, which is an achievable size for beginners and perfect if your workspace is small.

Make sure everything on this list is within reach. For tips on how to organize your workspace, see page 16.

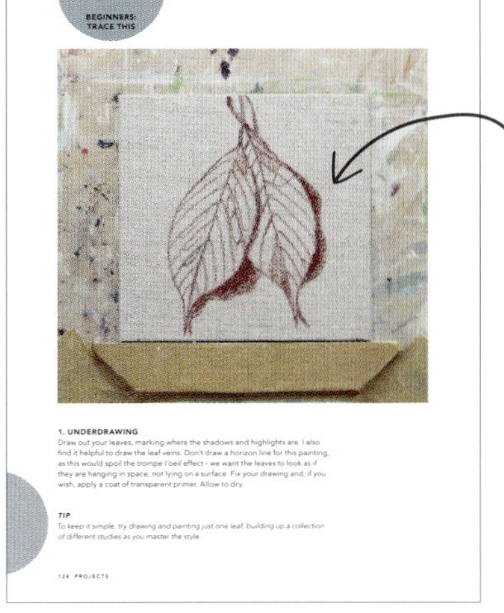

If you want to try painting exactly the same subjects as those in the book, you can use this feature to trace the underdrawings (see page 20). Though it is always better to work from life, this method works well for absolute beginners as every step of the painting process can be followed faithfully, while practising different techniques.

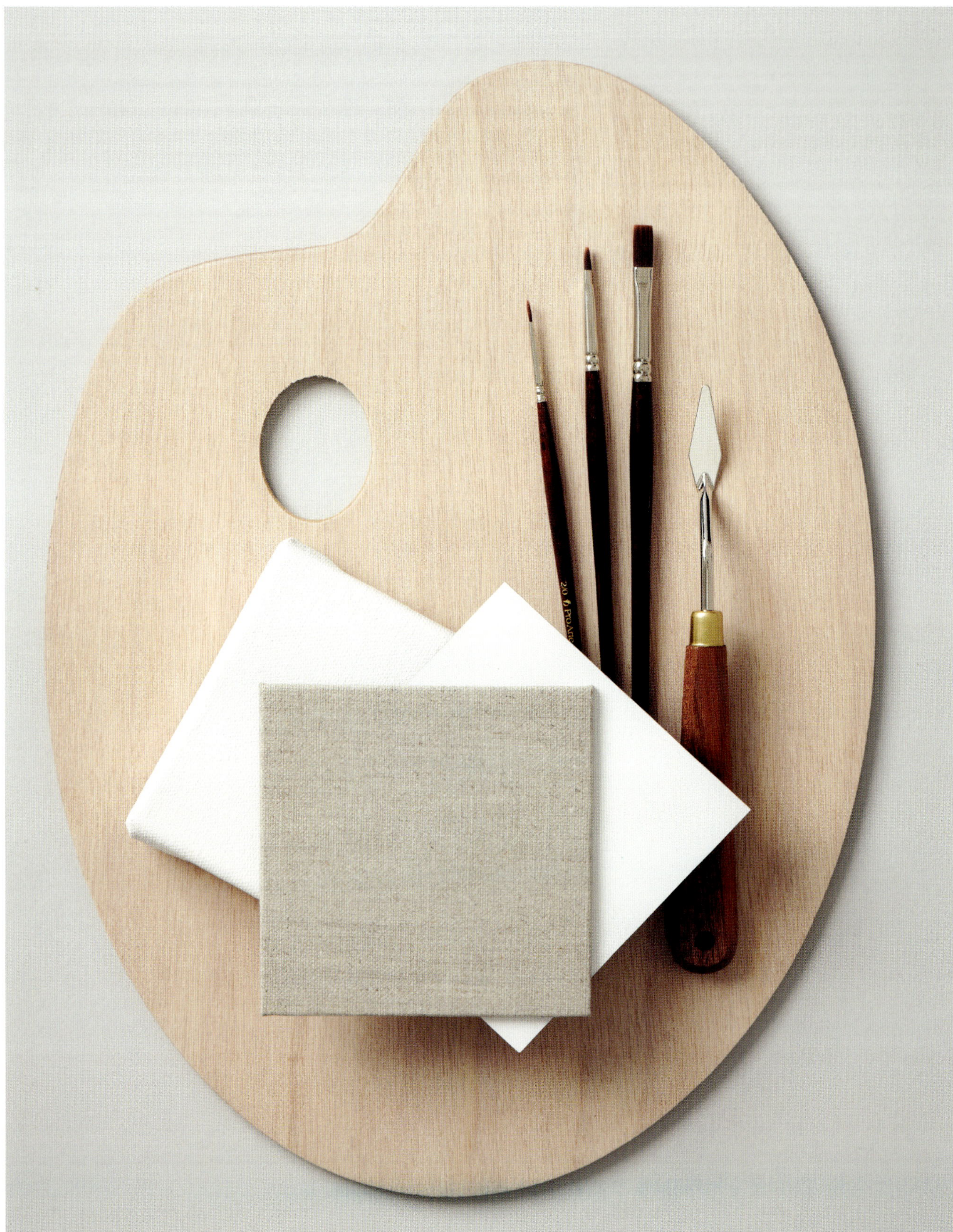

PAINT, SUPPLIES, WORKSPACE

If you've never used oil paints before, this chapter will help to demystify which paints, brushes and other equipment are essential for the projects in this book. Here you will also find advice for setting up a workspace.

Paint choices

It can be confusing walking into an art shop and seeing row upon row of colourful tubes of paint – there are so many to choose from and it isn't always easy to know which ones to pick, especially if you are new to oil painting. In this section, I will explain the different qualities of the many types of oil paints that are available. Listed below are the paints that form my basic palette, and their different qualities.

1 **Titanium White PW6:** This slow-drying, opaque white is really useful for bright highlights and for mixing with other colours to create solid backgrounds and foregrounds. I recommend getting a larger tube of this paint as it is probably the one you'll use most. **(1)**

Ivory Black PBK9: It's useful to have a small tube of this even though we can mix our own chromatic blacks. This is perfect for those really, really dark occlusion shadows. **(2)**

Raw Umber PBR6: This fast-drying, semi-transparent brown pigment has greenish undertones and is one of the fundamental 'Earths*'. Perfect for roughly painting compositions and blocking in shadows. **(3)**

Burnt Umber PBR6: Fast-drying and semi-transparent, this Earth has more red-brown undertones than Raw Umber and is brilliant for underpaintings. **(4)**

Cadmium Red PR108: This fast-drying, rich colour can be expensive but I love its warmth and opacity – ideal for making red apples pop! **(5)**

Permanent Magenta PV19: This is a rich, deep red-violet colour that makes lovely pinks and purples and can also be used as a glaze. **(6)**

Cadmium Yellow PY35: Another more expensive colour, but I find it indispensable because of its intensity and ability to create warmth. It is very opaque and has rich undertones – ideal for painting lemons. **(7)**

Lemon Yellow PY3: Unsurprisingly, this is a great yellow for painting lemons! A transparent, slow-drying pigment with green undertones; when mixed with white it is beautifully luminous. **(8)**

Cobalt Blue PB28: This fast-drying, semi-transparent and fresh blue is, in my opinion, one of the 'cooler' blues. It is fairly expensive but is lightfast and mixes well, creating beautiful greens. **(9)**

Ultramarine Blue PB29: This warmer blue is one of my favourites, with rich and intense undertones – it produces lovely violets. **(10)**

Permanent Green Light PG7, PW6, PY74: This mixed pigment, semi-transparent colour is extremely lightfast and permanent. It is a vivid bright green that I love using when I'm painting green pears or apples. **(11)**

Yellow Ochre PY42: This greeny-gold Earth colour is always on my palette. Great for darkening yellows. **(12)**

*'Earths' are, as the term suggests, brown colours that exist naturally in the earth and are considered the oldest pigments, going back to prehistoric times. They include umbers, siennas, and ochres.

Optional extra colours: This list has suggestions for a starter set, but as you become more familiar with oil paints, you can add or replace colours with your favourites. As an extra (but not an essential extra) to the above colours, I also like to have a tube of **Kings Blue Deep** because I use it so frequently. Other colours I love include **Burnt Sienna**, **Indian Yellow** and **Alizarin Crimson**.

ARTIST-QUALITY AND STUDENT-QUALITY PAINTS

As you browse through tubes of paints, you will notice that there are two kinds of oil paints – artist-quality (or Professional) and the less expensive student-quality range. If you are new to oil paints and do not wish to spend too much initially, then the student-quality paints might be a good option to begin with. Less expensive than the artist-quality tubes, they will allow you to get a feel for oil paints and experiment without worrying too much about waste. As you become more accustomed to working in oils, consider switching to artist-quality paints. This range costs more but the paints are more vibrant, more permanent, and there is a much wider choice of colours on offer. Here are some recommended brands that are of high quality:

- **Winsor & Newton:** *Artists'* range and *Winton* range (this is the budget student-quality range).
- I use mostly Michael Harding Oils and some Winsor & Newton artist-quality paints.
- There are many other reputable oil paint brands worldwide, so visit your local art shop – the employees are generally artists themselves, so can offer help and guidance.

Ready-made oil paints consist of pigment bound in linseed oil. The pigment gives the paint its colour, and it is the quality of the pigment that is important when selecting your paints and is reflected in the price and type of paint. Other considerations include the paint's transparency, its permanence, and lightfastness, all given on the paint tube's label.

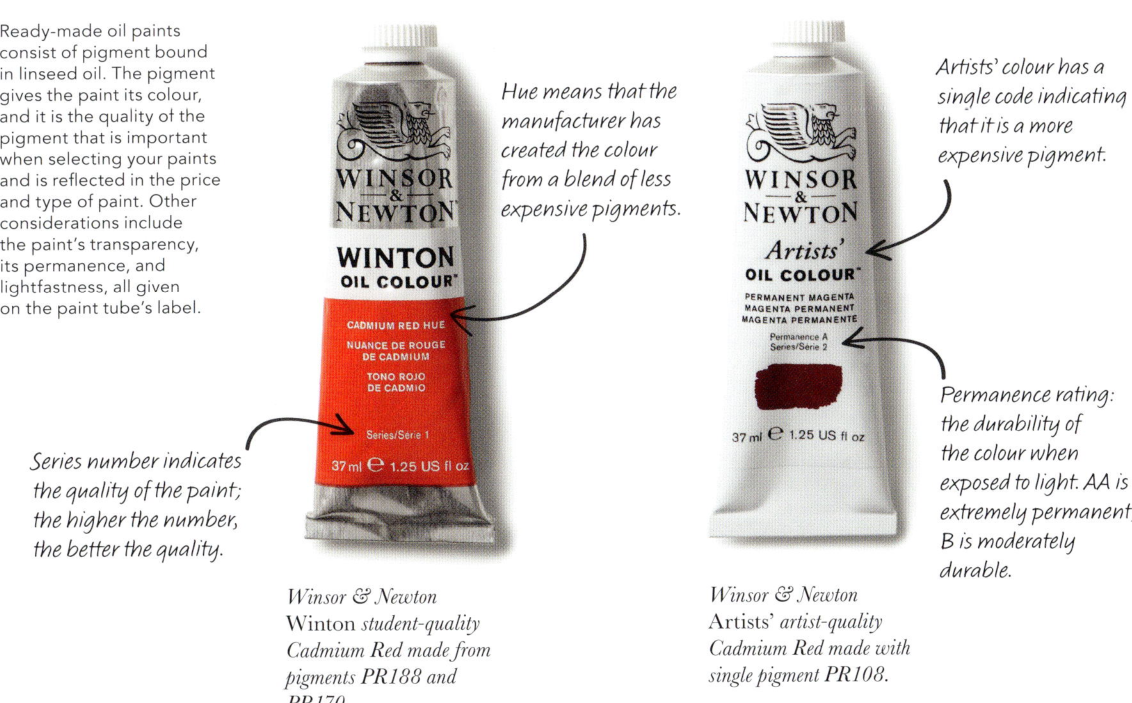

Hue means that the manufacturer has created the colour from a blend of less expensive pigments.

Artists' colour has a single code indicating that it is a more expensive pigment.

Series number indicates the quality of the paint; the higher the number, the better the quality.

Permanence rating: the durability of the colour when exposed to light. AA is extremely permanent; B is moderately durable.

Winsor & Newton Winton *student-quality Cadmium Red made from pigments PR188 and PR170.*

Winsor & Newton Artists' *artist-quality Cadmium Red made with single pigment PR108.*

TIP

The pigment number is the chemical description of the pigment, not the manufacturer's colour code. It is useful to differentiate the two, as you can then switch between brands and buy the same colour from a different oil paint manufacturer if you take note of the pigment number you need.

Canvases & other materials

CANVASES

All the projects in this book are painted on small linen boards, measuring 10 x 10cm (4 x 4in.), which are available in art shops and online. The natural linen colour provides a warm undertone to paint over (rather than bright white), and I also like the texture of the canvas. They often come in packs of three and are economically priced.

OTHER SUPPORTS

Stretched canvases: These come primed, but you can also buy raw canvas fabric and stretch your own canvases onto a wooden frame.

Wooden boards: These come unprimed and are usually made from plywood or hardboard (you can cut your own boards if you have the right tools).

Primed gesso boards: Though slightly more expensive, these boards are ready to be painted on (although I personally always add one or two coats of my own gesso for good measure).

RECOMMENDED OIL PAINTING MATERIALS

It can be quite daunting when you realize how many different oil painting products are available and hard to know which ones you really need, especially if you are a beginner. When you're new to using oil paints it is best to keep it simple.

Odourless or citrus-scented diluent: This is used to clean brushes and thin oil paints. Avoid using turpentine or white spirit – they might be cheaper in price, but the odourless/citrus-scented diluents are a safer option. Care should still be taken when using them: make sure the room you are working in is well-ventilated and avoid direct contact with your skin and eyes.

Gesso: This is used to prime the surface before painting. Never paint straight onto canvas, paper or board that hasn't been primed first – providing a good 'ground' for your support is really important. Gesso creates a smooth surface and acts as a sealant, stopping the oil being drawn out of the paint over time, which would result in a dull finish.

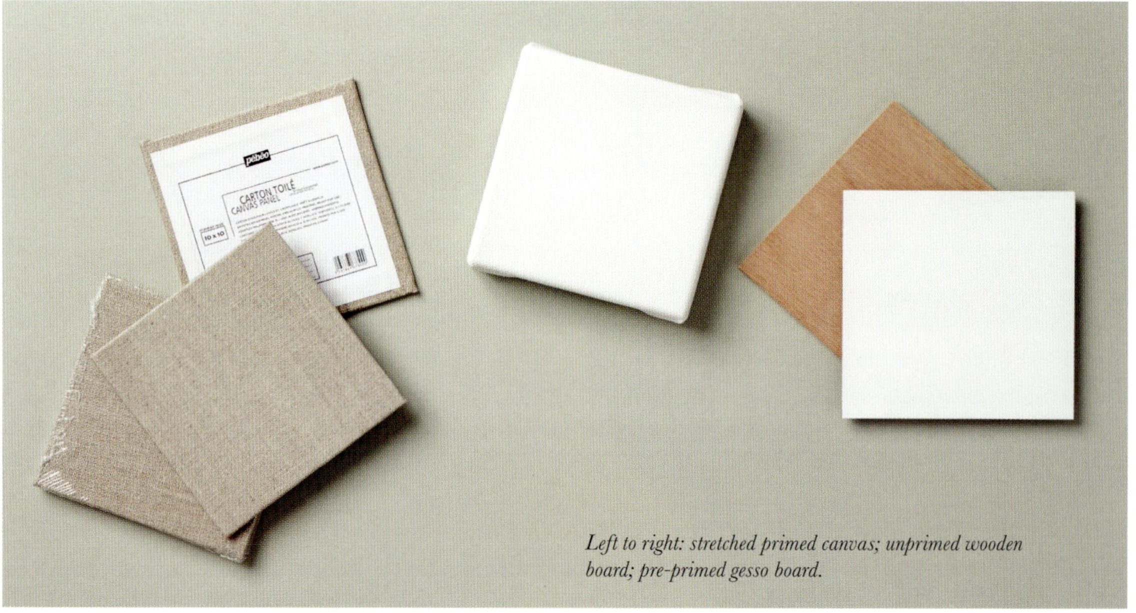

Left to right: stretched primed canvas; unprimed wooden board; pre-primed gesso board.

It also gives a surface 'grip' – even though the linen boards that I use are pre-primed, I always give them a coat of my own transparent gesso, as I find the surface a little slippery for my preference. Applying gesso is simple – take a wide flat brush (a utility one is fine) and apply a thin layer onto your surface. Some artists leave visible brushmarks in the gesso to give extra texture to the surface, but I paint it on smoothly, making sure I don't leave any lumps. To clean your brush, remove any excess gesso from the bristles with a paper towel and then rinse with warm water. Gesso becomes touch-dry very quickly and you can apply another coat at this point if you wish. Let it dry overnight before applying any oil paint.

Fixative: This is a colourless spray used to 'fix' drawings in graphite, pastel or charcoal in order to stop them from smudging. I use this spray to fix my underdrawings on my linen boards, so that when I start painting, the drawing doesn't smudge. It is useful because if you are not happy with your painting (which does happen), you can wipe off the paint and your original drawing will still be underneath. I add another coat of gesso after I have fixed my drawing and before I start painting, just for good measure!

Glazing medium: This is not an essential medium but good to have if you plan on trying out 'glazing'. I demonstrate how to glaze on page 28, but I don't actually use this technique in any of the projects in the book. I love this technique and it is definitely something worth exploring once you have developed more confidence in using oil paints.

Palettes: You will need a palette to mix your paints. There is a huge variety of palettes available, made of wood, glass, ceramic and plastic – all of which are fine, but I highly recommend paper palettes to start with (I still use them sometimes). They are convenient as there is no cleaning up to do once you have finished painting; you simply tear the used palette sheet out of the pad and dispose of it. If I haven't finished my painting and I still have paint mixes left, I put my palette inside an airtight palette box, which helps stop the paints drying out.

Other materials: You will need some paper towel and/or old rags, for any spills and for wiping brushes. A solvent pot or an empty jar with a lid to keep your diluent in is also essential. Art wipes are useful to keep nearby; they are perfect for removing oil paint from hands and surfaces.

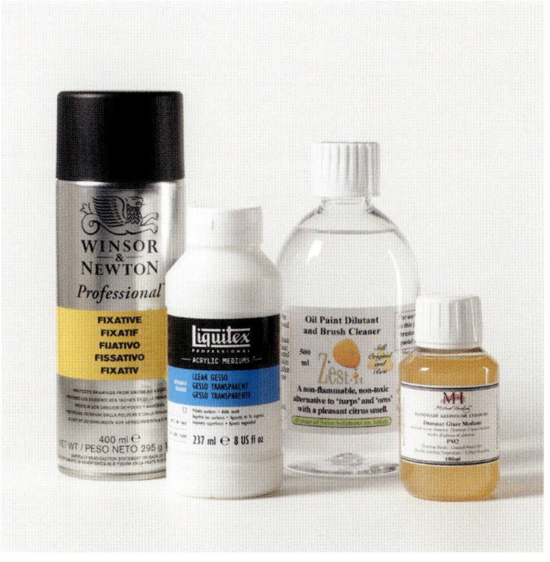

Left to right: mediums and fixative spray; wooden palette and pad of disposable paper palettes.

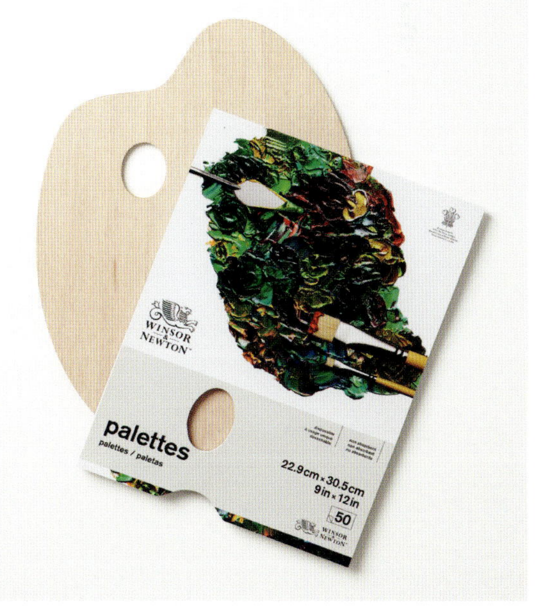

Drawing materials & brushes

BASIC DRAWING MATERIALS

A selection of drawing materials, such as pencils, a ruler and eraser, are essential, whether for sketching ideas or plotting an underdrawing. For general purposes, HB (#1) and B (#2) graphite pencils are ideal. I use a sanguine pastel pencil for my underdrawings, but graphite works just as well.

I also recommend keeping a sketchbook – it is great practice to sketch regularly, even just one quick sketch daily will help to train your eye and improve your observational skills. A viewfinder can be useful, too, to help check the composition of your set-up; either make your own from card or buy online.

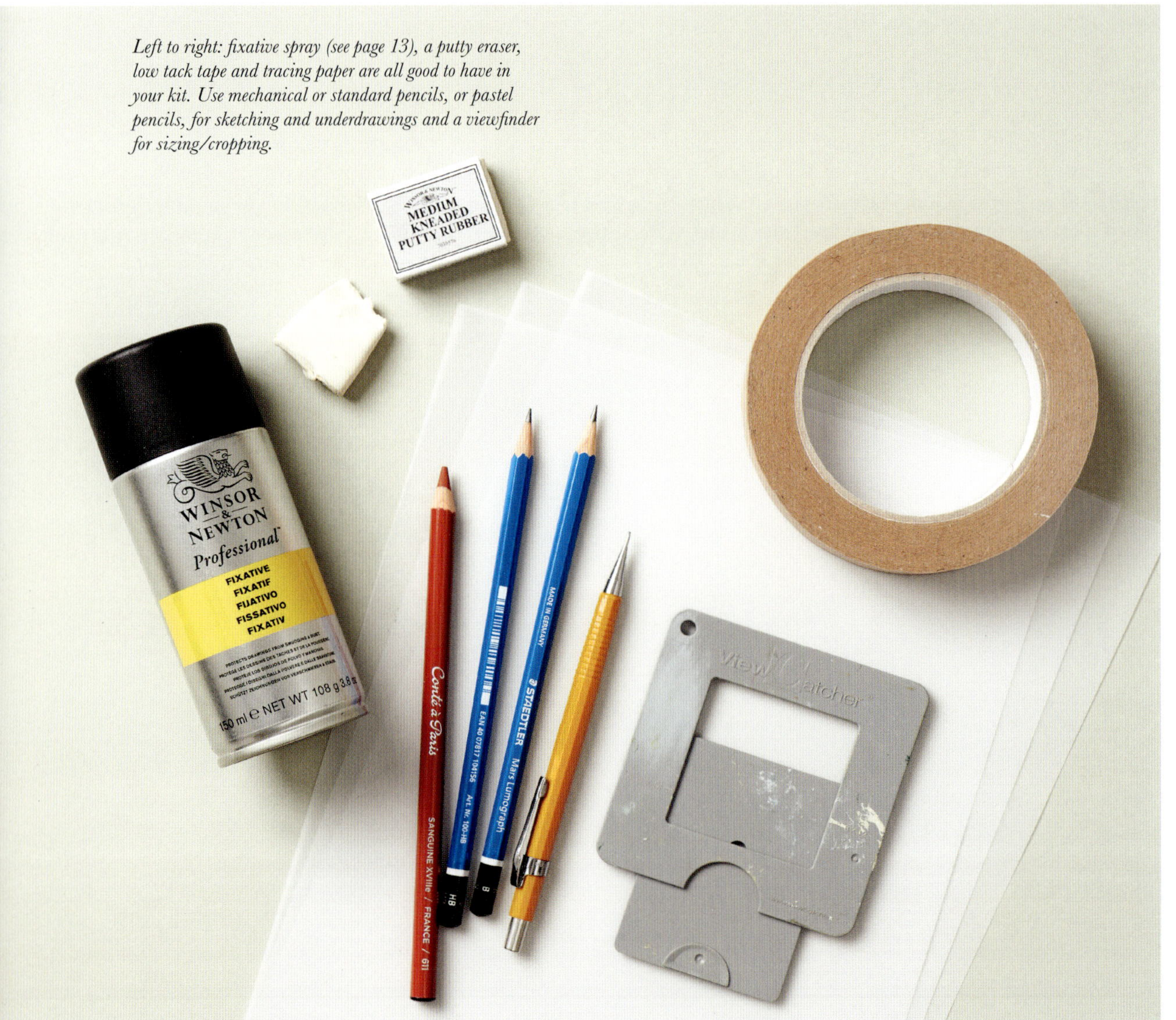

Left to right: fixative spray (see page 13), a putty eraser, low tack tape and tracing paper are all good to have in your kit. Use mechanical or standard pencils, or pastel pencils, for sketching and underdrawings and a viewfinder for sizing/cropping.

PAINTBRUSHES & MORE

There are many types, shapes and sizes of brush to
choose from. For beginners, I recommend synthetic
brushes as they are a less expensive option than natural
fibres. I use the following selection in the projects:

- **Flat brushes** are useful for applying broad strokes
  of colour to cover large areas, such as blocking in
  backgrounds, while also giving clean edges. **(1)**
- **Filberts** are a really useful 'all rounder' brush; have
  more than one in different sizes. **(2)**
- **Round brushes** have a more traditional shape, which
  comes to a point and can produce a range of marks;
  the smaller ones are great for finer details. **(3)**
- **Old brushes** are useful for dry brushing. **(4)**
- **Utility brushes** don't need to be expensive as you only
  need to use them to apply gesso to your canvas. **(5)**
- **Palette knives** can be used to mix paints on your
  palette, and to apply paint thickly or to scrape paint
  off the canvas. **(6)**

*Right, from top to bottom: ¼in. flat, ³⁄₁₆in. flat, Size 0 filbert, Size 1
round, Size O round, Size 2/0 round, Size 3/0 old round, splayed brushes
for dry brushing and utility brushes for applying gesso. Brushes are graded
by size: the higher the number, the larger the brush.*

CLEANING YOUR BRUSHES

Brushes need to be cleaned after every painting
session. Start by squeezing the excess paint off the
brush by pinching the bristles carefully through a
rag or paper towel (don't scrub your brush as this
will damage the bristles). Next, clean your brush
in diluent by swirling it around. Wipe your brush
again to check that there is no more paint left in the
bristles. To make sure they are thoroughly clean,
rinse them in warm water and use soap, such as
artists' brush soap. Squeeze any water out and at
the same time you can reshape the bristles. Brushes
that have been used to apply gesso do not need to
be cleaned using diluent. Remove the gesso first
using a rag or paper towel, then rinse the brush
thoroughly in warm water. Clean your brush straight
after use, before the gesso dries and hardens.

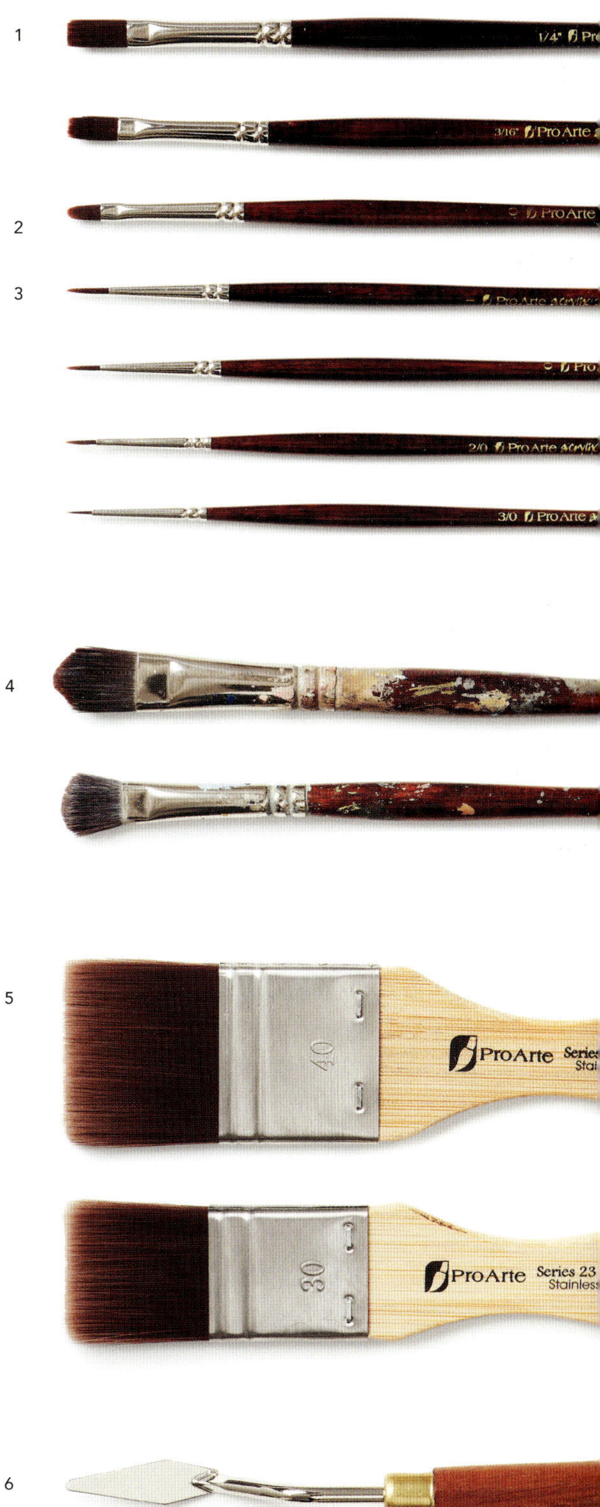

Setting up a workspace

The advantage of working on a smaller scale is that your work area doesn't have to be huge. For many years, I painted in the dining room of our family home – I bought a small table, a chair and a trolley, and this became my workspace. Having a dedicated area and being able to keep all my art paraphernalia in one place made a big difference to my productivity. Whether you have a similar set-up or a studio, there are a few things to keep in mind in order to get the most out of your workspace.

Lighting: It is important to remember that not all light is the same – it can have different temperatures and hues that affect how we perceive colours. In an ideal scenario, an artist's studio has neutral, even lighting that is constant and bright enough to work in without being dazzling. Although achieving the perfect lighting isn't always easy, we can control it as much as possible, which is crucial when painting still lifes. Curtains or blinds can regulate sunshine if it is too bright, and if the space is too dark, then investing in a daylight lamp can really make a difference – it also allows you to work at night. Whatever lighting you choose, make sure that both your still-life set-up and your easel or board are lit with the same temperature of lighting.

Table: When I am working on small paintings, I like to be seated at a table rather than standing. I find it more comfortable, and I am more able to keep a steady hand when painting finer details. Depending on how large your table is, you may also be able to place your shadow box on it (see page 48).

Easel: I use a table easel with a drawing board, and I can keep my palette and pot of diluent next to me, within easy reach. If I am working on larger paintings, I use a radial easel or an A-frame easel.

Chair: You don't need a specific type of chair, just make sure it is comfortable – when you are immersed in your painting, you may be seated on it for a long time. Some artists like to have chairs with wheels so that they can scoot backwards and assess their work from a distance. An adjustable chair might be a good idea so that you can raise it, lower it or alter the back rest. Even if you decide to work standing up, or if you don't have the space for a table, I recommend getting a stool to perch on.

Storage: As well as keeping your space tidy, storage is also important so that you can stow away any harmful materials – a lockable cabinet or box is preferable if you have young children around.

Trolley: This is really useful for storing jars of brushes, mediums, paints and any items that you need within easy reach while you are painting.

Workstation: Space permitting, a preparation area for priming boards and varnishing is really useful. I use an old sideboard for this purpose – the height is ideal and it has cupboards and drawers for storage.

SAFETY: *Oil painting can involve working with substances that may be harmful.*

- Ensure your workspace is well-ventilated – fumes from solvents can cause headaches, dizziness and nausea. If you get any solvents on your skin, wash immediately with soap.
- Some paints contain harmful pigments (for example, Cadmium), so wash your hands thoroughly (including under your nails) after each painting session or wear protective gloves. It is best not to eat and drink in your workspace to avoid accidentally ingesting something harmful – and don't put the end of the paintbrush in your mouth!
- Fixative sprays should only be used in very well-ventilated areas or outside – the particles they release into the air can be very harmful when inhaled.
- Any toxic or flammable materials and substances should be stored away, preferably in a lockable unit.

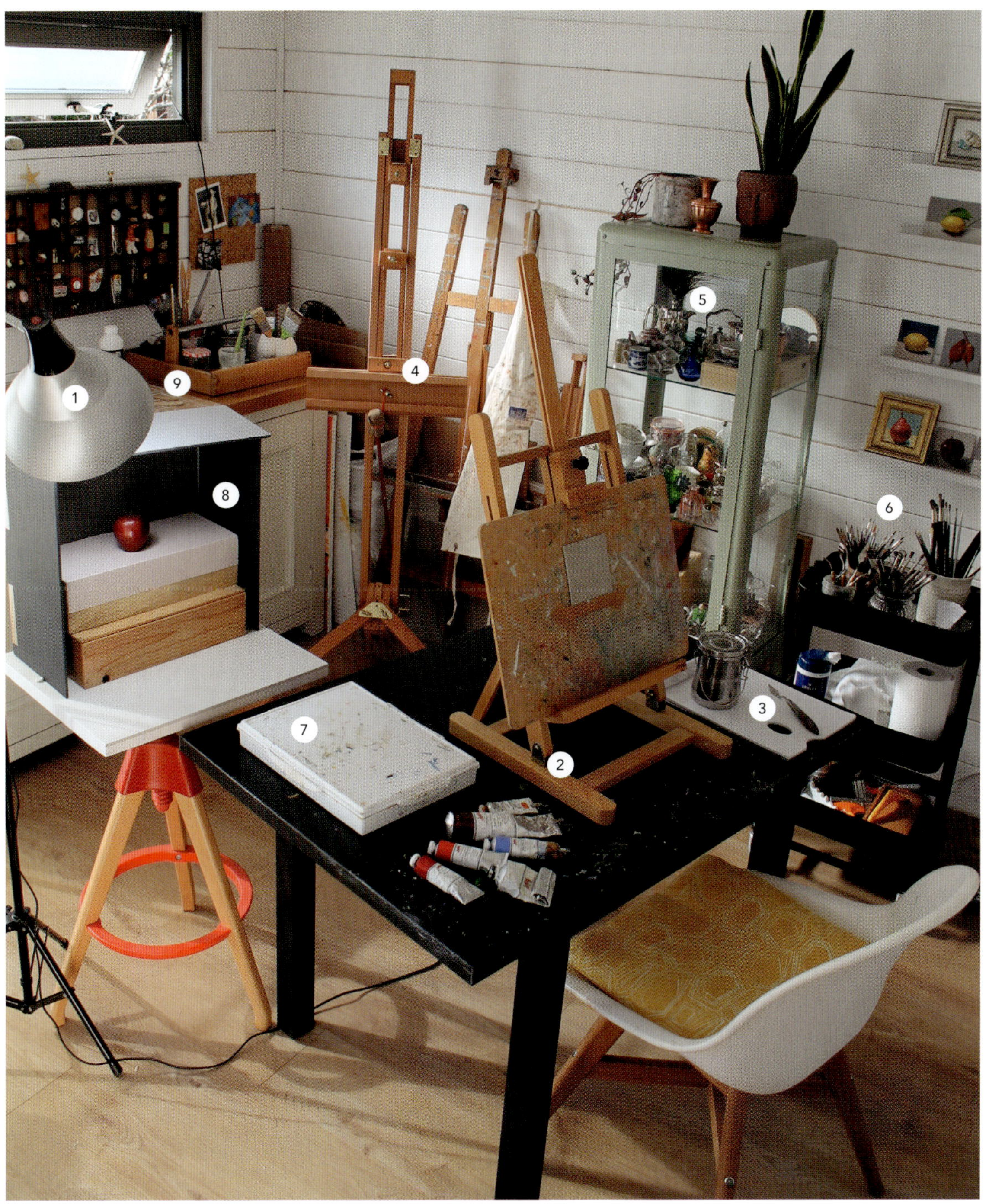

Daylight lamp **(1)**

Table easel and wooden board **(2)**

Palette, palette knife and pot of diluent **(3)**

Radial easel and A-frame easel **(4)**

Storage **(5)**

Trolley **(6)**

Airtight palette box **(7)**

Shadow box **(8)**

Workstation **(9)**

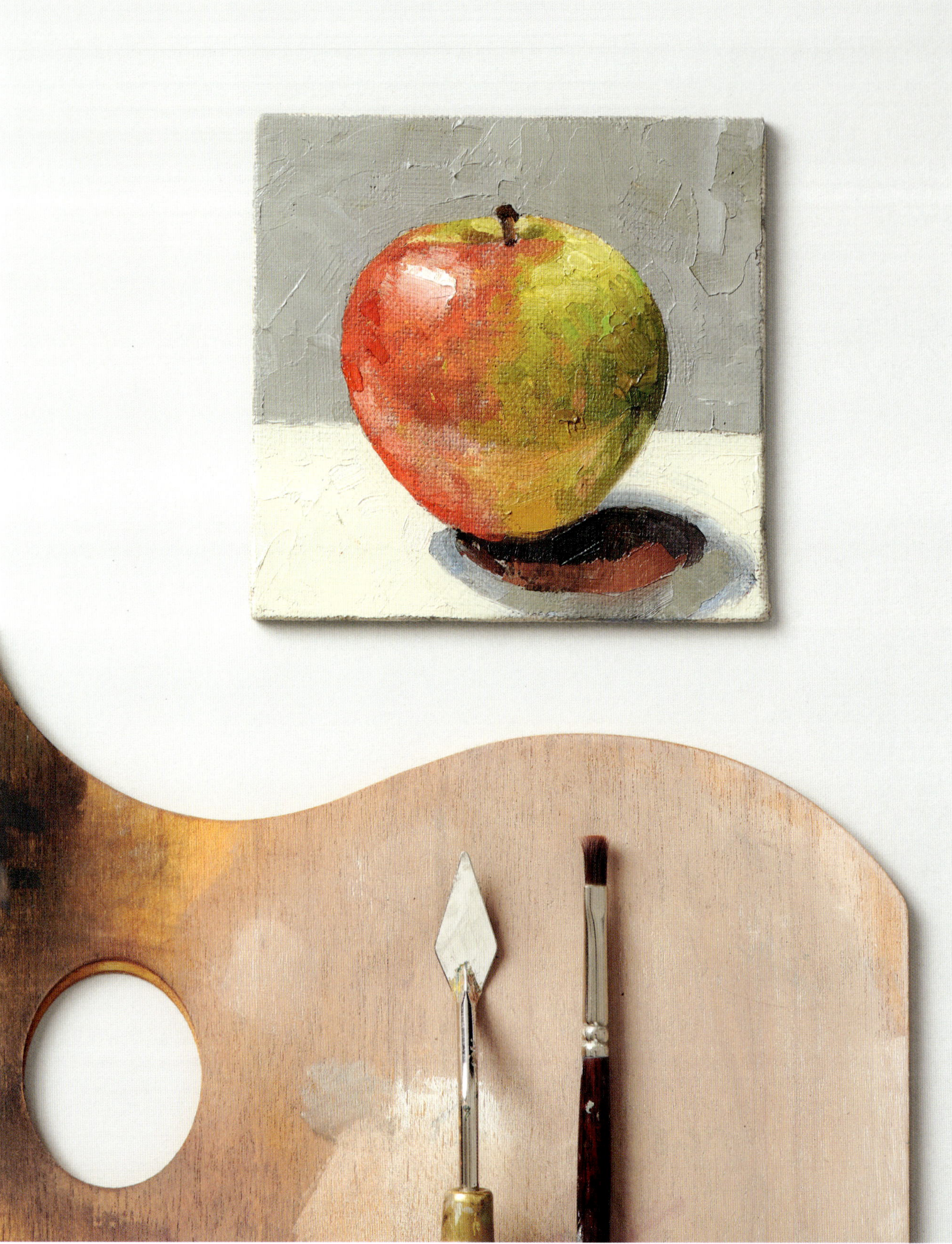

CHAPTER 2

TECHNIQUES

If you need to know more about a technique or want to expand your skills,
the detailed explanations in this chapter will help you to feel confident with
the building blocks of oil painting.

Transferring a drawing

Prior to starting a painting, I will often do an underdrawing straight onto my linen or wooden board (after it has been primed), using a pastel or graphite pencil. Occasionally, however, I will also transfer drawings from my sketchbook as this saves me having to redraw the subject from scratch and therefore saves time. This is particularly useful if I am embarking on a more complicated still life with more than one object in the composition.

There are other methods for transferring your drawings, such as the 'grid' method, or 'squaring up', if you want to enlarge your drawing, but this approach is best suited for the exercises in this book.

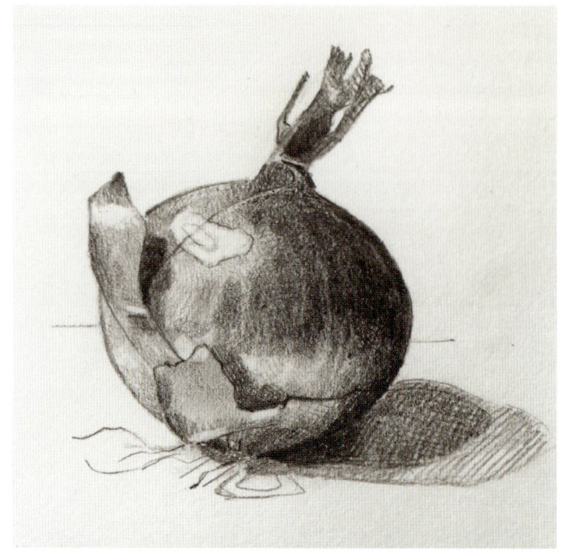

A preparatory drawing of an onion from my sketchbook.

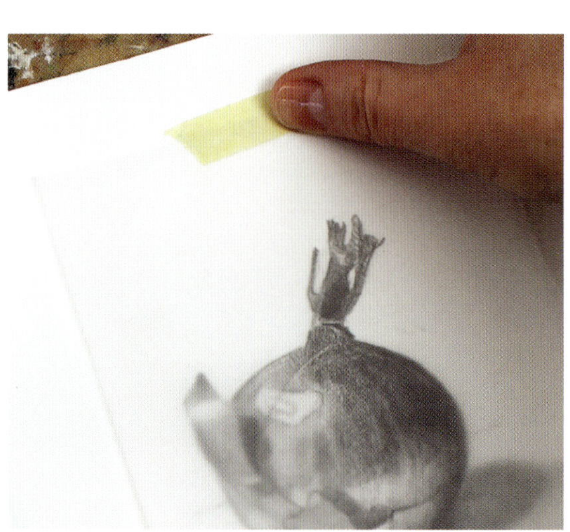

1. Place a piece of tracing paper over the drawing that you wish to transfer. Use masking tape to secure it in place and stop it moving around.

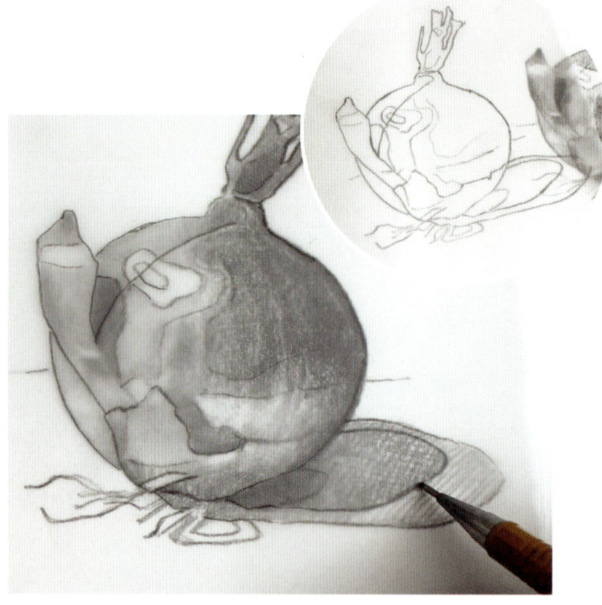

2. Use a pencil to trace the outline of the drawing, making sure you include key information; for example, the outline of the highlight, cast shadow, and edges that mark areas of different tones. Follow the main outlines; there's no need to include details.

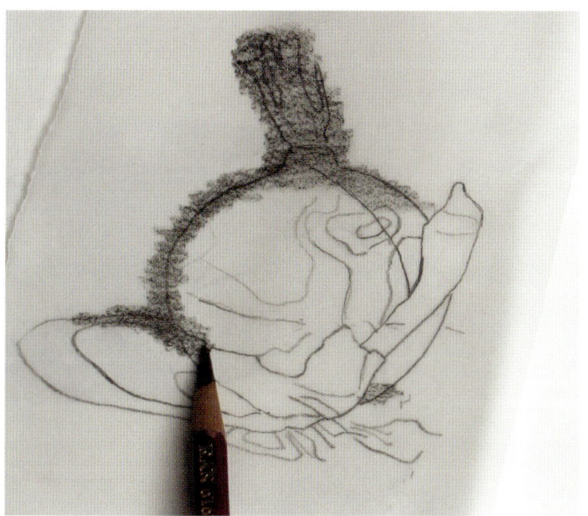

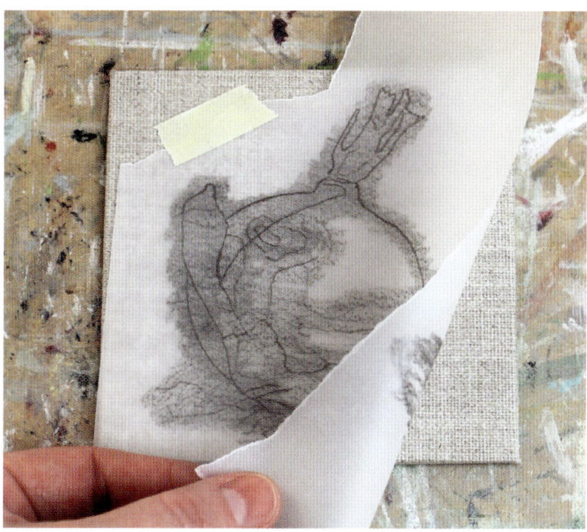

3. Remove the tape and flip the traced drawing over so that the traced lines are facing down. Using a soft pencil, shade the reverse side of your traced drawing, making sure you shade over all your lines.

4. Tape the tracing paper (the correct way round) to your linen board, making sure that you are happy with its position. The shaded marks are now on the underside and your original tracing facing up.

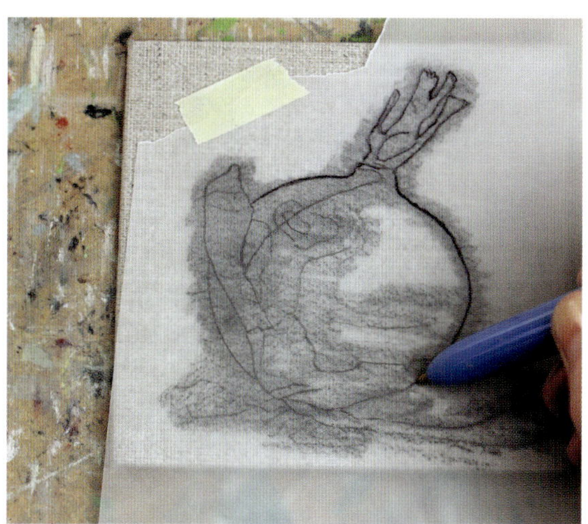

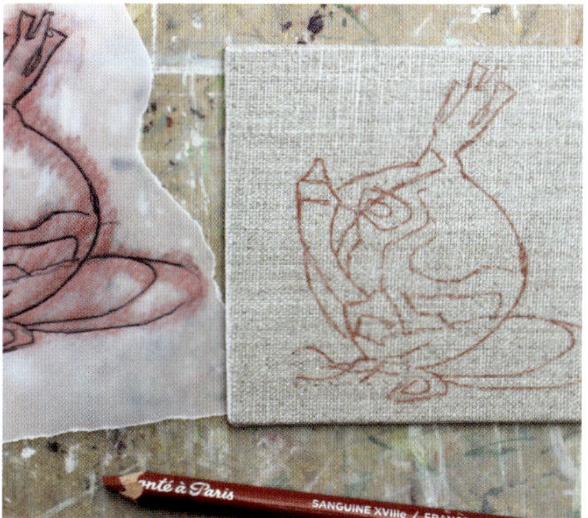

5. Using a pen, begin going over your traced drawing, following the outlines. The resulting impression left on your linen board/surface acts as a good starting point for your painting. I always 'fix' my drawings before I paint (see page 13).

6. You can also employ this technique to transfer a drawing using charcoal or pastel, as shown in the photo above.

Underdrawing

Underdrawings can be incredibly useful, especially if you are embarking on a complicated still-life composition. There is no rule to say that you should always do an underdrawing first – but even the simplest of outlines on your canvas can really pay off. I find that I can begin painting with much more confidence knowing that I have already figured out the most important elements of my subject, and there is much less chance of my painting going wrong from the start!

An underdrawing can be approached in a number of ways, using various materials, including charcoal, pencil, pastel and diluted oil paint – it really comes down to personal choice and whatever works best for you.

Each project in this book focuses on a single everyday object, which automatically makes the composition more straightforward. Even so, I will always begin by looking at my subject through a viewfinder (see page 14) to check that I am happy with how it looks aesthetically.

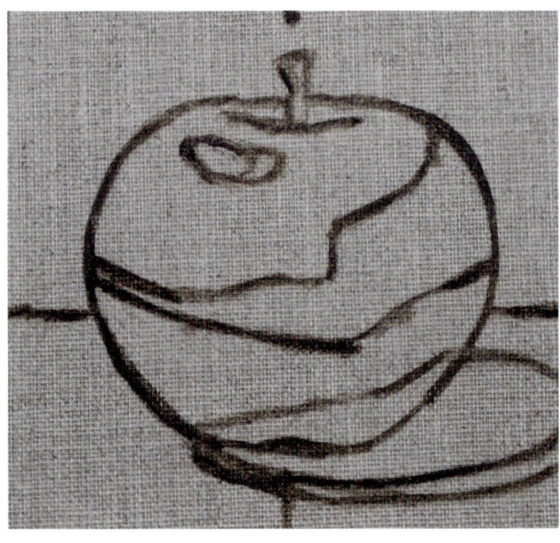

In this underdrawing of an apple, I used a filbert brush and diluted Raw Umber paint, a fast-drying colour, to establish the key elements – the main outline of the apple, the highlight, the core shadow, etc.

1. Start by measuring the vertical halfway point of the canvas and, using a sanguine pastel pencil or graphite pencil, make little marks at the top and the bottom; these will help you to position your subject, here an apple, in the centre. I also mark out the horizon line, just off centre – on my 10cm (4in.) square canvas this falls 4cm (1½in.) up from the base. You can now begin to draw the outline of your subject's shape.

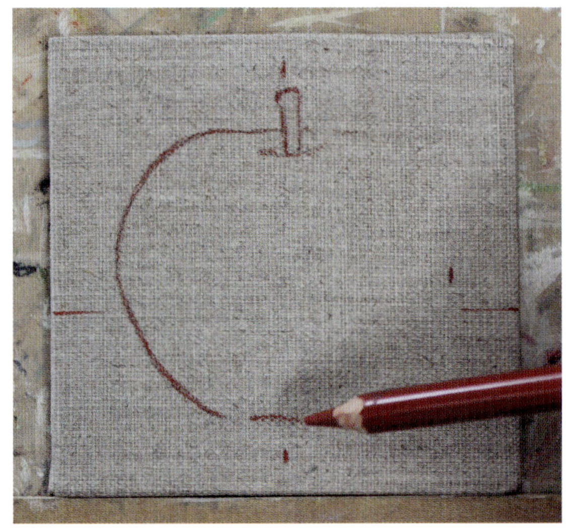

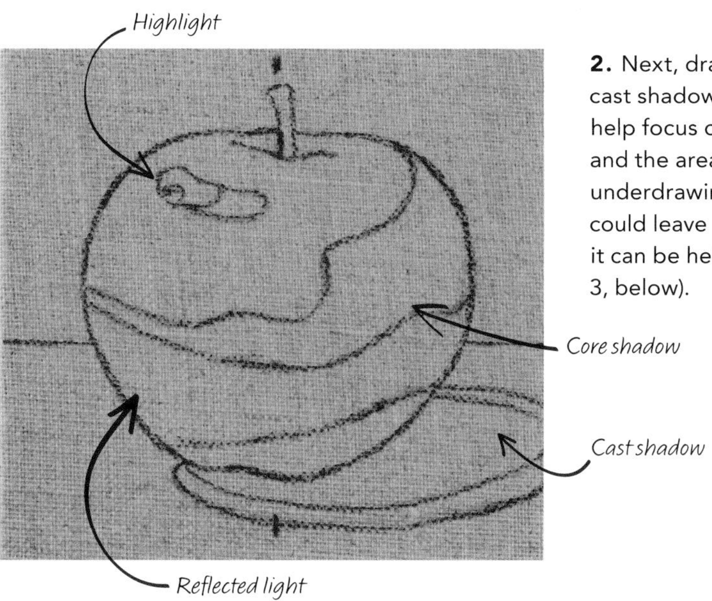

2. Next, draw the outline of the highlight and the cast shadow and, after squinting at the subject to help focus on the tones, mark out the core shadow and the area of reflected light. At this point, the underdrawing contains plenty of information and you could leave it here and begin your painting. However, it can be helpful to add some shading too (see step 3, below).

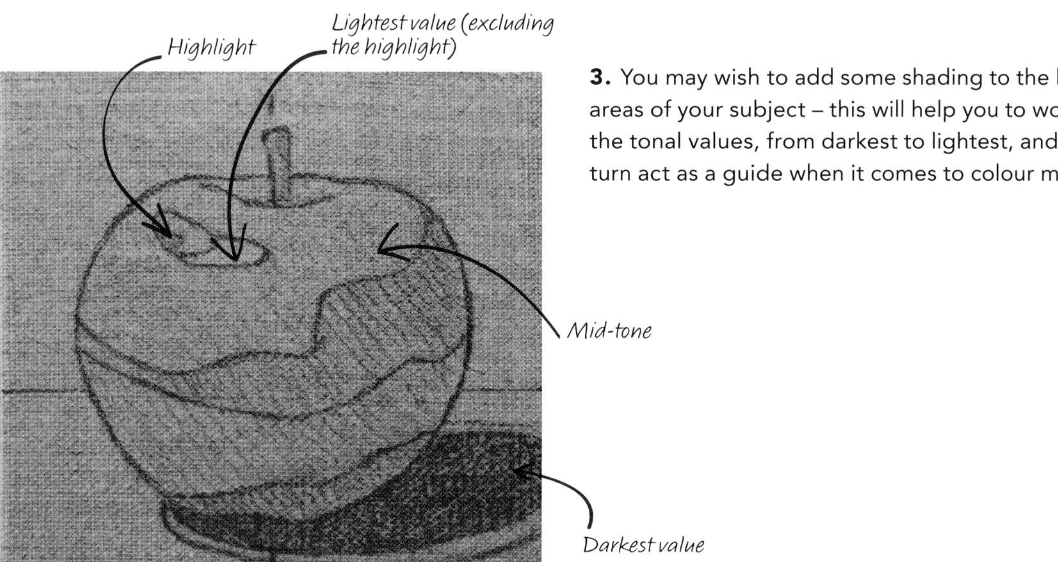

3. You may wish to add some shading to the key areas of your subject – this will help you to work out the tonal values, from darkest to lightest, and will in turn act as a guide when it comes to colour mixing.

TIP

If you have used pencil, pastel or charcoal, remember to 'fix' your underdrawing so that it doesn't smudge when you begin painting. Once the fixative spray has dried, I recommend applying another coat of transparent gesso on top of your drawing (see page 12).

Underpainting

As with underdrawings, it is not compulsory to always begin your work with an underpainting. However, they do serve as an extremely useful way to help you figure out the all-important values of your subject (see pages 38–39), allowing you to control the tonal balance of your work from the very beginning. Usually, an underpainting is made using faster drying, earthy colours, such as Raw Umber. Probably the most commonly known form of underpainting is the simple 'grisaille', where one of these fast-drying colours is gradually diluted to create a range of values – the more the paint is diluted, the 'lighter' in value it becomes.

Alternatively, a more elaborate approach to the grisaille involves mixing your chosen colour with white paint, instead of diluting it. This form of grisaille allows you to create a full range of values and results in a more opaque underpainting; it therefore takes longer to dry.

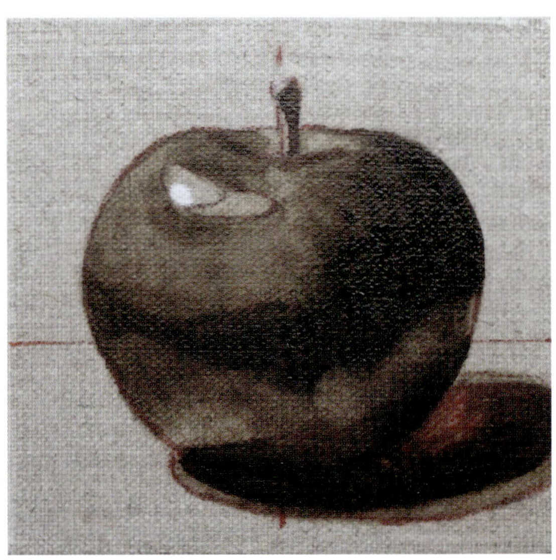

1. My personal preference is to paint the darkest values first. Start with Raw Umber that has been very slightly diluted, almost straight out of the tube. Using a filbert brush, block in the darkest areas, following the guides on the underdrawing.

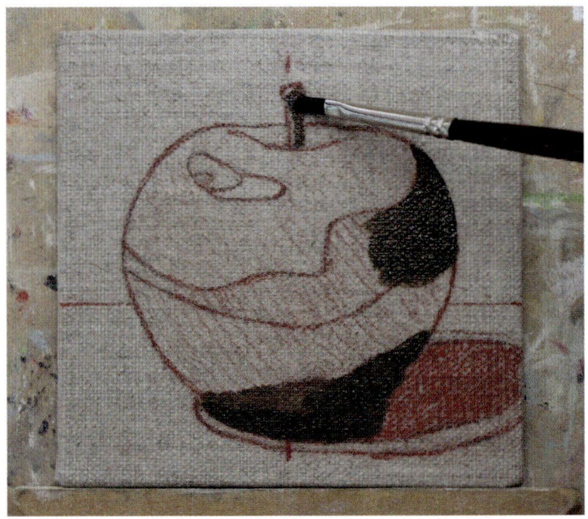

TIP

Due to the paint being diluted, corrections to an underpainting can easily be made by 'tonking' (see page 33) and, if necessary, the whole thing can be wiped off, allowing you to begin again. Your underdrawing (if you have one) won't be affected as long as it has been fixed.

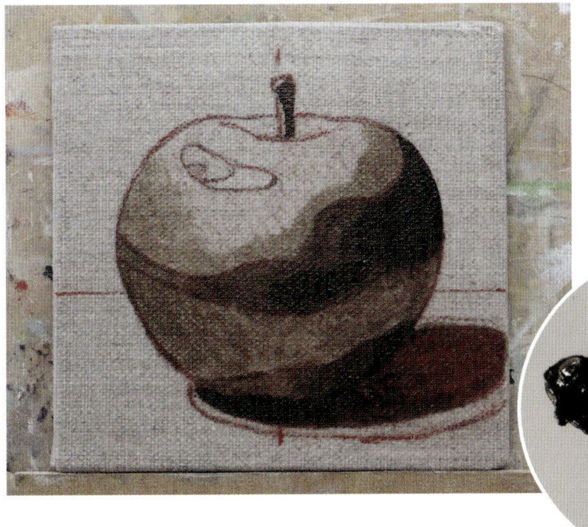

2. Dilute the paint further as you work from dark to light values. Here, the area of reflected light on the underside of my apple is blocked in with a much more diluted mix than that in step 1.

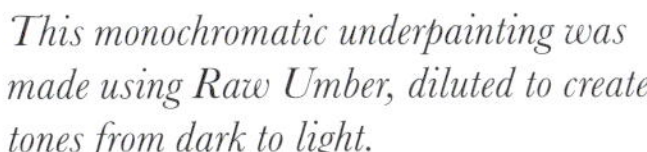

This monochromatic underpainting was made using Raw Umber, diluted to create tones from dark to light.

TIP

Remember that an underpainting is intended to be painted over once it has dried, so it doesn't matter how neat it is. The important thing is to establish the main areas of dark and light.

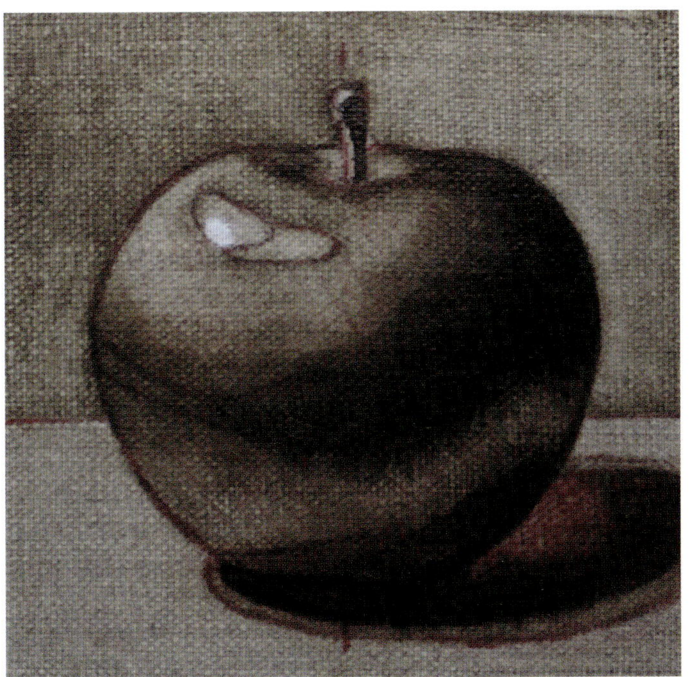

3. Block in the rest of the apple as well as the background and the foreground. You now have a monochromatic version of the apple painting and a really good understanding of its values. I should only have needed one colour (Raw Umber) for this underpainting, but I have put a sneaky little spot of white paint where the brightest highlight is. This has helped me achieve a wider range of values.

Your finished underpainting should take no longer than 24 hours to dry before it can be painted over.

Fat over lean

If you want to build up layers in an oil painting, you need to follow one of the golden rules, known as working 'fat over lean'. This technique helps guarantee a painting's longevity; not following the process can result in the surface of your painting cracking in the future.

Oil paint dries and hardens gradually on exposure to air (oxidisation). Initially, after a few hours or so, the paint will be a bit tacky but still workable. After a day or two, the oil paint might be 'touch dry', meaning that, although the surface of the paint feels dry, the paint beneath is still wet. After 6 months or more, oil paint can usually be considered dry, or 'cured', but this will depend on how thickly the paint has been applied.

Cracking can happen when thin, or 'lean', paint has been applied over thicker, or 'fat', paint. The thin layer will dry quickly, while the fat layer beneath dries gradually – as it does so, it contracts and causes the hardened top layer of lean paint to crack and even flake off.

To prevent this, with each layer that is applied, the oil content of the paint should increase, or become 'fatter'. The first layer of paint should be made with thinned-down paints, either using a diluent, or ideally with 'lean' paints that have a low oil content (such as Raw Umber). Progressive layers should increase in 'fat' content – some colours have more oil content than others and can be used straight from the tube, or a medium such as linseed oil can be added to 'fatten' them.

- As you build and develop your painting skills, you will get to know which paints have a higher and lower oil content.
- Explore different mediums to find which give you the effects you are aiming for in your own work.

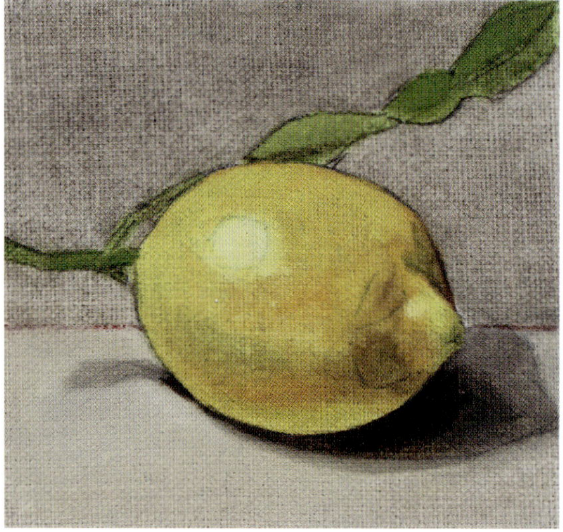

1. I painted the first layer of this painting using thinned and 'lean' oil paints. Once dry, I can then build on this layer with 'fatter' paint.

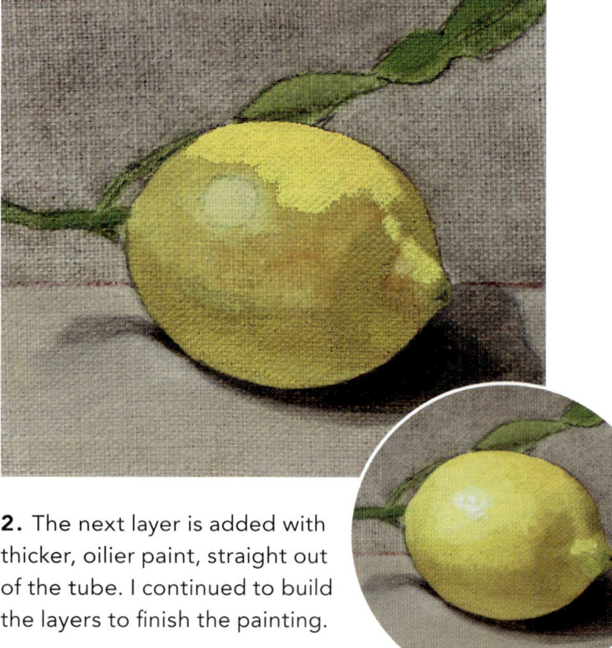

2. The next layer is added with thicker, oilier paint, straight out of the tube. I continued to build the layers to finish the painting.

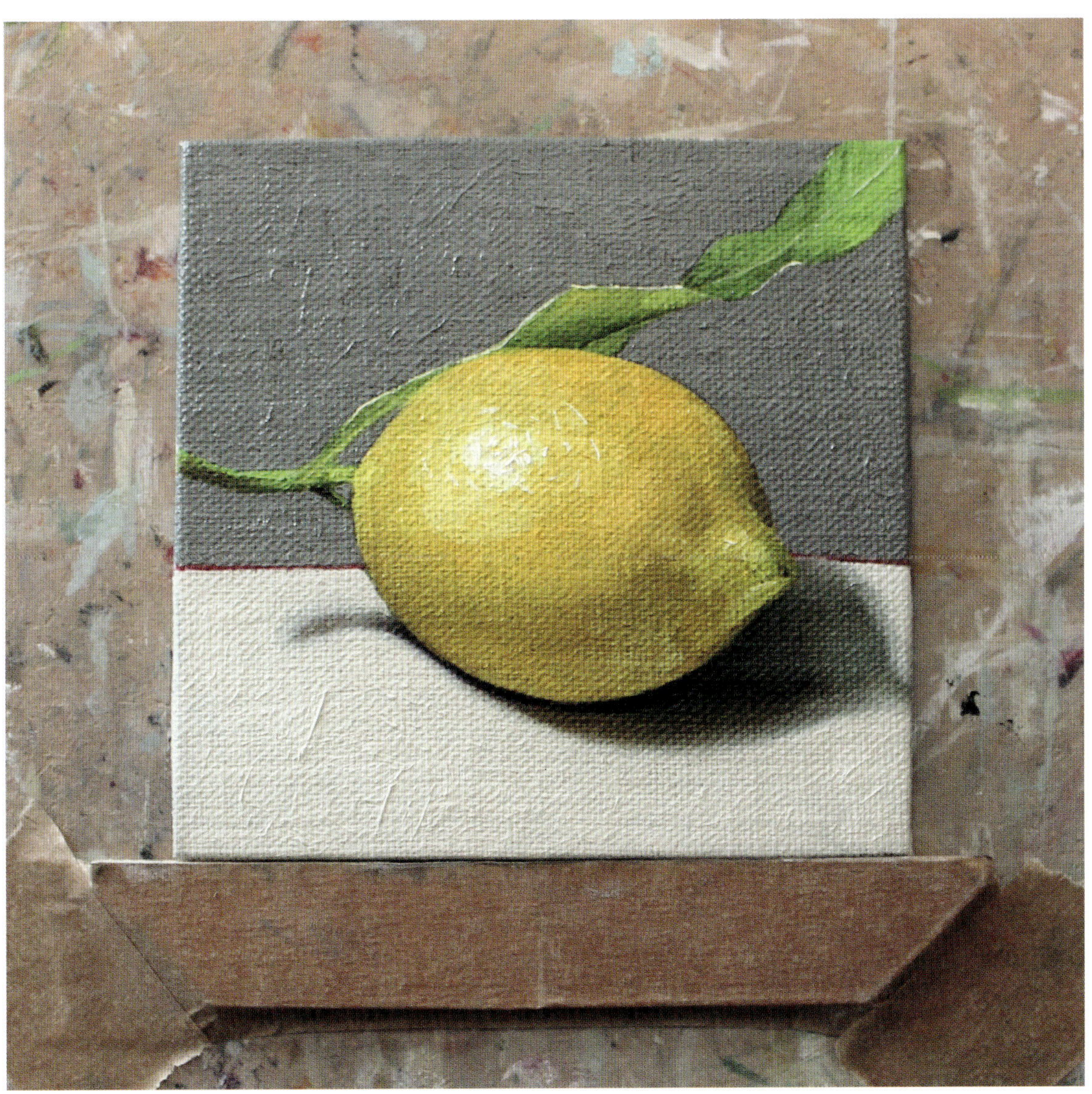

The finished painting using the 'fat over lean' method. As time goes on and the paint ages, the surface should not crack because the paints have been applied in the correct order.

Glazing

Glazing is a technique where a thin layer of paint (made transparent by mixing it with a medium) is painted over the top of an existing layer of dry paint. The paint layer beneath the glaze remains visible and no detail is lost; however, the glaze alters its colour. Make sure the paints you use for glazing are transparent (or at least semi-transparent) – paint tubes state the level of opacity on their labels.

The effects of glazing on a painting can be subtle yet luminous, and colours can be made even more vibrant by building up successive layers using this technique. Artists such as Rembrandt and JMW Turner are known to have used glazing in their paintings, and Renaissance painters achieved beautifully glowing reds and blues by building up layer after layer of rich colour.

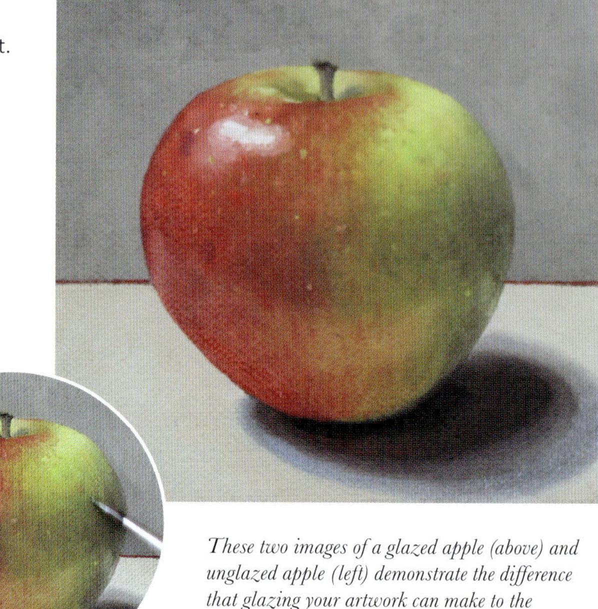

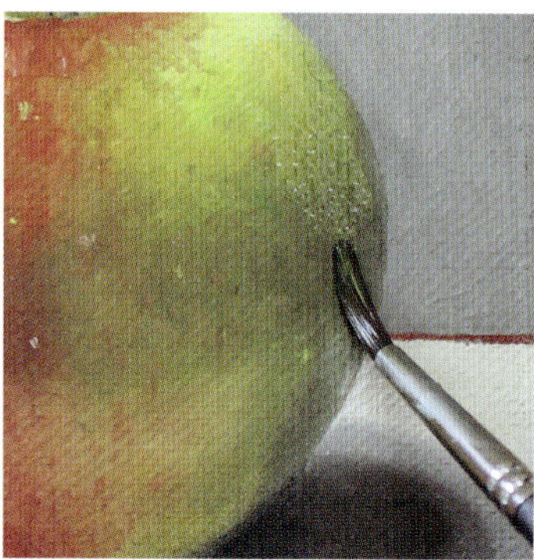

These two images of a glazed apple (above) and unglazed apple (left) demonstrate the difference that glazing your artwork can make to the vibrancy of a finished painting.

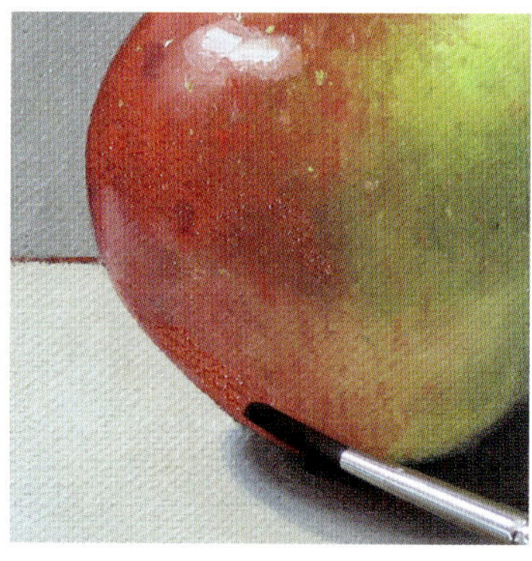

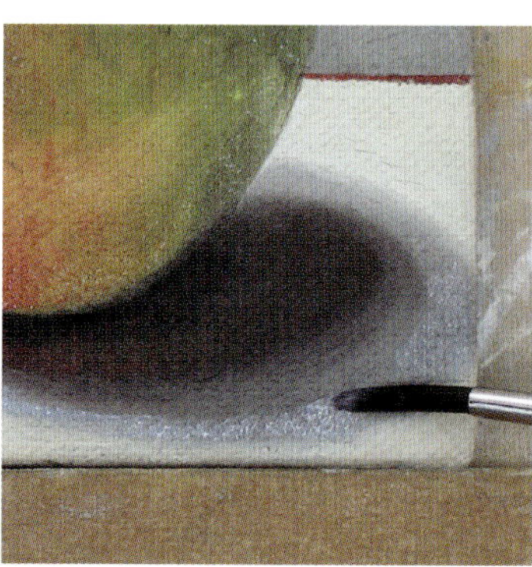

1. With a soft brush, apply thin, even layers of glaze using a small amount of paint mixed with glazing medium. Here, I glazed the right-hand side of my apple with a yellow glaze that alters the shadowy colours beneath, making them less grey.

2. Next, I painted a deep yellow-orange glaze over the dark red areas, which adds warmth.

3. Lastly, I applied a blue glaze over an existing blue layer, to intensify the colour.

Blending

Blending is a technique used when an artist wants to soften any hard edges between colours or tones, and it is acheived by gently merging the boundaries together. If done meticulously, an artist can achieve imperceptibly smooth gradations between colours. Alternatively, an artist whose brushwork is more loose may choose to keep blending to a minimum – the degree to which you choose to blend is down to personal choice and depends on your style.

- To achieve an even smoother finish, just use a finer brush.
- For the projects in this book I used an old, soft brush for blending but you can achieve looser blended effects with your fingers or palette knife.
- If you are hesitant about trying this technique on an area of your painting, try testing the colours you want to blend on an old canvas or some primed paper first so you can see the results.

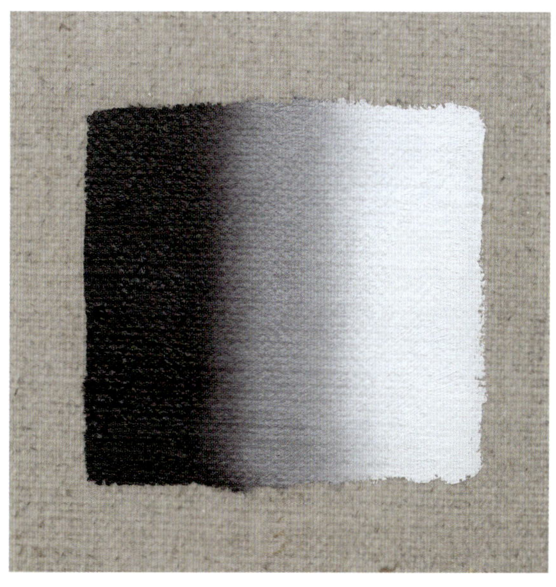

Blending results in much softer boundaries between colours, creating subtle transitions.

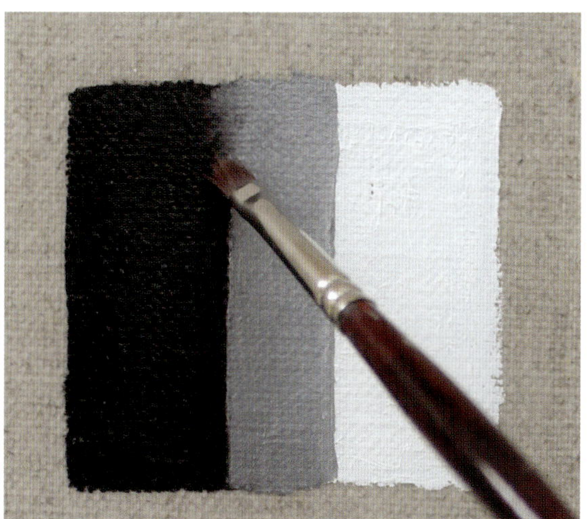

1. To demonstrate the effect, I have painted three strips of colour, the boundaries of which are butting up to one another with clear edges. Using a fairly soft, small, dry brush, gently brush along the boundary with small, light strokes, working back and forth.

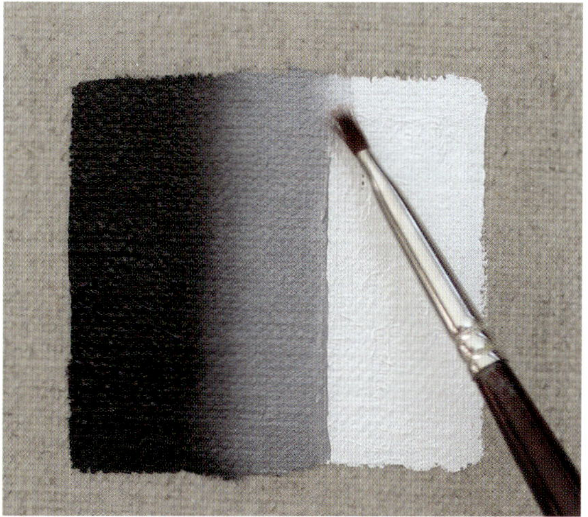

2. With a clean brush, repeat the blending process between the grey and white boundary. The edges are now merged and the transitions between colours are soft and subtle. Remember to wipe your brush regularly to avoid muddying the colours.

Alla prima

The term 'alla prima' means 'at first attempt' in Italian, and this lively, loose approach can result in your work feeling fresh and spontaneous. Alla prima is a direct method of painting, working 'wet-into-wet', which means that wet paint is painted on top of wet paint, without having to wait for the layer beneath to dry first, and any modifications to your painting are kept to a minimum. Paintings are completed quickly in one session (or sitting) with little or even no underdrawing, and each colour is laid down with confidence, the strokes remaining virtually unaltered.

- If you prepare and mix your colours in advance, you will be able to lay them down quickly and confidently, without the need for adjustments.
- Working alla prima means that all your colours are laid at once into a wet painting, so that the 'fat over lean' rule (see page 26) doesn't apply. Your painting will dry at the same rate, at the same time.

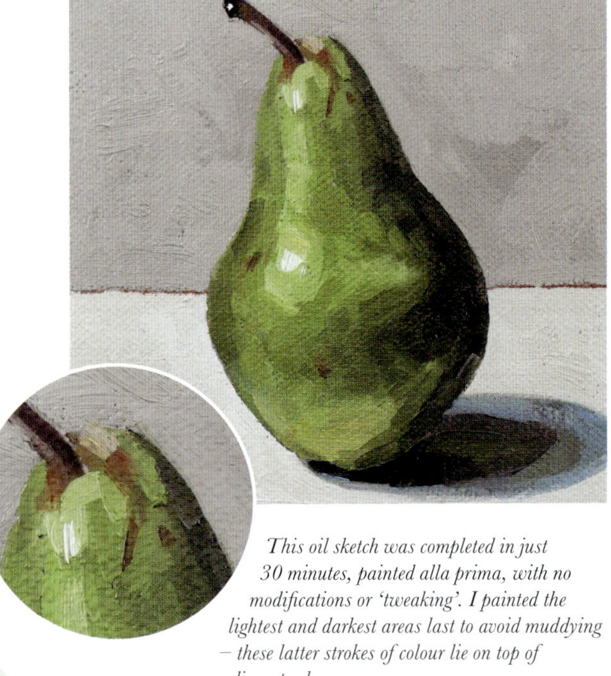

This oil sketch was completed in just 30 minutes, painted alla prima, with no modifications or 'tweaking'. I painted the lightest and darkest areas last to avoid muddying – these latter strokes of colour lie on top of adjacent colours.

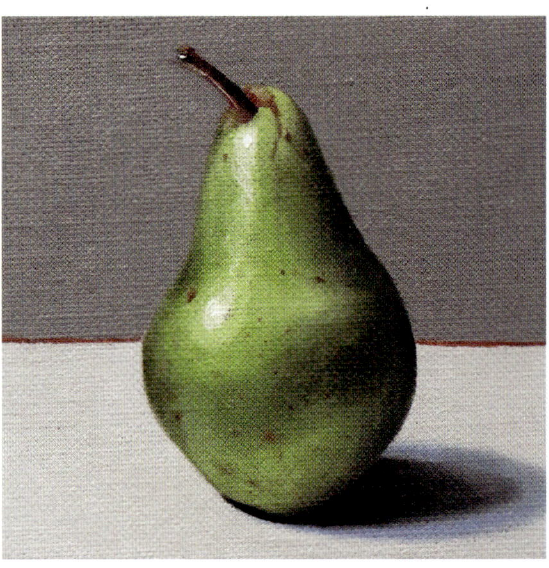

For comparison, here is the same pear, painted in my usual, more detailed and deliberate style.

TIP

Plan ahead, either using a tonal sketch as a reference or an underdrawing to map the main areas of different value that correspond to your paint mixes.

Impasto

To me, impasto is a way of almost sculpting with paint – it offers the artist an opportunity to apply thick paint using anything from a brush, a palette knife, their fingers or even squeezing paint directly onto the canvas from the tube! Oil paint is particularly suited to this technique as its rich composition lends itself to expressive mark making.

The red and green apple on the right has been painted using impasto. Admittedly, this technique is best suited to larger painting surfaces; however, I used it here to illustrate the effects that can be achieved using this technique in a simple way.

Famous artists known for their use of impasto include Vincent Van Gogh, Jackson Pollock and Frank Auerbach. The technique is even noticeable in the works of Renaissance artists such as Titian and Tintoretto.

- Brushmarks, ridges and 3-D peaks can be created on the painting's surface, building texture and adding dimension.
- Impasto marks often use the thickest paint, so remember to save these effects until last (see Fat over lean, page 26).
- Impasto is a great painting technique if you like to work quickly, and the visual effect is one of liveliness and energy.

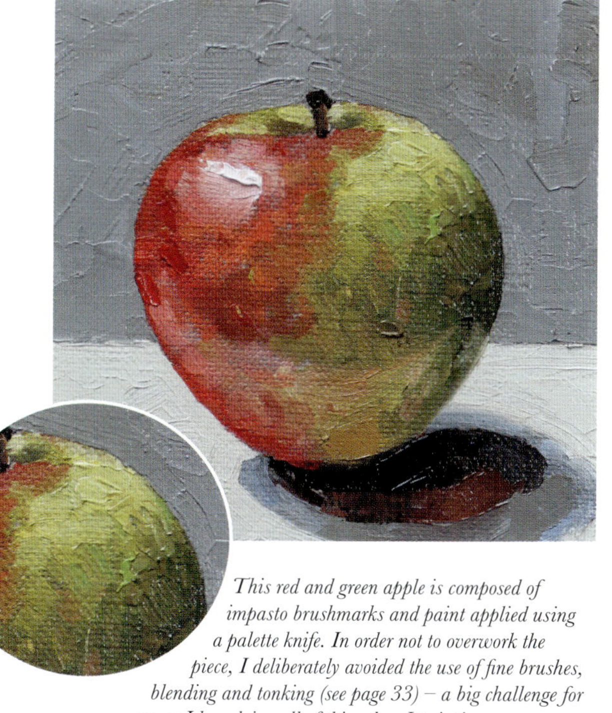

This red and green apple is composed of impasto brushmarks and paint applied using a palette knife. In order not to overwork the piece, I deliberately avoided the use of fine brushes, blending and tonking (see page 33) – a big challenge for me as I love doing all of this when I paint!

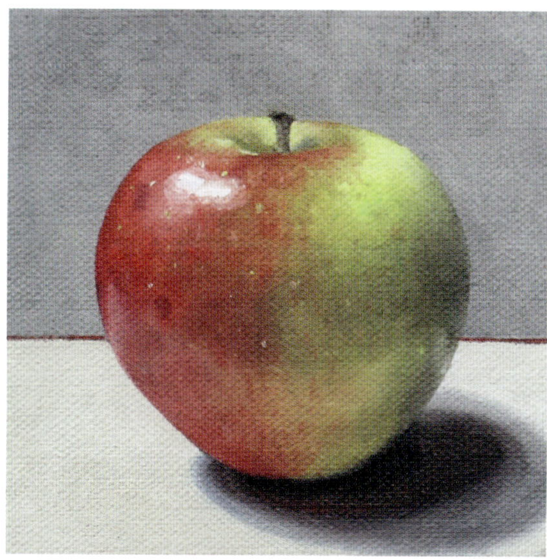

For comparison, here the same apple is painted in a more refined and detailed style, the only use of impasto being in the highlight.

TIP

Plan ahead, either using a tonal sketch as a reference or using an underdrawing to map the main areas of different value that correspond to your paint mixes.

Dry brush

The dry brush technique is a useful method of suggesting texture in a simple and effective way and can be used to add visual interest to areas of solid colour. Only a small amount of undiluted paint is used on the brush and quick, light strokes should be made, allowing the dry surface below to remain visible through the scratch-like brushmarks.

I recommend doing a little test brushstroke on a separate surface (a piece of paper will do), just to be sure that you have the desired texture before you work directly on your painting.

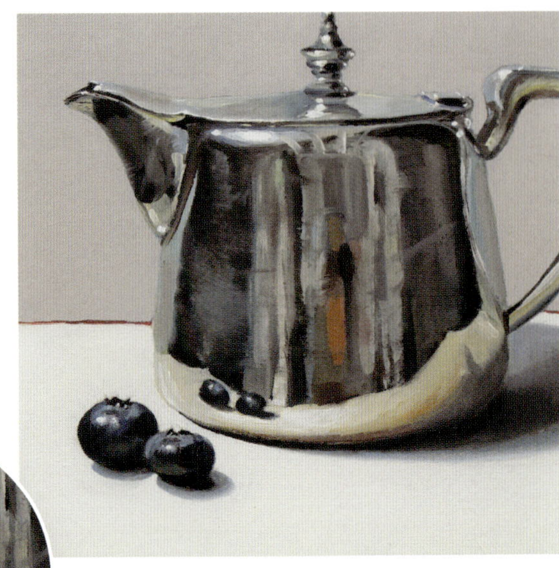

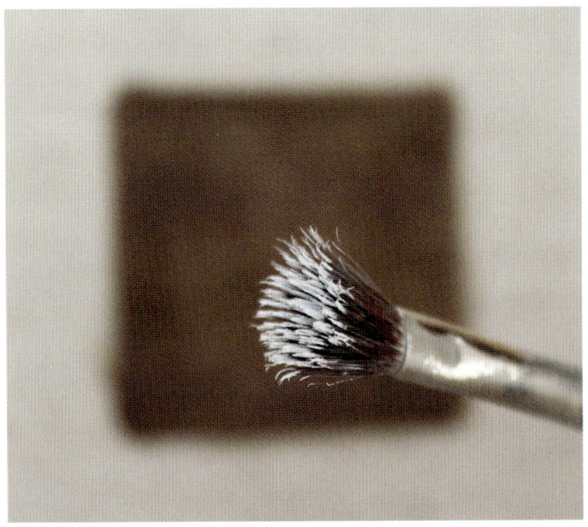

In the painting above, the dry brush technique was used to create the worn silver effect on the teapot. On the left is the same teapot before the dry brushing.

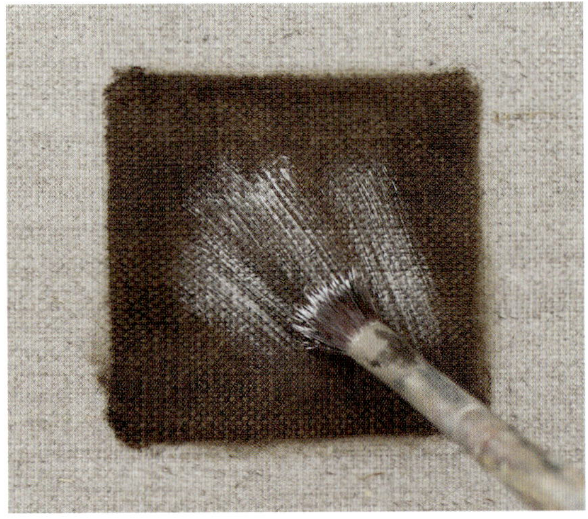

1. Only a small amount of paint is needed for this technique and just the tip of your brush should be very lightly loaded with some undiluted paint. Fan brushes are ideal or you can use an old brush with splayed bristles, as I have here.

2. Using confident, light strokes, brush the paint onto your dry surface. The colour beneath should still be visible through the brushmarks.

Tonking

This technique, named after former Slade Professor Henry Tonks, can be used if excess paint needs to be removed from a painting – for example, if there is too much paint on the surface and the paint risks becoming muddied if you continue to work into it.

A sheet of absorbent paper, such as paper towel or newspaper, is placed on top of the painting – either over a particular area or over the whole surface – and the paper is smoothed over the surface. As the paper is slowly peeled away, a layer of paint is lifted off with it, leaving a thinned-out version of the original painting on the canvas.

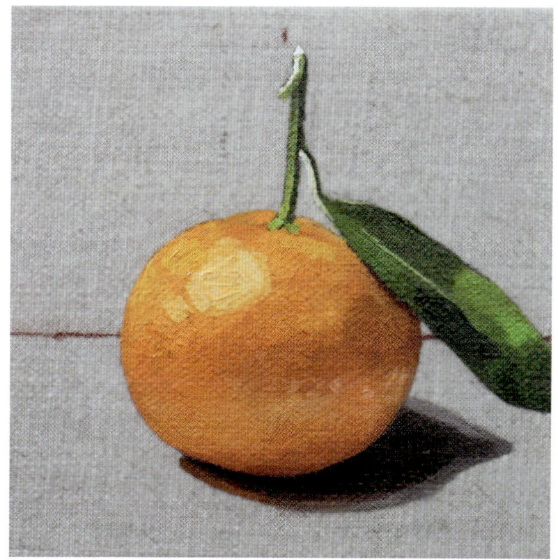

After tonking, the surface of this painting has become much smoother and more workable, reducing the likelihood of the final painting becoming muddied.

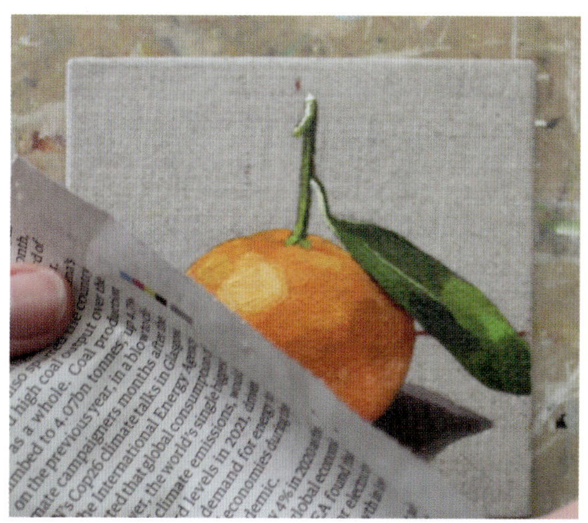

1. I had painted the first stages of this clementine too thickly and needed to remove some paint as it was becoming difficult to work with.

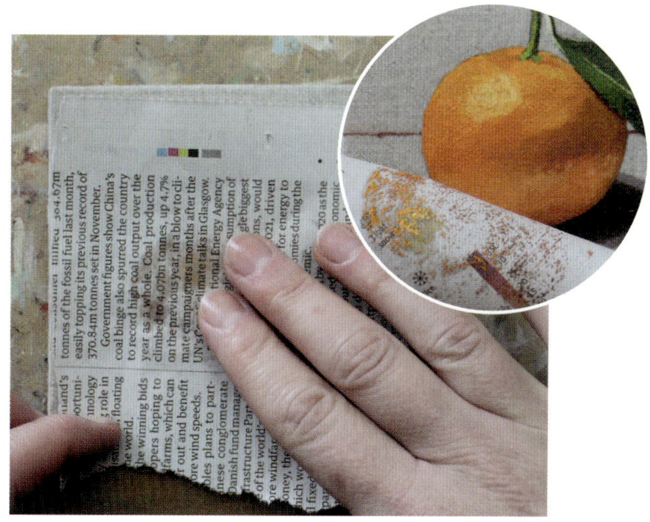

2. By gently pressing a piece of newspaper over the problem area, I 'tonked' by rubbing with flattened fingers, or you can use the palm of your hand. [Inset] Carefully peeling the paper back removes the excess paint.

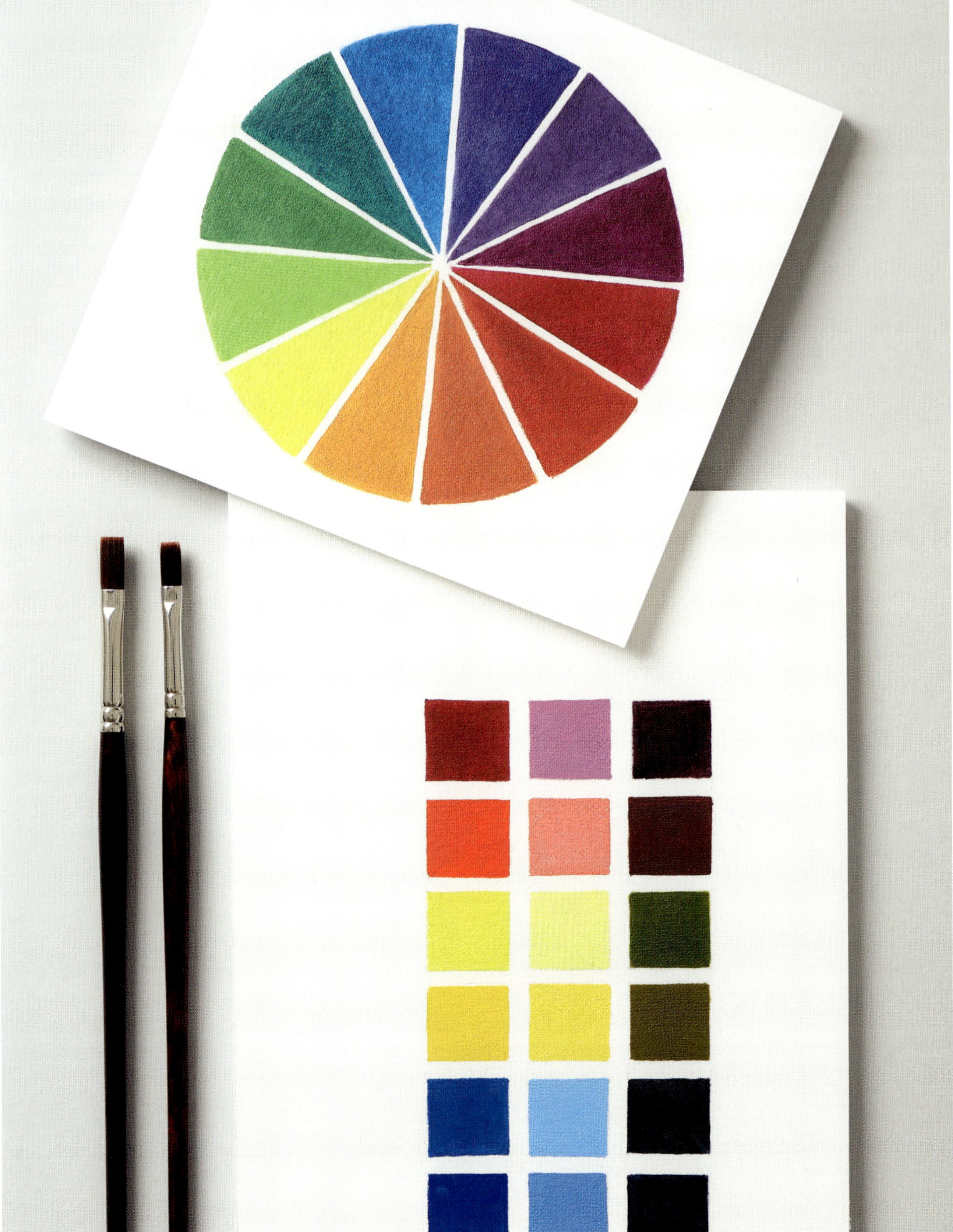

CHAPTER 3

UNDERSTANDING COLOUR

Colour theory is a fascinating world and can be explored at your leisure. This chapter seeks to explain simply why certain colours work well together, how to mix paints and how to arrange a palette.

How to look at colour

The subject of colour is endlessly fascinating, and can seem a little daunting! Countless books have been written about the theory of colour – everything from the science behind our perception of colour, to the way we apply this knowledge to colour mixing and painting. So much of what we know about colour is down to Sir Isaac Newton and his experiments in the late 1600s, on light and prisms. When refracting white light through a glass prism, he saw that it is made up of seven colours (red, orange, yellow, green, blue, indigo and violet). When light waves hit objects the colours that we see are the result of certain waves being reflected back to us.

When we look at a painting, these waves of light throw back colours that are determined by the pigments within the paints.

The following terms are used in colour theory to describe colour attributes:

- **Hue** describes which colour group a colour belongs to – for example, Ultramarine, Cobalt and Kings Blue Deep are in the blue hues group.
- **Value** *(also referred to as tone)* describes how light or dark a colour is.
- **Saturation** *(also referred to as chroma)* describes a colour's intensity and vibrancy.

PRIMARY, SECONDARY AND TERTIARY COLOURS

In the world of art, we use visual charts and wheels to help us organize colour. The colour wheel is used to illustrate the relationships between colours. Red, blue and yellow are the three primary colours, and are so called because they are the only three colours that cannot be mixed from other colours. Primary colours are the source from which all other colours are derived.

By mixing primaries together we can create secondary colours: green, orange and violet. By further mixing these secondary colours, we can create tertiary colours: red-orange, yellow-orange; yellow-green, blue-green; blue-violet and red-violet.

When painting, you will come across different paint versions of each primary colour. For example, you can choose from reds such as Vermillion, Cadmium Red or Magenta, or a blue from Ultramarine, Cobalt, Phthalo and so on. The different attributes, such as saturation and temperature, mean that you can choose a paint colour to refine your palette and suit your subject.

These colour wheels have been created with different paint versions of the primary colours. I used the paint colours that I chose for the projects to demonstrate the subtle differences you can achieve with your palette selection.

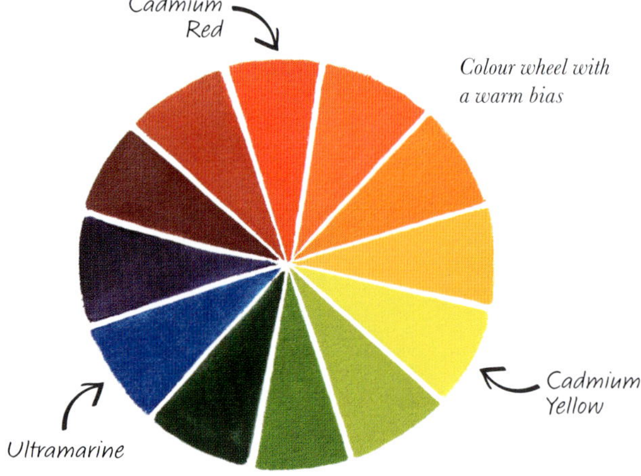

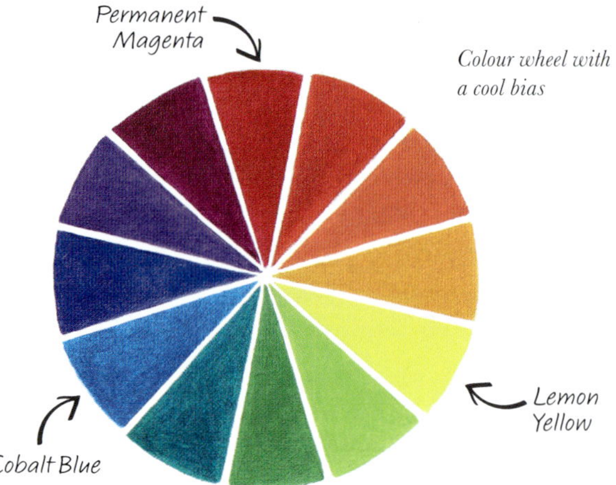

ANALOGOUS COLOURS

Analogous colours are found sitting right next to each other on the colour wheel. They work well together and so painting with them can result in a more coherent and harmonious piece of work.

Red-orange, orange and yellow-orange are analogous colours, as are blue-violet, violet and red-violet.

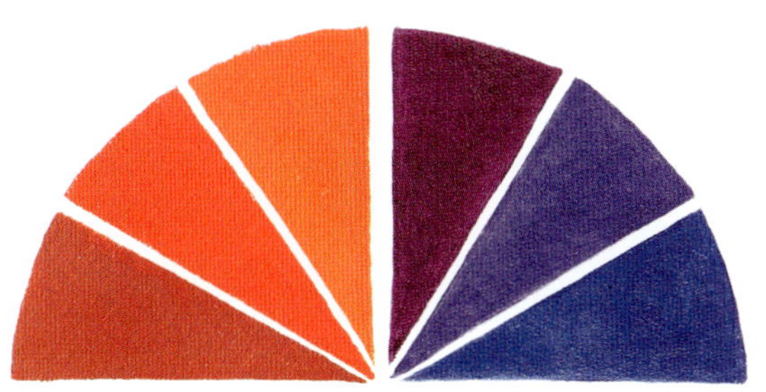

COMPLEMENTARY COLOURS

Complementary colours are opposites on the colour wheel: red and green; yellow and violet; blue and orange. When mixed together they will produce muddy, neutral colours. However, if you place them side by side, they appear brighter, enhancing the intensity of each other.

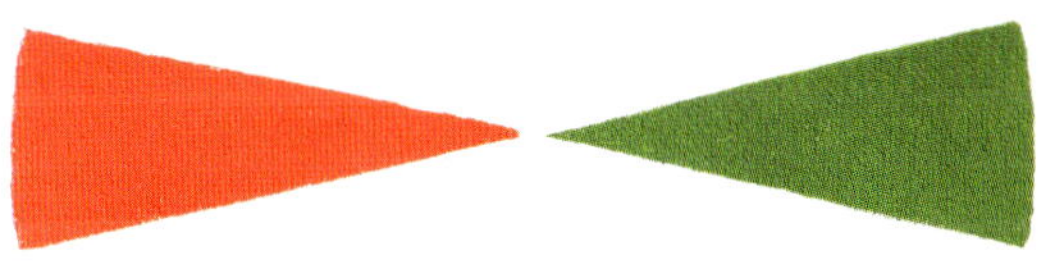

Complementary pairing: red and green

CONTRASTING COLOURS

You can create impact with your choice and placement of colours. Strong contrasts using opposites on the wheel will look dramatic, or use a touch of a warm colour in an otherwise cool palette to add visual interest.

COLOUR TEMPERATURE

Colour wheels can be split into two halves – the 'cool' icy hues (blues, greens and purples) in one half and the 'warm' fiery, hot colours (reds, yellows and oranges) in the other. You can use these colours in your work and make the most of their visual effects; warm colours are usually more vibrant and the eye is drawn to them first, while cool colours are more soothing to the eye. If you look at the two colour wheels (opposite), you may notice that the colours in the top one feel warmer whereas the colours in the second wheel feel cooler. That is because colours within their hues can be thought of as warmer or cooler too, known as colour bias. Compare the two reds: Cadmium Red leans more towards orange/yellow, making it warmer; Permanent Magenta leans towards blue, making it cooler. Lemon Yellow has a more green/blue bias whereas Cadmium Yellow leans more towards orange. Using these paints as the base for your mixes will create a palette with a warm or cool bias.

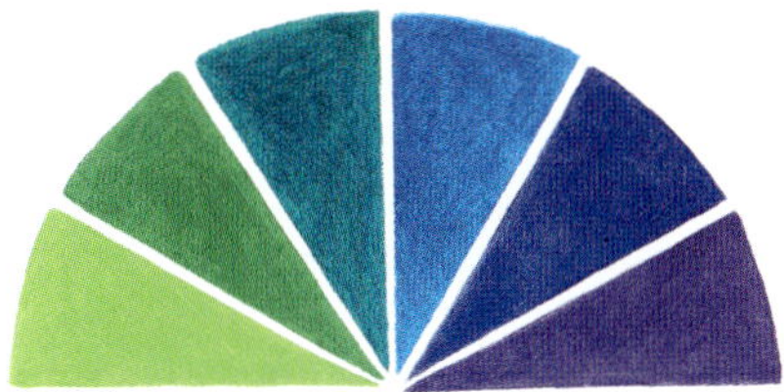

Cool 'icy water' half of the colour wheel

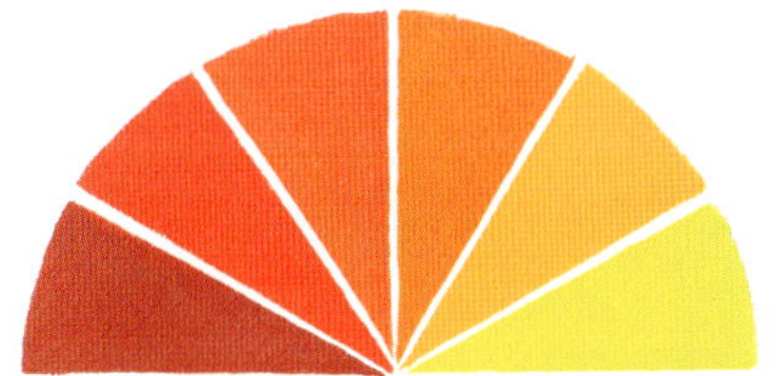

Warm 'fiery' half of the colour wheel

Tonal range & value

Understanding value, or tone, is so important if you want to achieve a successful painting. Tonal variations give subjects their form and shape, and without them your painting will look flat. Tones vary from light through mid to dark, and although you can use tones of one hue, it is important to understand that tonal range is found across all colours in a painting. Getting your head around values means that you can be freer with your choice of palette, allowing you to create dynamic and expressive work with more exaggerated colours. I would go so far as to say that as long as your values are accurate, you can pretty much get away with anything!

ASSESSING VALUE

Creating a greyscale, or looking at your image in black and white, can help you to easily figure out the values of all your colours and make sure that you have strong contrasts from highlights to shadows. A greyscale (left), numbered from 1 to 10, shows a tonal range with values from No. 1, the lightest (white), to No. 10, the darkest (black). By comparing paint colours to the categories on the scale, you can determine their value and whether they are appropriate for the strength of tone required. For example, the two yellows – Cadmium Yellow and Lemon Yellow – sit at the lighter end of the scale because this hue is lighter in value. I would describe Lemon Yellow as being highly saturated and very light in value.

When we look at Cadmium Red, it sits approximately halfway on our greyscale at No. 6. If we mix a little white with Cadmium Red, it becomes less saturated (less vibrant and colourful) and it lightens in value (becomes less dark), moving up the greyscale to No. 4. By mixing tints and shades (see page 40), you can extend the range of a colour.

MAKING A GREYSCALE

To make your own greyscale, draw out 10 equal boxes (about 2.5cm/1in. squared) onto primed oil paper. Number the boxes from 1 to 10. Starting with the first box, No. 1, paint it with some pure Titanium White. Skip to box No. 10 at the opposite end and paint this with Ivory Black. On your palette, take some white paint and add a very small amount of black to create the lightest grey and use this to fill in box No. 2. Continue to add increasing amounts of black to your white for each box. You should end up with a scale showing an even gradation from white to black – or light to dark.

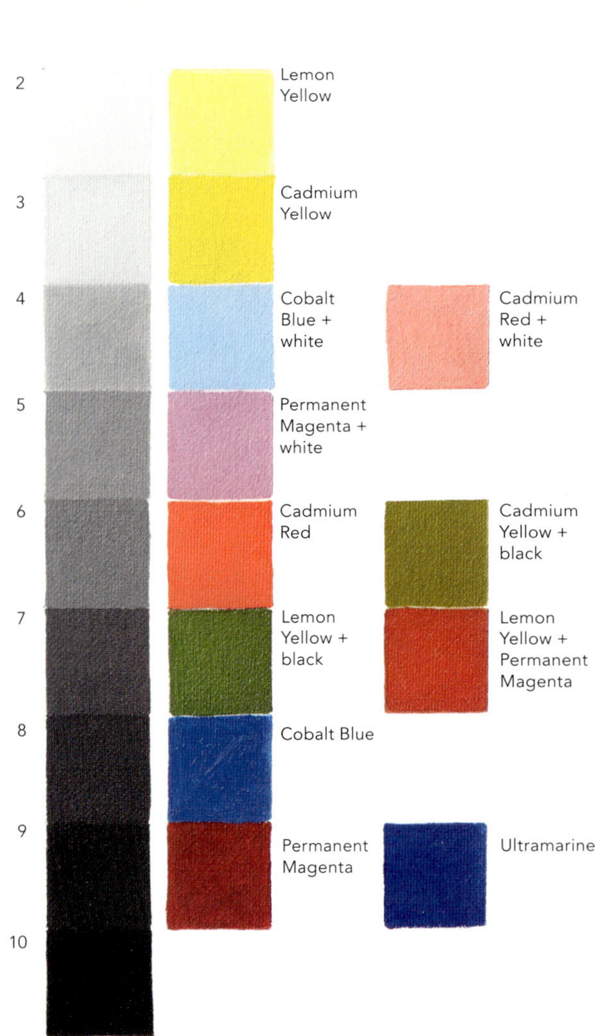

USING YOUR GREYSCALE

To help assess the range of values you need for painting your subject, start by holding your greyscale next to your set-up or reference. Squint your eyes – this helps you to notice things in less detail as we just want to see the most important shapes. Look for the darkest and lightest areas or shapes. Next, look for the values that fall in between, the mid-tones. Where do they land on your scale? Look at the main focal point of your set-up; is it going to stand out or will it be lost because its value is too similar to that of its surroundings? Question whether you might need to rearrange the objects in your set-up or change the position of your light source; a more dynamic arrangement with strong light and shade will result in a more interesting and eye-catching painting.

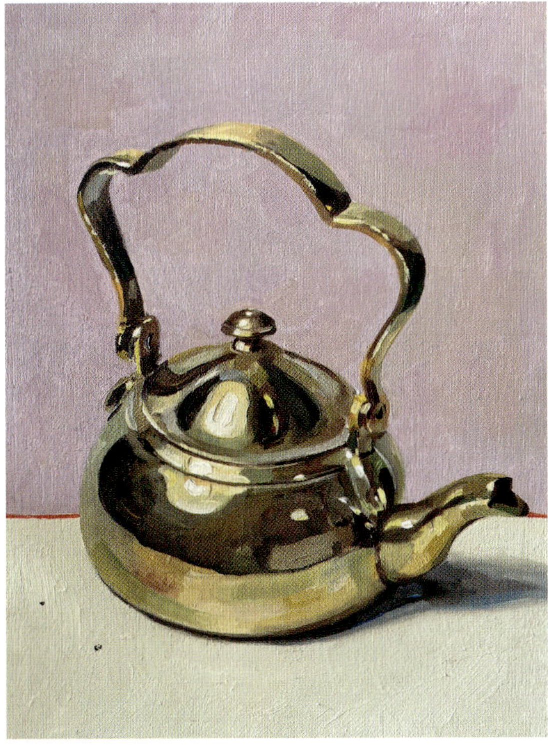

Try to identify the tonal range from lightest to darkest in this image, plotting the colours next to those on a greyscale.

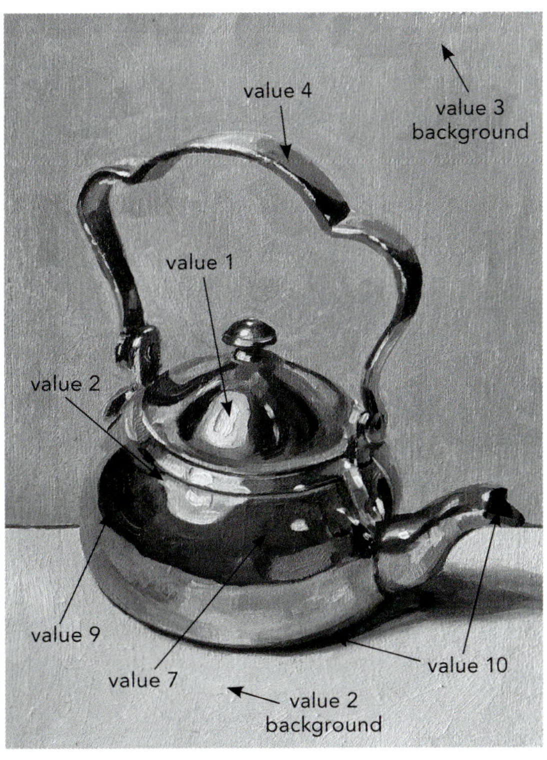

When viewed in black and white it is simpler to assess the tonal range, regardless of the different hues.

Colour mixing

It will take some time to master colour mixing but there are a few things to keep in mind to help you avoid wasting too much paint! Although there is nothing wrong with using paint straight out of a tube, more often than not the colour that comes out needs adjusting – it may need lightening, darkening, toning down. Being able to mix colours effectively means we can achieve a more accurate palette.

TINTS AND SHADES

Start by mixing different values, using white and black to create tints and shades (below) and combining paint colours to mix new colours (opposite). Make your own tints and shades chart with your preferred palette, varying the amounts of white or black to achieve a range of tones, then progress to mixing colours with each other to see where it takes you. Bear the following in mind as you experiment with colour:

- Be cautious when mixing colours with white paint; the results are not always as expected. The saturation of a colour can be zapped with only the tiniest amount of white.
- Adding black to any colour will darken its tone, but you run the risk of ending up with a muddied mess.
- To maintain vibrant colours, use analogous colours to lighten or darken your mixes. For example, to darken an orange mix, add red; to lighten it, add a little yellow.

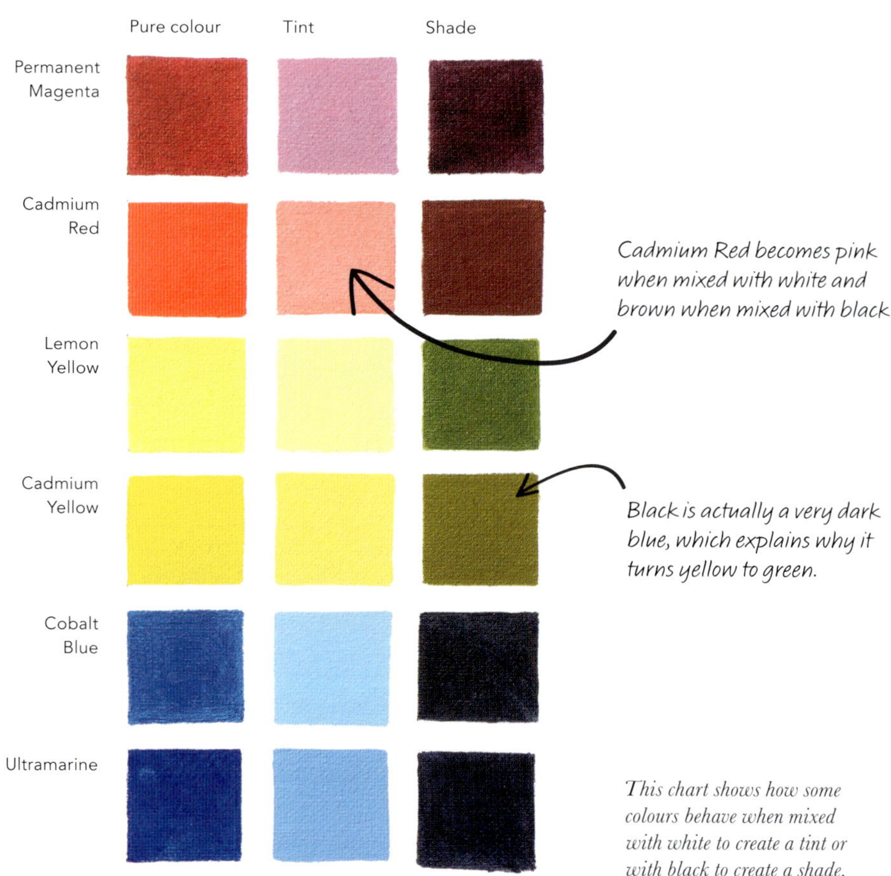

Cadmium Red becomes pink when mixed with white and brown when mixed with black.

Black is actually a very dark blue, which explains why it turns yellow to green.

This chart shows how some colours behave when mixed with white to create a tint or with black to create a shade.

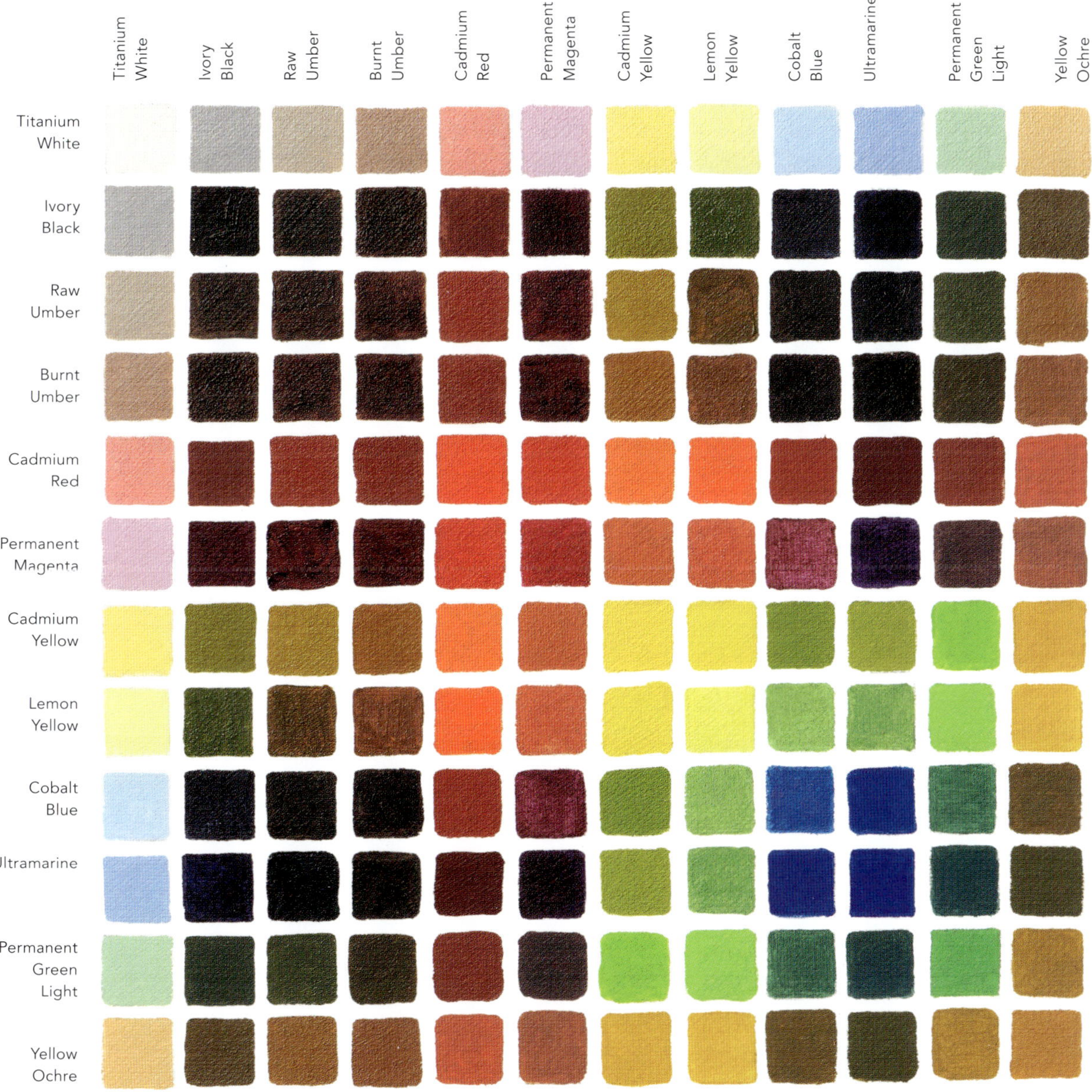

This colour chart is based on all 12 paint colours used for the projects in this book. It illustrates how each colour behaves when mixed with the other colours and gives you an idea of the range that you can achieve with this palette.

TIP

Different brands of oil paint can have different names to describe the same colour, which can be really confusing! To ensure you have the right colour, check the standard Pigment Number on the side of the tube (see page 11).

Arranging a palette

It's a good idea to have a well-organized palette when you're painting. Every artist will have their own personal way of arranging paints on their palettes – the important thing is to keep the arrangement consistent so that you can quickly and easily find the colour you need. Most often, the blobs of paint are placed around the edge, leaving the centre of the palette clear for mixing colours together. I like to organize my palette as pictured below.

Obviously, the choice of colours on your palette will depend on what you are painting – you won't necessarily need lots and lots of colours as this can just make things confusing. Before squeezing any paint onto my palette, I always take some time to study the set-up in front of me first, so that I can work out which colours I think I'll need.

I can generally mix the colours I need from my usual selection of paints shown on the palette below, but I sometimes add other colours depending on what I'm painting. For example, although it can be replicated by mixing Ultramarine and white, I always have a convenient tube of Kings Blue Deep to hand.

A STARTER PALETTE

A good starter palette should include at least one of each primary hue: a red, a blue and a yellow, so that you can mix some good secondary and tertiary colours (see page 36), plus white. I also recommend Raw or Burnt Umber because brown is hard to mix. Additional colours can be accumulated over time.

Working with a limited palette is great practice when starting to paint, as it forces you to figure out how far you can stretch each colour and which mixes you can (or can't!) achieve from only a few tubes of paint – all while simultaneously helping you produce a harmonious painting.

TIP

Keep white away from the darker colours as this lessens the chances of accidental cross contamination.

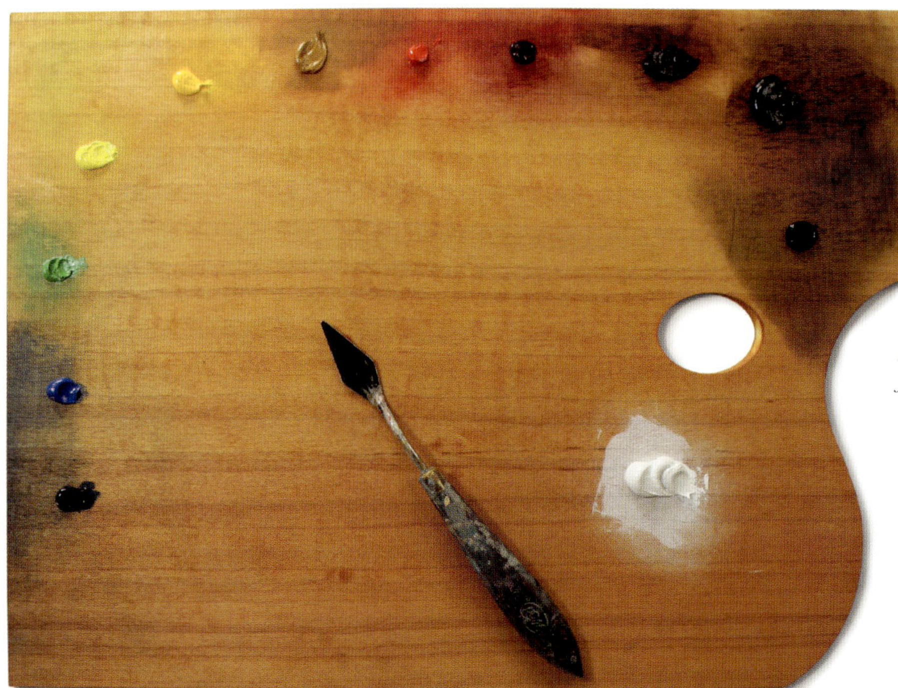

My palette layout, clockwise from lower left: Ultramarine, Cobalt Blue, Permanent Green Light, Lemon Yellow, Cadmium Yellow, Yellow Ochre, Cadmium Red, Permanent Magenta, Burnt Umber, Raw Umber, Ivory Black and Titanium White.

HOW TO MIX ON A PALETTE WITH A KNIFE

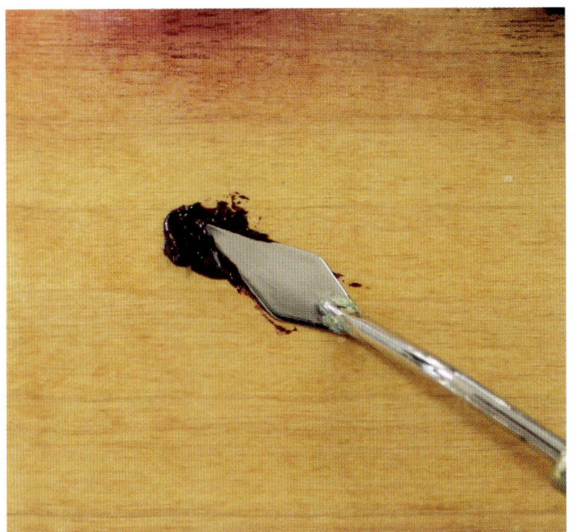

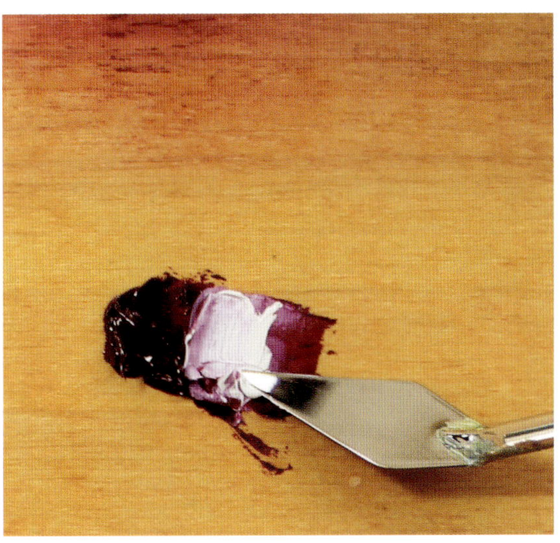

1. Using a palette knife, take some of your chosen colour, in this case Permanent Magenta, and place it nearby, by spreading the paint and squashing your knife flat onto the palette.

2. After wiping your palette knife, take a little of the second colour, in this case Titanium White (just a tiny amount is needed), and press it firmly into the first colour.

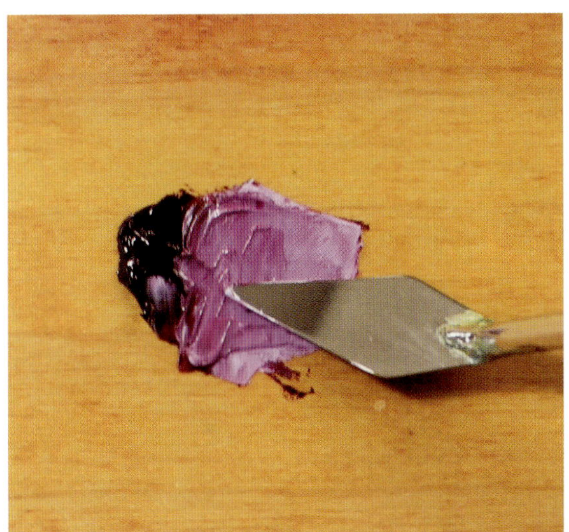

3. Next, begin scraping up all the paint and squashing it down flat onto the palette, mixing the two colours together in a back and forth motion. Repeat until smoothly blended, without streaks.

4. The same can be done using a paintbrush, using circular movements to blend the paints. The mix will not change colour as it dries. You can add mediums to adjust the consistency of the paint.

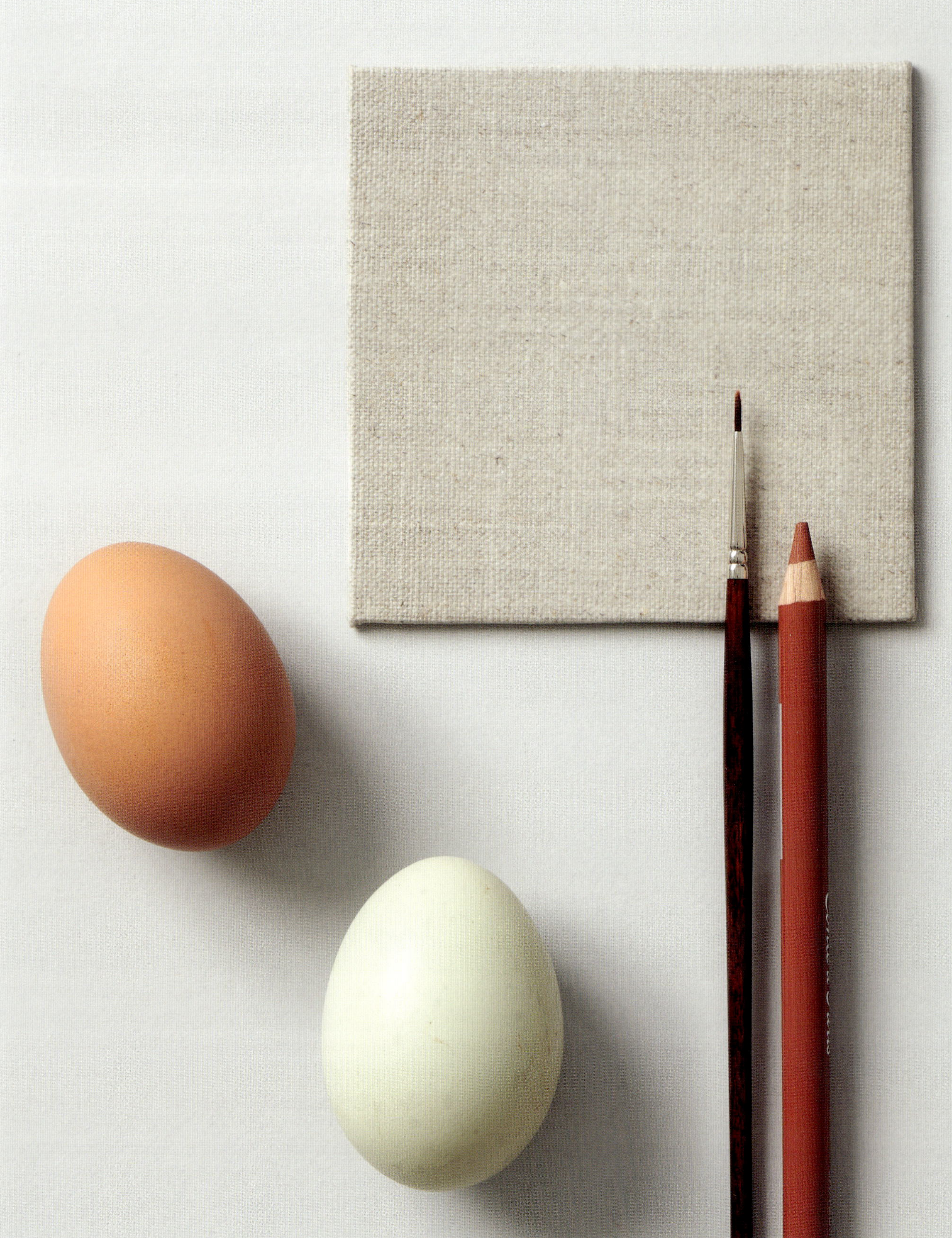

CHAPTER 4

SUBJECTS

You will be ready to start painting after reading this chapter, which will help in choosing a subject, how to set up a still life and how to observe local colour.

What should I paint?

A still-life set-up doesn't need to be complex in order for it to be beautiful and interesting. A painting with a single object can be just as powerful and evocative as a painting with a really complicated composition. With only one object to look at, the viewer is able to observe it more closely and with greater concentration. As for the artist, they may be drawn to an object simply because it has interesting textures or shapes. Perhaps it evokes strong memories or is metaphorical in meaning. Painting a still life can become quite an intense experience – you really get to know the object well after spending hours scrutinising it closely! We don't have to look far for something to paint either. Our homes are full of potential still-life subjects (you'll probably have a few things in your fridge that are crying out to be painted!) and if you're anything like me, then you'll find it hard to resist collecting interesting, beautiful or unusual little treasures from thrift shops and antique markets.

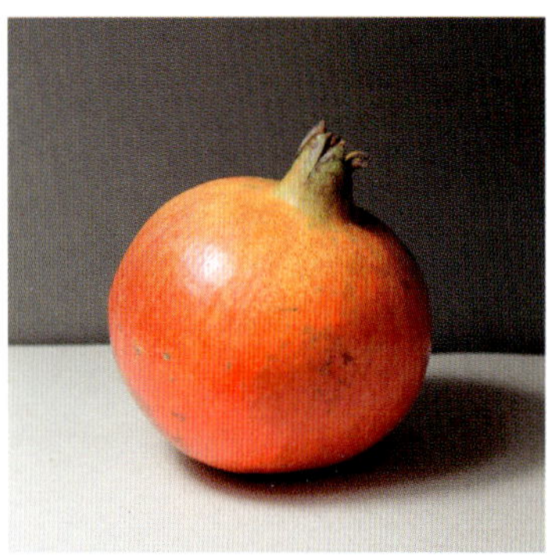

A pomegranate is a great subject for experimenting with blending, with shades ranging from deep red to yellow-green.

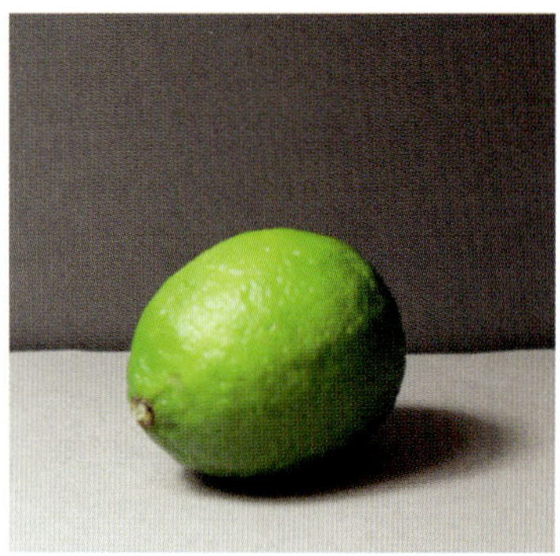

The gnarly texture of citrus fruit skin encourages you to take your time over the speckled highlights and shadow details.

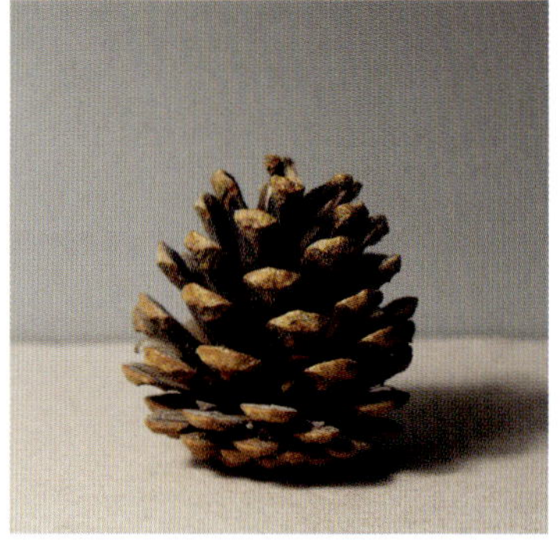

Pine cones are such fascinating organic forms, with deep shadows, rough textures and complex shapes providing plenty of inspiration for the oil painter.

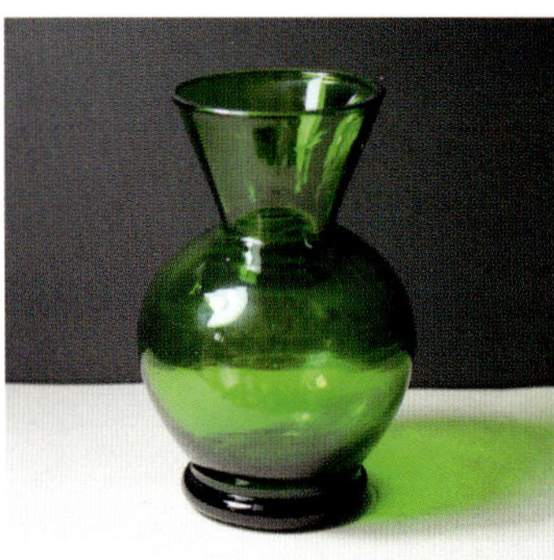

A coloured glass vase allows beautiful coloured shadows to be cast on surfaces, as well as plenty of highlights in different shades of green.

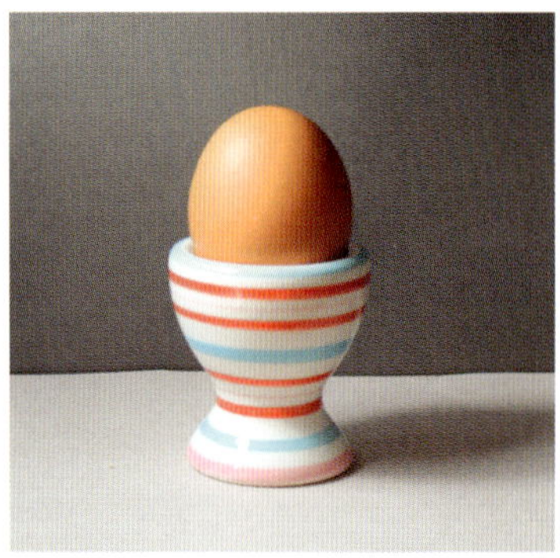

A balanced composition can be created from the most simple of everday objects. Here, symmetry and colour create a playful scene.

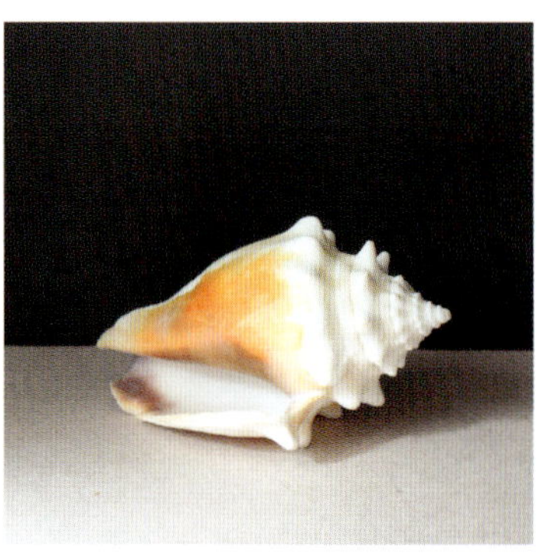

Shells are arresting organic forms, often with textures, colours and shapes that are unique to them.

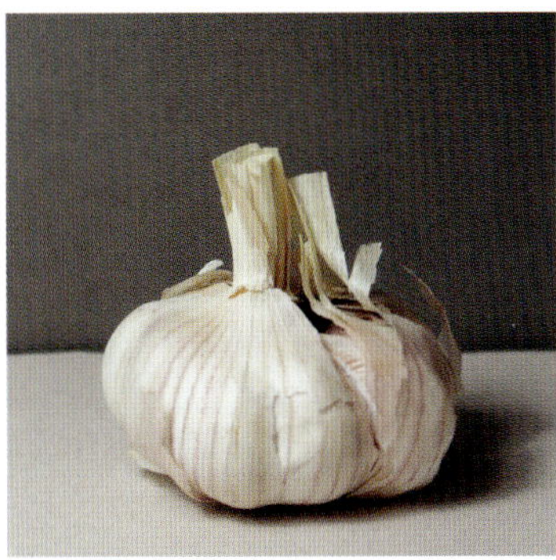

Painting a bulb of garlic is very meditative; the outer layers are very delicate and papery, while the pink, grey and purple lines are very subtle.

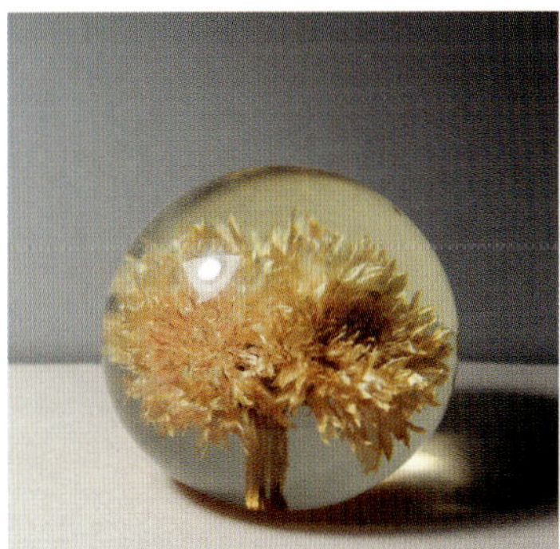

The object captured in this paperweight is a dried flower, but viewed through the distorting glass, it would make for a valuable exercise in close observation.

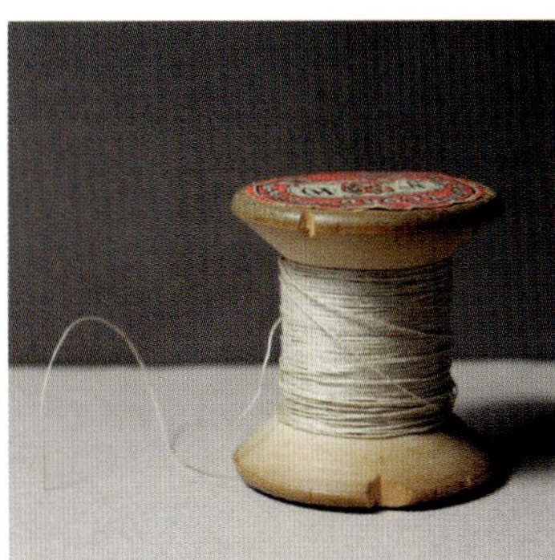

A deceptively simple object, the thread unspooling from the wooden bobbin would be a great way to practise steadiness of hand when painting with a very thin brush.

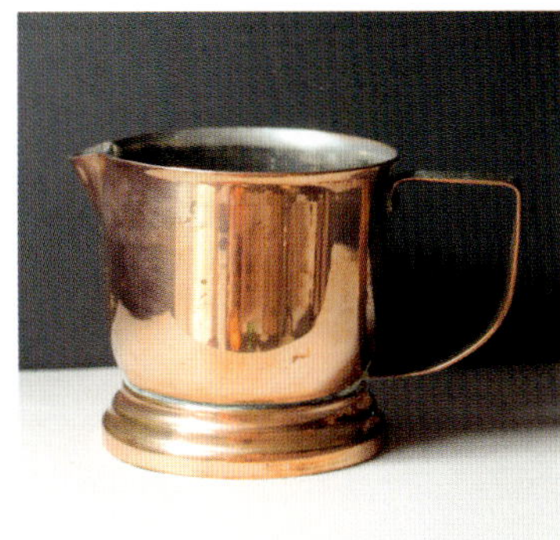

An antique copper jug with age spots, scratches and plenty of reflections presents a unique challenge. Try this one when you are feeling more confident.

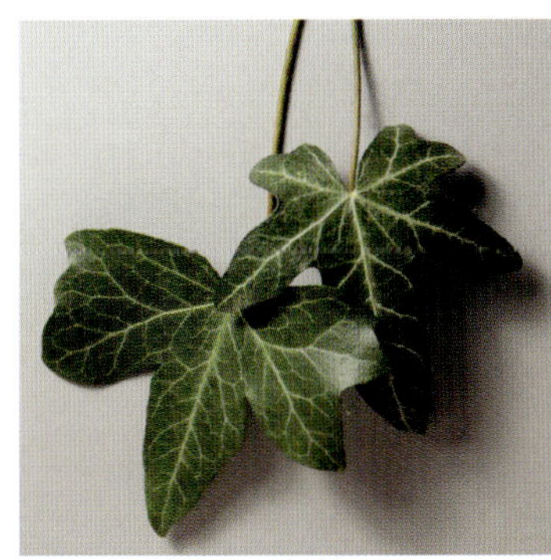

Two leaves taped to the back of a shadow box hang suspended for a *trompe l'oeil* effect. The veins in the leaves are interesting to paint and the smooth surface rewards patience.

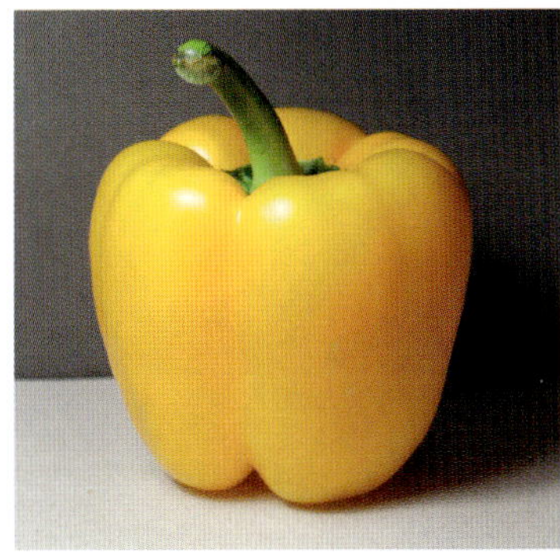

The smooth, almost wax-like texture of a sweet pepper is a challenge, as all your paint strokes have to be smooth and gentle to capture the glossy surface.

TAKE A CLOSER LOOK – 45 MORE EVERYDAY OBJECTS TO PAINT

1. Apricot
2. Artichoke
3. Avocado
4. Brussels sprout
5. China ornament
6. Cookie
7. Crystal shot glass
8. Draped fabric
9. Dried flower
10. Dried leaf *trompe l'oeil*
11. Feather *trompe l'oeil*
12. Fig
13. Ginger root
14. Grapes
15. Green apple
16. Green pepper
17. Jar of jam
18. Lipstick
19. Marble paperweight
20. Mushroom
21. Nectarine
22. Old key
23. Perfume bottle
24. Physalis
25. Pink apple
26. Plum
27. Pomegranate
28. Radish
29. Reading glasses
30. Red pear
31. Rose bud
32. Scotch bonnet pepper
33. Sea glass
34. Silver spoon
35. Small antique book
36. Small bowl
37. Small candle
38. Small toy car
39. Billiards/pool ball
40. Stoneware mug
41. Strawberry
42. Tennis ball
43. Tomato
44. Tulip
45. Walnut in shell

Creating a still-life set-up

Using a shadow box for your still-life set-up gives you lots of control over the setting, from background colours to light and shadow. Using a lamp allows you to control the lighting, meaning you're not at the sun's mercy and working against the clock. A shadow box will also block out any distracting things that are in the background and enable you to focus more easily on the object that you are observing.

On the page overleaf you can see how different background colours and changing the position of your light can dramatically alter the appearance and mood of your set-up.

MAKING YOUR OWN SHADOW BOX

YOU WILL NEED

  Thick cardboard or foamboard
  Ruler
  Utility knife
  Tape

1. Start by cutting your cardboard or foamboard into one 42cm (16½in.) square piece and three 21 x 42cm (8¼ x 16½in.) pieces. Two of the narrower pieces will be the 'wings' on either side of the shadow box, and the remaining piece will be the loose 'lid' of the shadow box.

2. Take one of the wings and tape it to the side of the larger back panel, leaving a slight gap of approximately 5mm (¼in.). Do the same with the other wing. These act like hinges, which means the box can be folded flat and stored away when you're not using it.

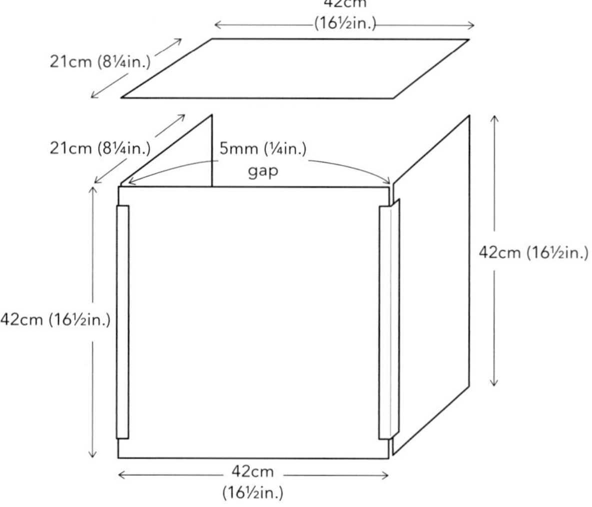

Arranging your set-up: To adjust the level of the objects that you are painting, place them on some old wooden boxes (like the ones shown opposite). You can remove the boxes to paint larger objects. The boxes and the back of the shadow box can be covered with coloured paper or fabric to create different moods (see page 50).

Lighting and shadows: Temperature, angle and strength of lighting will produce very different effects. Here, the lamp is on the left and a piece of loose foamboard is placed on the top and can be moved around to manipulate the amount of light/shadow in the box. Artists' daylight lamps can be expensive but you can also use a regular desk lamp. The light bulbs you choose will affect the temperature in your shadow box. The direction of your light source will create both shadows and highlights. A shadow can have several characteristics, picking up local colours and varying in intensity. It is helpful to be able to identify these elements and adjust your lighting to get the best effects. See the labels in the photograph opposite to identify the occlusion shadow (darkest shadow) **(6)**, penumbra (the outer edge of a cast shadow) **(7)** and the highlight (the lightest and brightest tone – where the light hits) **(8)**.

Where to position your shadow box: Your shadow box should be at eye level, placed on a table and no closer than a few feet away. Try to position the easel so that the canvas/board is at a similar level to your still-life set-up. This allows you to glance backwards and forwards easily between your painting and the object that you are observing. If you are right-handed, set the shadow box to the left of your easel and vice versa.

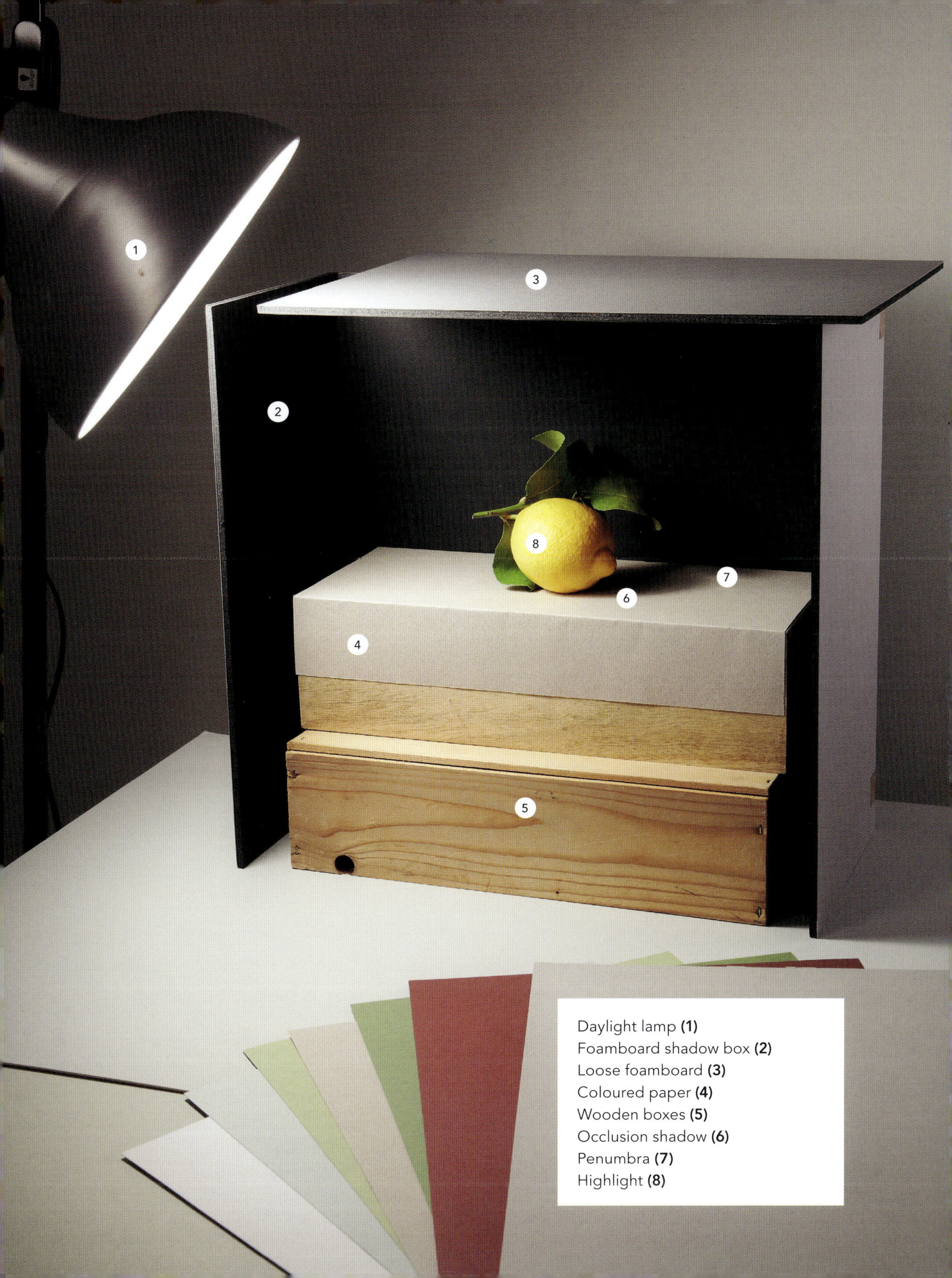

Daylight lamp (1)
Foamboard shadow box (2)
Loose foamboard (3)
Coloured paper (4)
Wooden boxes (5)
Occlusion shadow (6)
Penumbra (7)
Highlight (8)

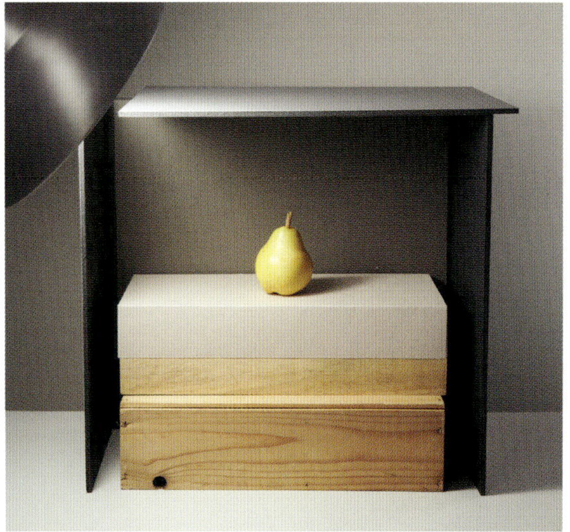

NATURAL

I have used neutral grey paper for the background and foreground. This gives the set-up a very soft, natural feel.

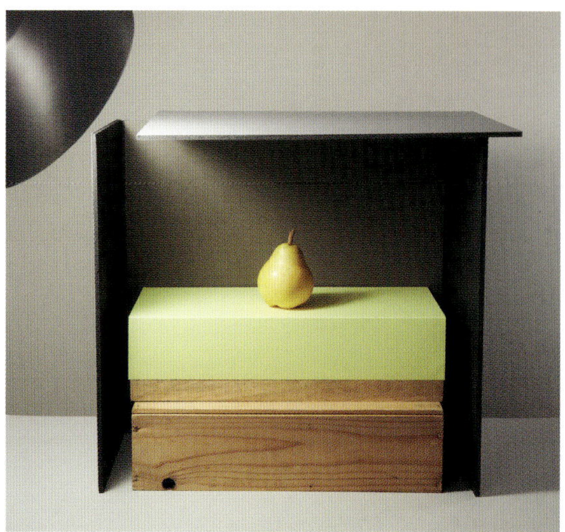

CONTRASTING

In this set-up, the pear stands out against the dark background and the vibrant green paper creates a nice contrast. Note the lovely cast shadow, too.

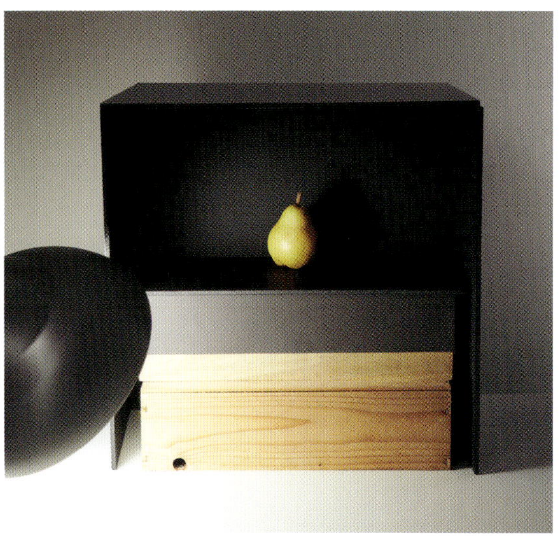

DRAMATIC

In this set-up, the pear emerges from the black background. I have lowered the lamp, so that the pear is lit up from below, creating wonderful form and cast shadows.

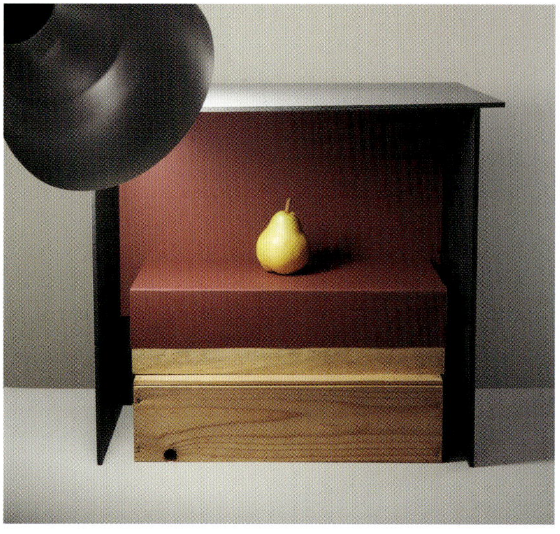

COMPLEMENTARY

This set-up exploits the effects that complementary colours have on each other (see page 37). The warmth of the plum-coloured paper allows the cooler, greeny-yellow pear to stand out brightly.

Local colour

When painting an object in a still life, one of the first things to look for is its 'local colour' – the object's overall colour as you actually see it (and not what you think the object's colour is).

Take a look at the first image of the pear (below left) – our brains might tell us that we are looking at a green pear but, in reality, it is more yellow in colour. Working out the local colour of an object requires close observation and the ability to trust what our eyes are seeing.

To figure out the pear's local colour, I ignored the shadowy part of the pear and the highlight. I found the local colour somewhere in between these areas, judging it to be the pear's overall colour.

When observing an object, we need to take into account the temperature of the lighting and how it affects the appearance of an object's colour. Is the lighting warm or cool? My perception of the pear's local colour varies greatly depending on the temperature of the lighting I use.

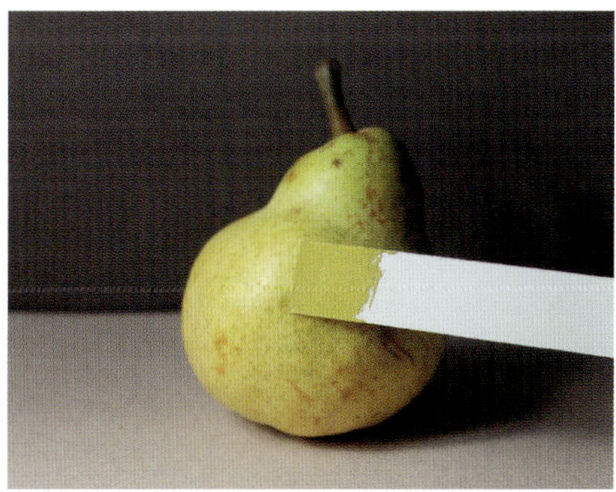

The local colour can be found somewhere between the shadows and highlights.

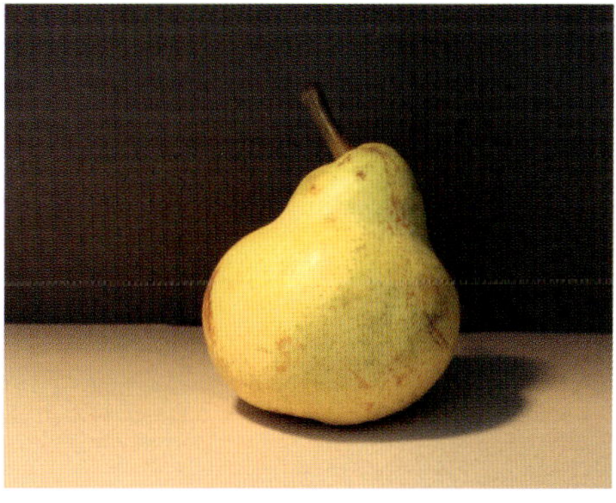

Note how the pear's local colour differs when warm lighting is used.

MAKING COLOUR STRIPS

Cut a piece of card into a rectangle measuring approximately 10 x 30cm (4 x 12in.). Then cut the rectangle into 15 strips, each measuring about 2cm (¾in.) wide. Using a utility brush, apply a coat of gesso approximately 2cm (¾in.) deep along the top of each strip, including the edges (don't cover the whole strip in gesso). Let the strips dry overnight.

Paint the gessoed end of your strip with your local colour mix (or any other colour mix that you wish to keep a record of). Use the rest of the strip to write down which colours you used and any other information (including the lighting conditions) that might be useful next time you paint that object.

In my sketchbook, I have used strips to keep a record of the local colour mix and the core shadow colour mix of the egg I painted, which means painting it again will be easy.

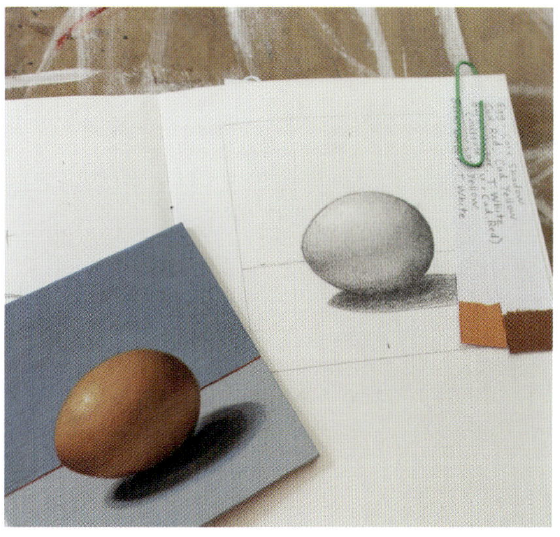

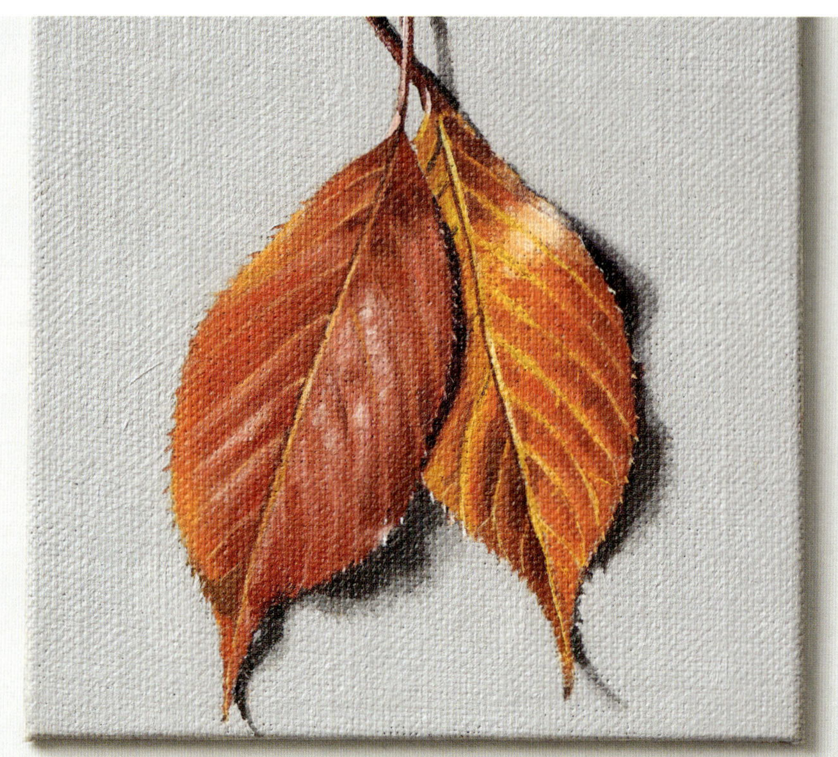

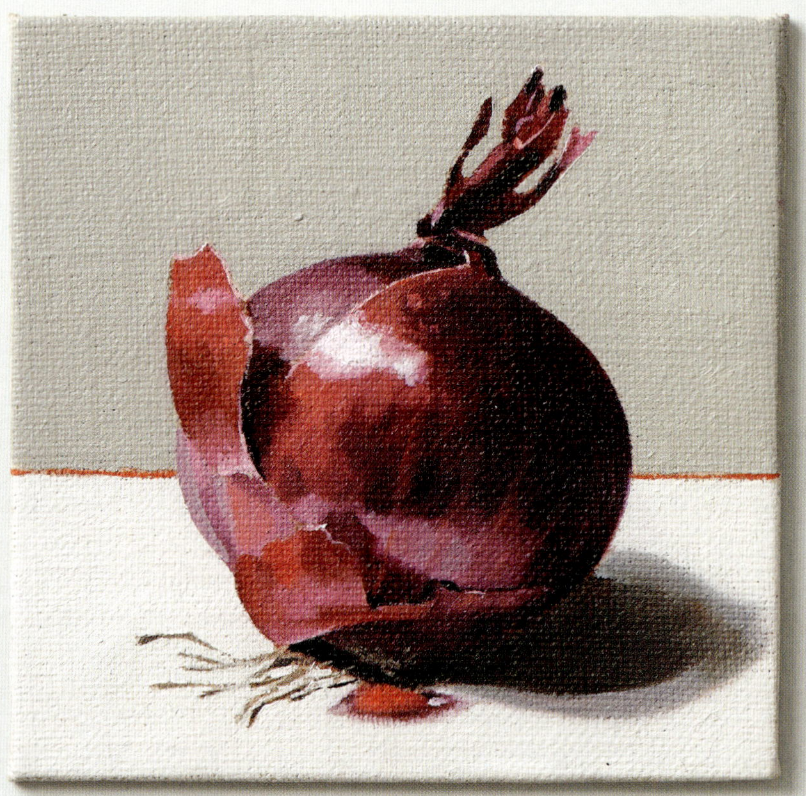

PROJECTS

Let's begin! The projects are organized so you can progress steadily as you go along, but feel free to dip in and out if you have more confidence.

EGG

Why an egg? It may seem like a rather simple thing to paint; however, it is much trickier than it first appears! Painting spherical or oval objects well usually takes a bit of practice. This project will help you learn how to look really carefully at light and shadow as well as subtle changes in value; key things that will give your egg its form and make it look three dimensional.

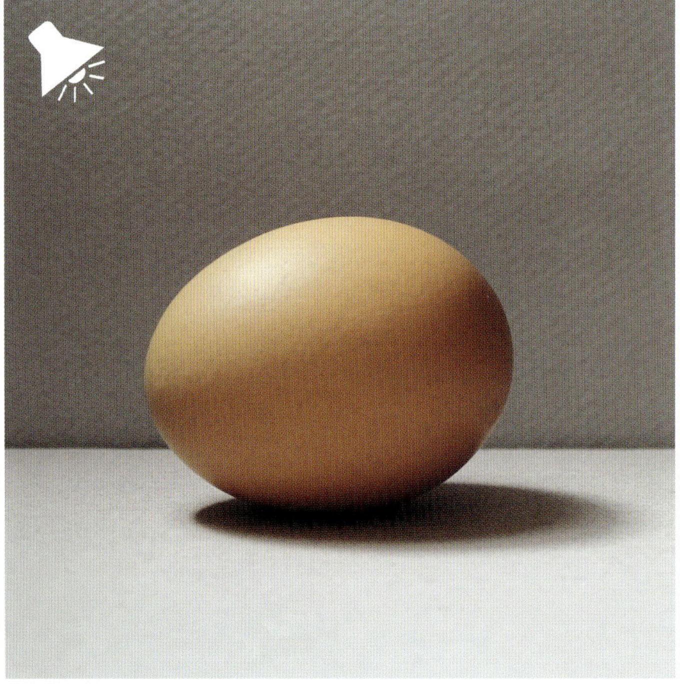

PAINT COLOURS

- Ivory Black
- Cadmium Red
- Titanium White
- Kings Blue Deep
- Cobalt Blue
- Burnt Umber
- Cadmium Yellow

TOOLS AND MATERIALS

- Linen board (10 x 10cm/ 4 x 4in.), primed with transparent gesso (see page 12)
- Graphite or pastel pencil
- Putty eraser
- Ruler
- Fixative spray
- Transparent primer
- Primed white card strips, for colour matching (optional)
- Small palette knife, for mixing
- Rag or paper towel
- Size 0 round brush
- Size 0 filbert brush
- ¼in. flat brush
- Soft brush, for blending and softening

SET-UP

I have placed my egg side-on in the shadow box, with my light source coming from the left. The background set-up was neutral in colour, which I found less distracting, and this then enabled me to focus clearly on the egg (artistic license later allowed me to alter the background colour of my painting to a shade of blue!).

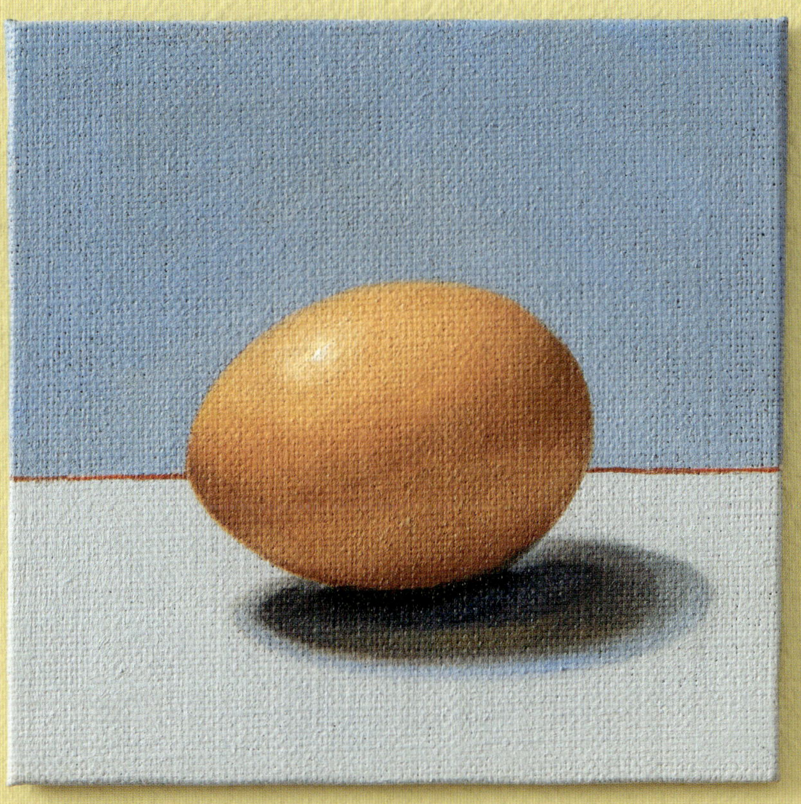

To help with the
composition I always
draw the horizon line, and
I like to leave this visible
in my final painting, but
you don't have to!

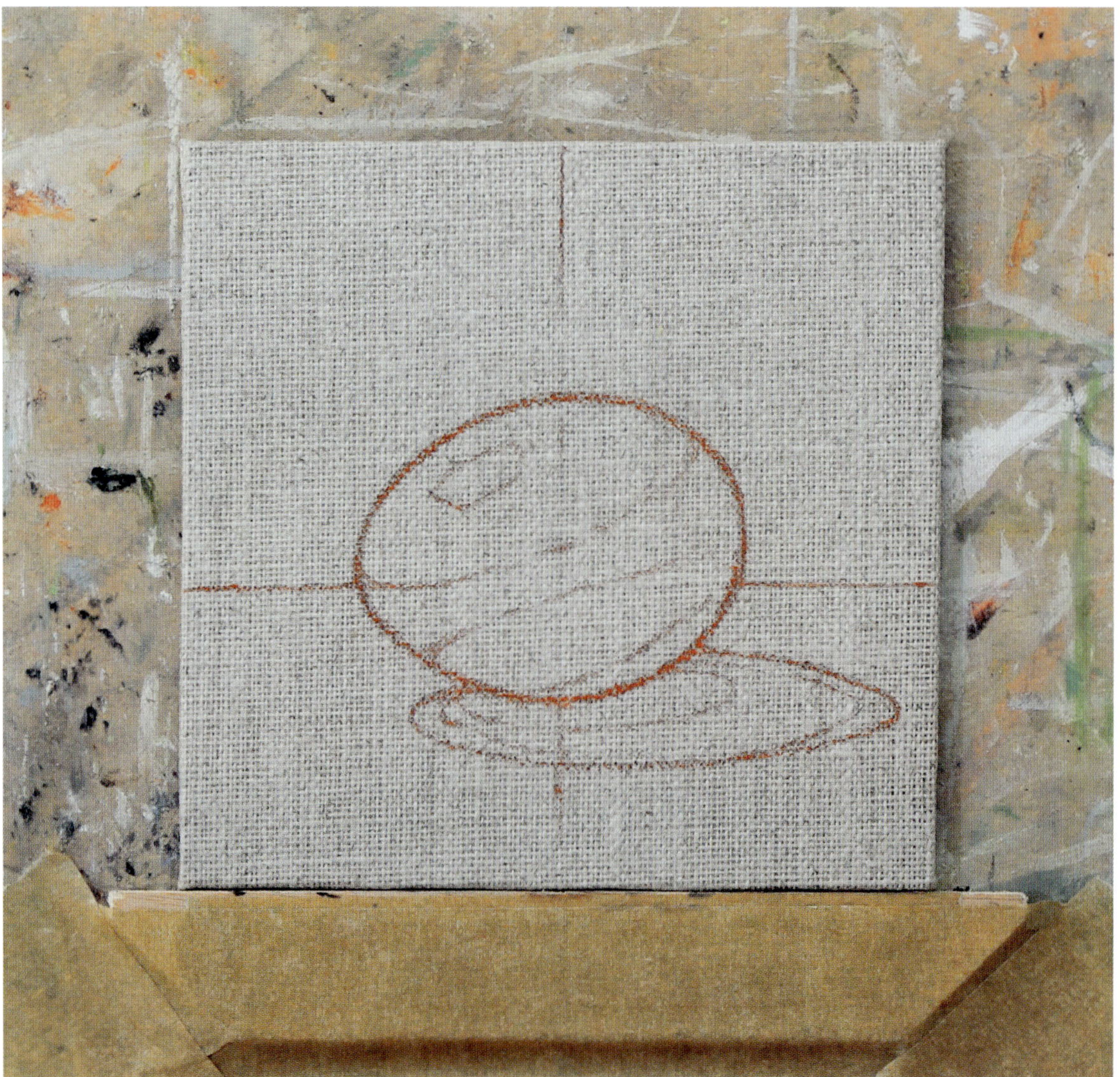

1. UNDERDRAWING

Add lightly drawn lines to divide the canvas into sections to help you place the egg centrally. Draw a vertical line halfway across the board and a horizontal line roughly a third up from the base. Add the oval egg shape, marking where the highlight and shadows fall on both the egg and the surface. Fix your drawing and, if you wish, apply a coat of transparent primer. Allow to dry.

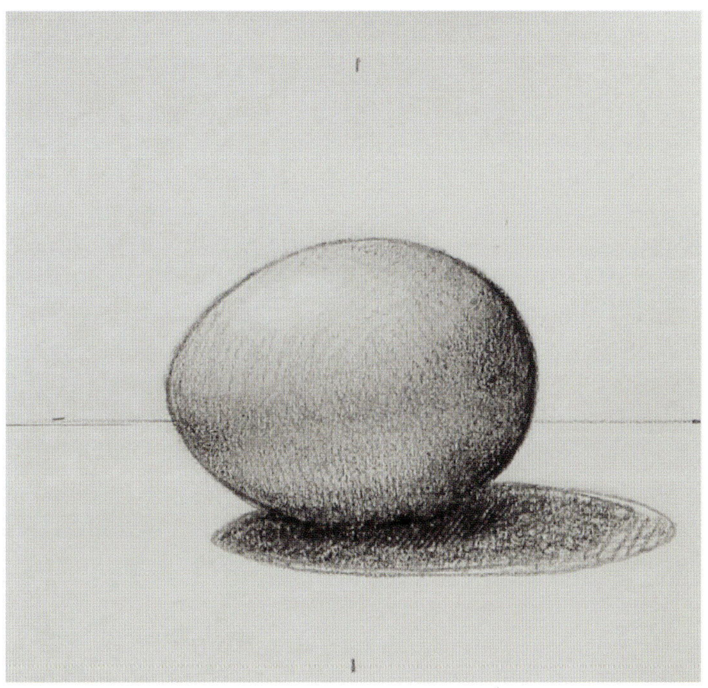

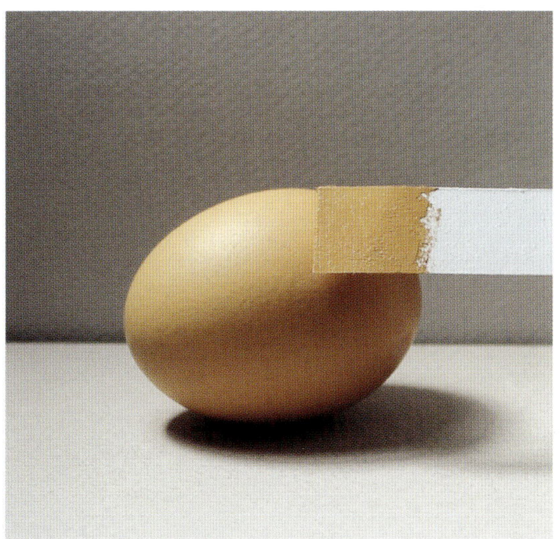

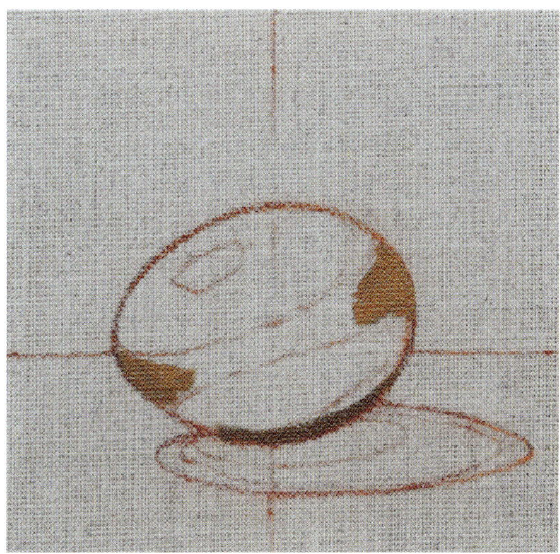

2. LOCAL COLOUR

Start by establishing the colour for the egg. Mix a small amount of Burnt Umber, Cadmium Red and Cadmium Yellow on your palette, adding a little Titanium White to lighten the mix, until you achieve a matching tone. As we work through this project, you will lighten and darken this local mix to create all the shades you need for your egg.

3. DARK AREAS

Put a small amount of the local colour to one side with a palette knife and add a little more Burnt Umber and Cadmium Red to the mix a bit at a time, to darken it. With a Size 0 round brush, begin to paint the core shadow and the darkest areas of the egg, starting at the outer edges.

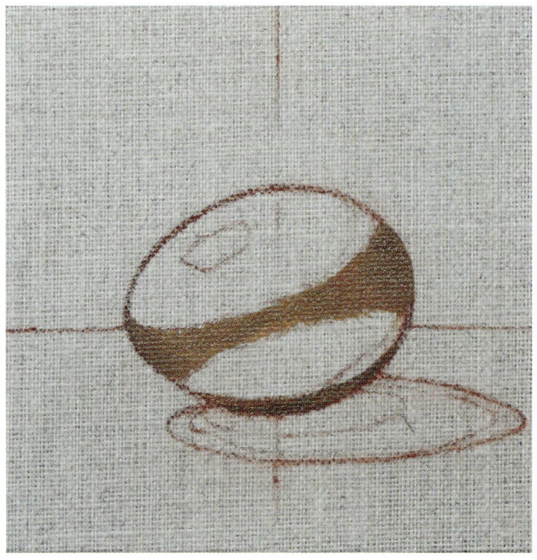 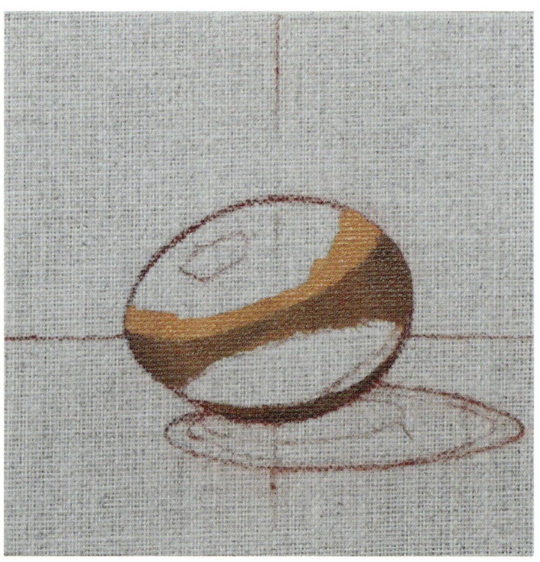

4. CORE SHADOW

I noticed that the core shadow lightens slightly as it curves around the egg, so I added a tiny amount of Titanium White to my paint mix and began to work my way across the middle. Look out for mirrored shapes to help you achieve the ovoid form.

5. MID-TONE

I then brought my attention to the area above the core shadow where the egg begins to lighten and transition into the mid-tones. With a Size 0 filbert brush, apply some of the original local colour mix from step 1, following the shape of the core shadow.

6. BLENDING

Wipe the brush and begin to very gently and slowly blend the hard edge at the terminator line, between the dark and light areas, being very careful not to overdo it and lose the distinction between the core shadow and the mid-tone.

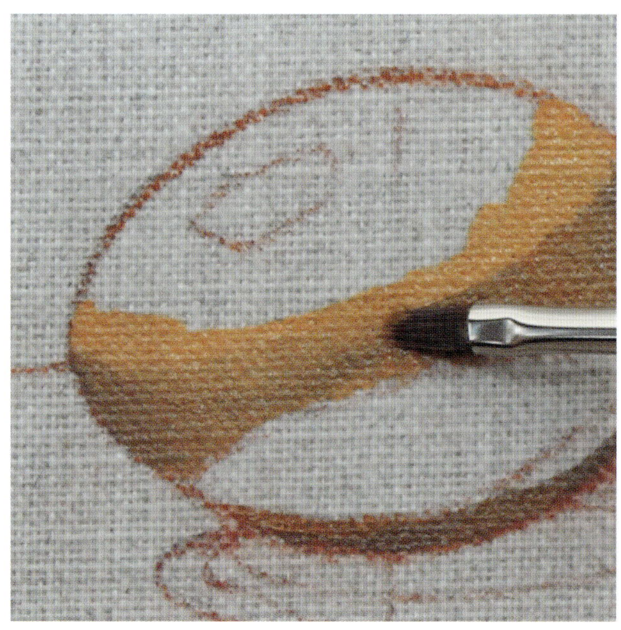

7. LIGHT-FACING PLANE

Now focus on the light-facing plane of the egg where the mid-tone begins to gradually lighten – ignore the brightest highlight for now. With the Size 0 round brush, work in sections or bands of colour that follow the shape of the egg (as in step 5). Each band lightens slightly as it gets closer to the light source, so adjust the local colour mix by adding very small amounts of Titanium White and Cadmium Yellow.

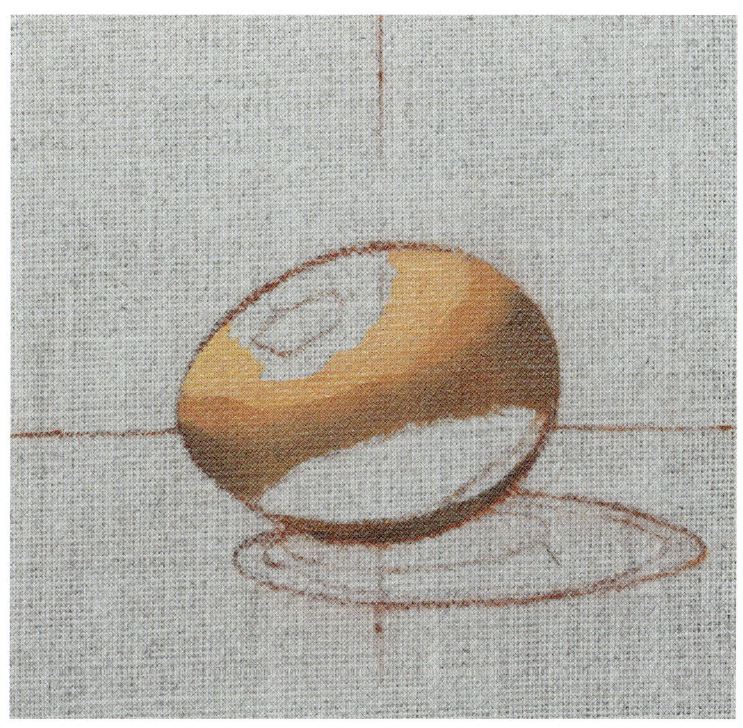

8. SOFTEN TRANSITIONS

Once I had finished blocking in the light-facing plane, I gently blended between each band using a clean, dry filbert brush, again being very careful not to overdo it. Don't worry, it doesn't need to look perfect at this point.

TIP

Take a moment to step away from your work – I find that giving my eyes and brain a rest for 5 minutes can really help, especially if I'm painting something particularly tricky! When I return to my work after a short break, I can usually see things more clearly and I will notice any adjustments that I need to make.

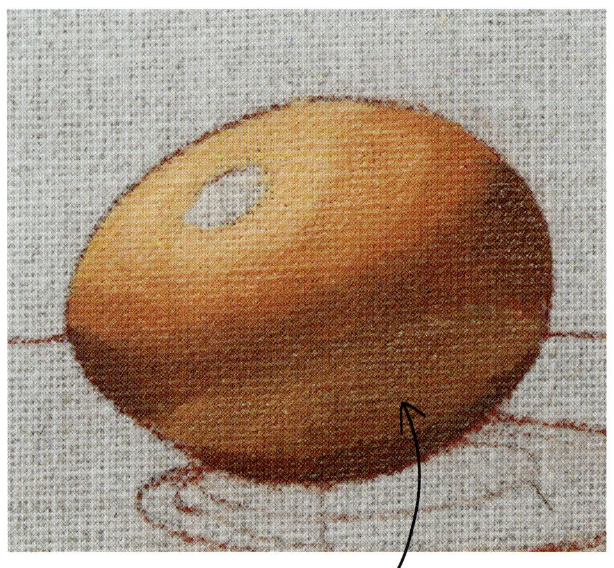

The form shadow is made up of subtle variations in shade where reflected light hits the surface.

9. FORM SHADOW

Now turn your attention to the shadowy underside of the egg. Observe the 'form shadow', below the core shadow. Notice that the form shadow is not one solid block of colour but is made up of subtle variations in shade. This is caused by light bouncing back from the surface upon which the egg rests – this is 'reflected light'. The form shadow is not as dark as the core shadow but looks slighter darker than the local colour – try squinting to help see these differences. Mix a slightly darker version of the local colour by adding a little Burnt Umber and apply it with the Size 0 filbert brush.

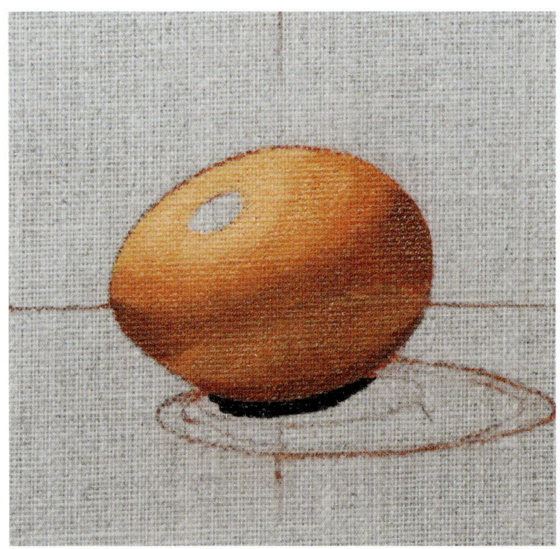

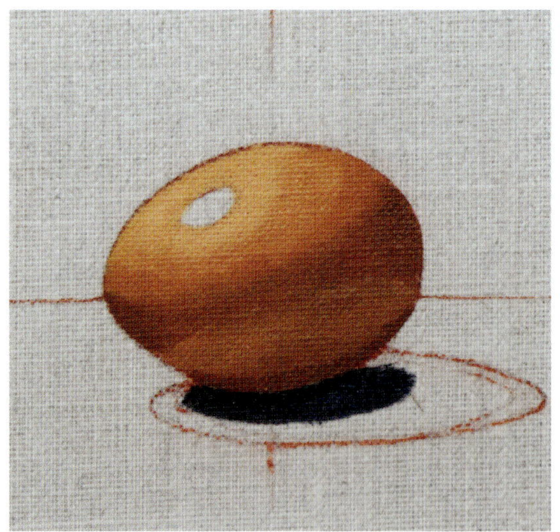

10. OCCLUSION SHADOW

Switch to a Size 0 round brush and paint the darkest part of the cast shadow – the occlusion shadow – using a mix of the Ivory Black and the Burnt Umber.

11. CAST SHADOW

Now add the darkest areas of the cast shadow, using a mix of Cobalt Blue with Burnt Umber. Block in with a Size 0 filbert brush, taking care to follow the ovoid shape.

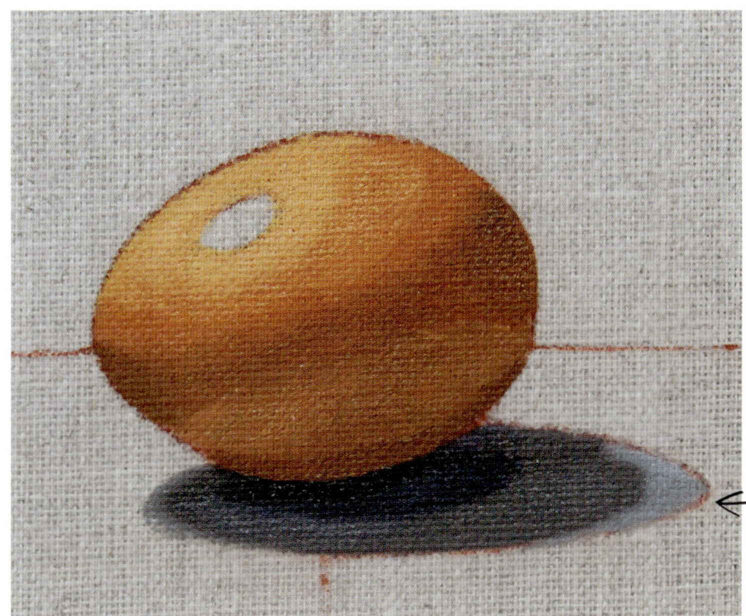

12. PENUMBRA

Add some Kings Blue Deep to the mix from step 11 and continue to block in the cast shadow, which you will notice lightens towards the edges (the penumbra).

13. SUBTLE DETAILS

I noticed that the egg is slightly reflected in the cast shadow so, with a clean, dry brush, I added the tiniest amount of local colour to this area and blended it in so that it is very subtle. I also noticed that there are two little areas of light creeping into the cast shadow on the left and right.

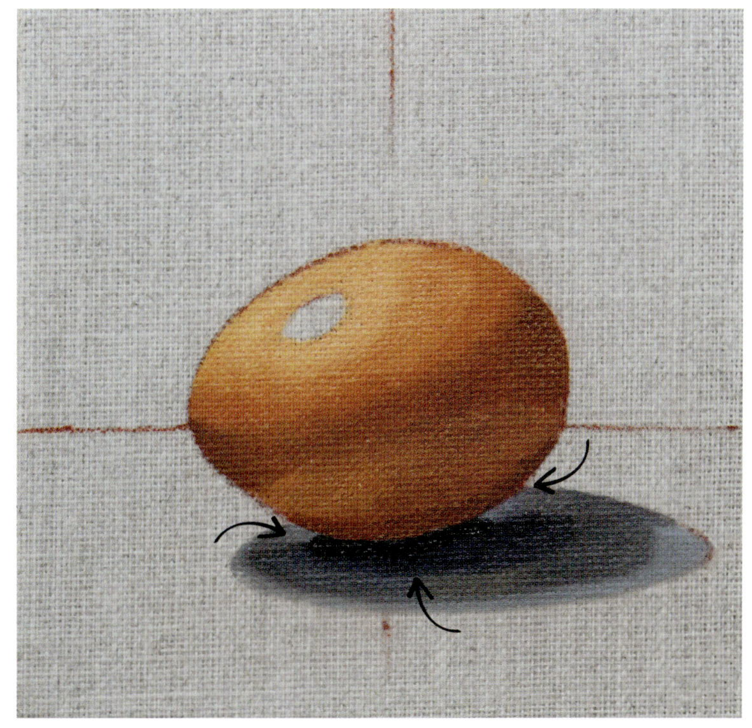

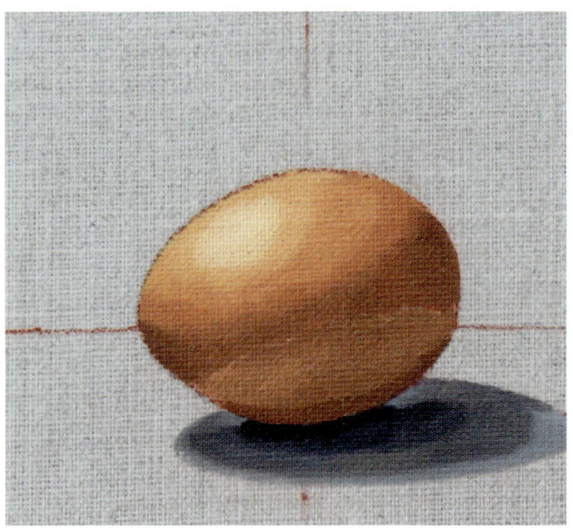 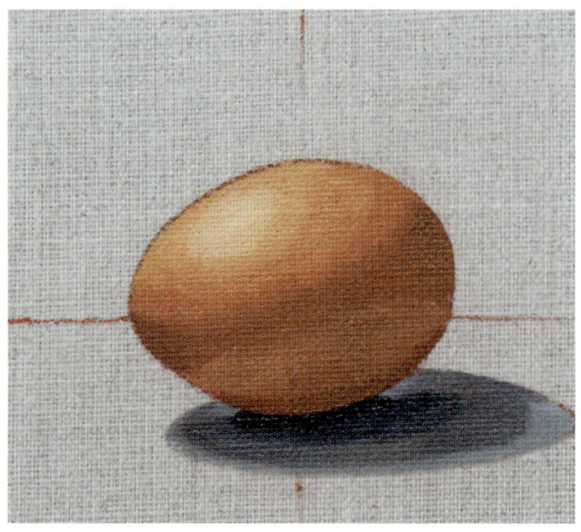

14. HIGHLIGHT

Return to the egg and look at the highlight. Mix some local colour with Titanium White and paint in the area with the Size 0 round brush.

15. ADDITIONAL BLENDING

Now that we have blocked in our egg, we can check any areas that may need blending and softening; for example, the area between the occlusion shadow and the base of the egg. Remember to do any blending with a soft, clean, dry brush – and don't overdo it!

16. SPARKLY BITS

Looking more closely at the highlight, I noticed some little spots of bright light at its centre and so, having wiped my round brush, I applied some tiny spots of pure Titanium White to add sparkle.

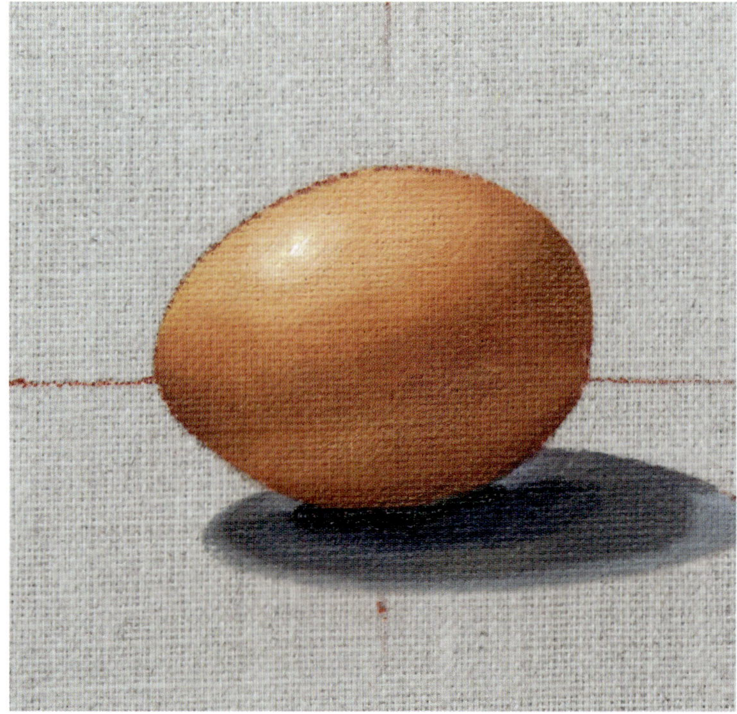

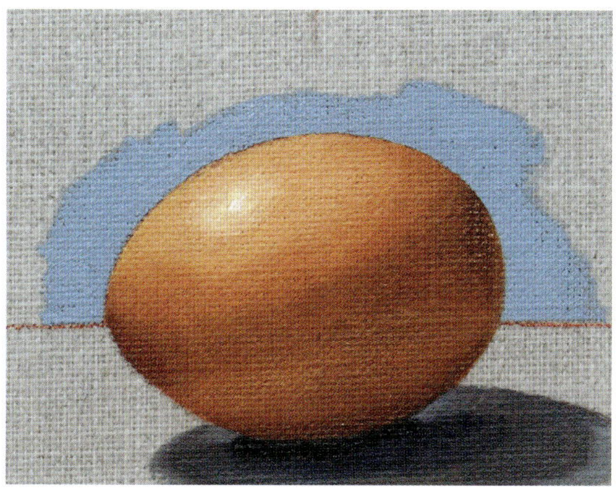

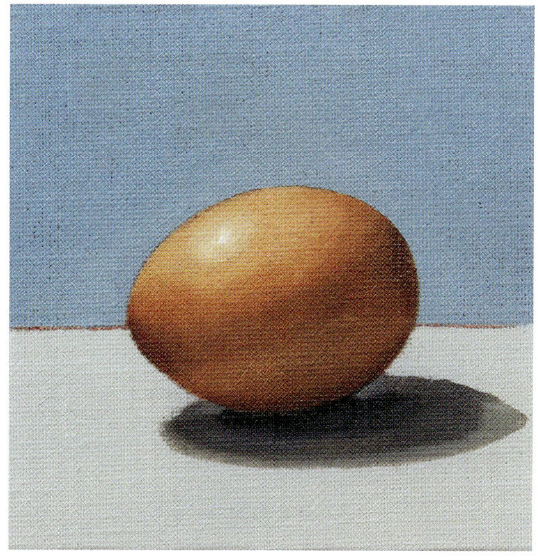

17. BACKGROUND

I wanted the egg to 'pop' so I decided to make my background more colourful than the neutral tones in my actual set-up. Using up the remaining mix from steps 11 and 12, add some extra Kings Blue Deep and Titanium White to create a blue that complements the egg. Carefully paint around the edge of the egg with the Size 0 filbert, using a wider brush to block in the remainder.

18. FOREGROUND

Use the same mix as in step 17, adding more Titanium White to create a lighter blue for the foreground. Apply the paint as before, starting with the outline and then blocking in.

19. FINAL ADJUSTMENTS

Using a clean, dry Size 0 filbert, gently blend the edges of the cast shadow and the foreground. Similarly, soften the hard edge between the egg and the background, being really careful not to smudge the painting and spoil the egg!

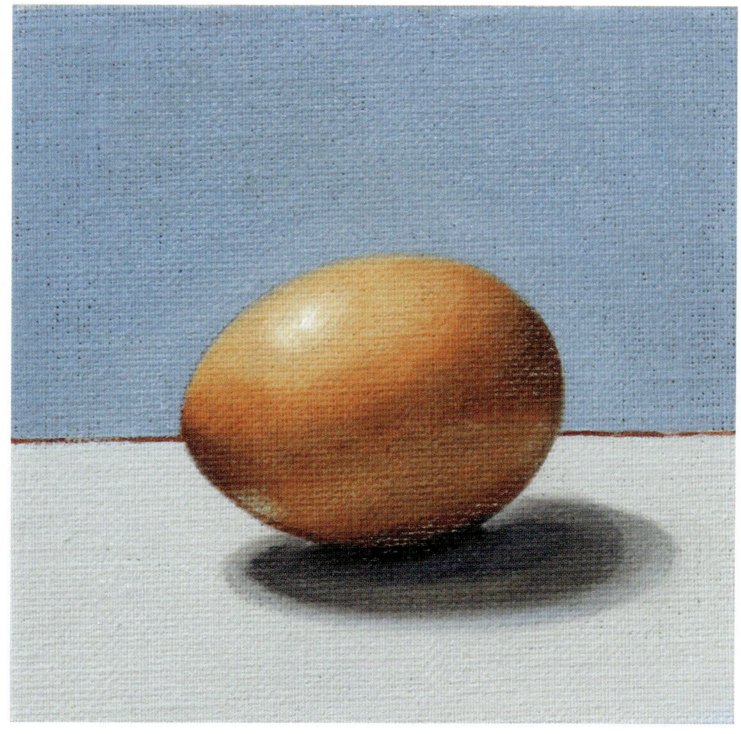

ESPRESSO CUP

For this project, I chose to paint a white espresso cup which, at first glance, seems rather plain and simple. However, as you look closer, you will see that it demonstrates beautiful and subtle transitions in value. By keeping the set-up monochrome without any distracting colours, you will learn how to observe and mix simple values from light to dark with a limited palette.

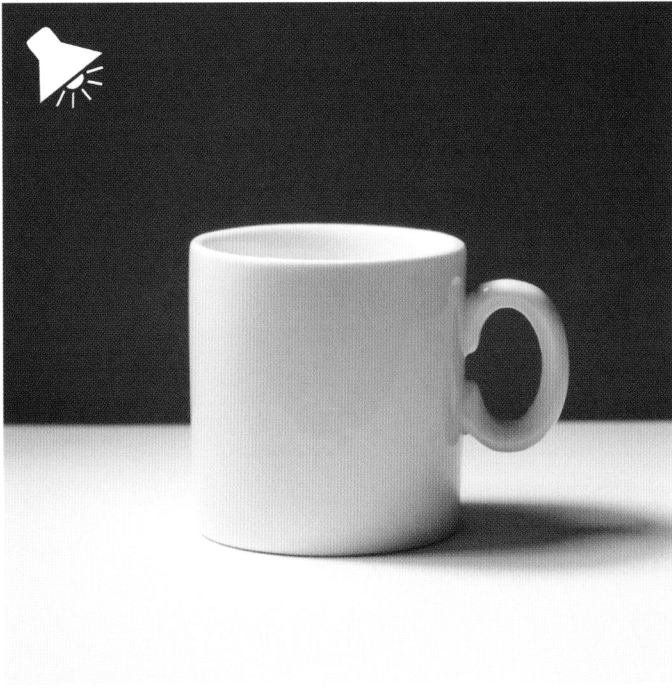

PAINT COLOURS

- ■ Raw Umber
- ■ Ivory Black
- ☐ Titanium White

TOOLS AND MATERIALS

- ☐ Linen board (10 x 10cm/ 4 x 4in.), primed with transparent gesso (see page 12)
- ☐ Graphite or pastel pencil
- ☐ Putty eraser
- ☐ Ruler
- ☐ Fixative spray
- ☐ Transparent primer
- ☐ Primed white card strips, for colour matching (optional)
- ☐ Small palette knife, for mixing
- ☐ Diluent (optional)
- ☐ Rag or paper towel
- ☐ Size 0 round brush
- ☐ Size 0 filbert brush
- ☐ Soft brush, for blending and softening

SET-UP

I placed the espresso cup on some white card and chose a dark grey card for the background, keeping to a monochrome scheme. Adjust the lighting to create contrasting shadows – here, the light on the left throws a dark cast shadow and an even darker occlusion shadow. The light is also reflecting off the lip of the cup, giving bright highlights; we have already established some of our lightest and darkest values!

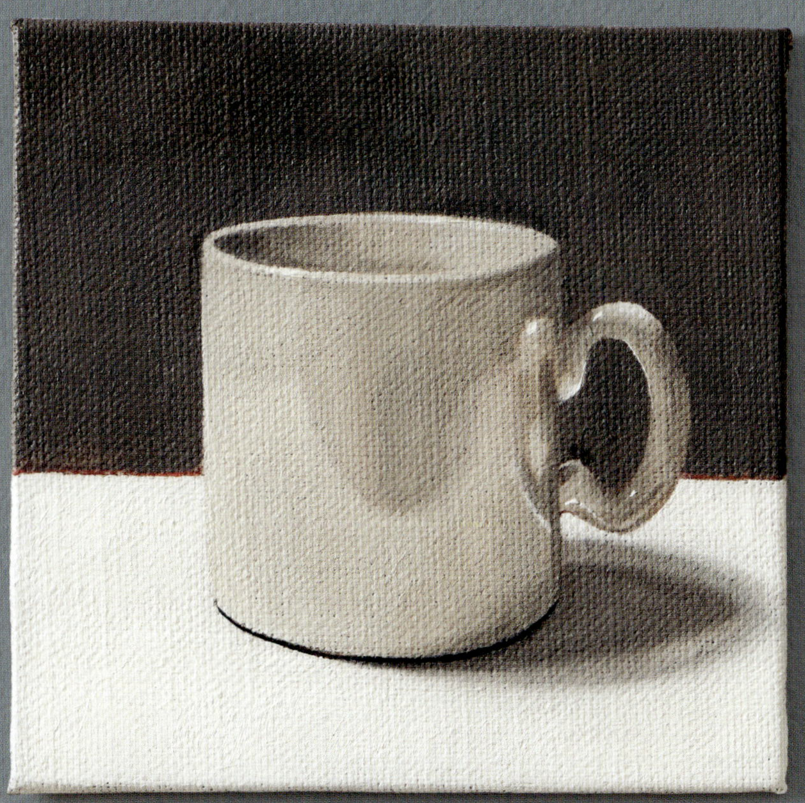

Remember to save
your purest white paint
for the most sparkly
highlights – the areas of
lightest value.

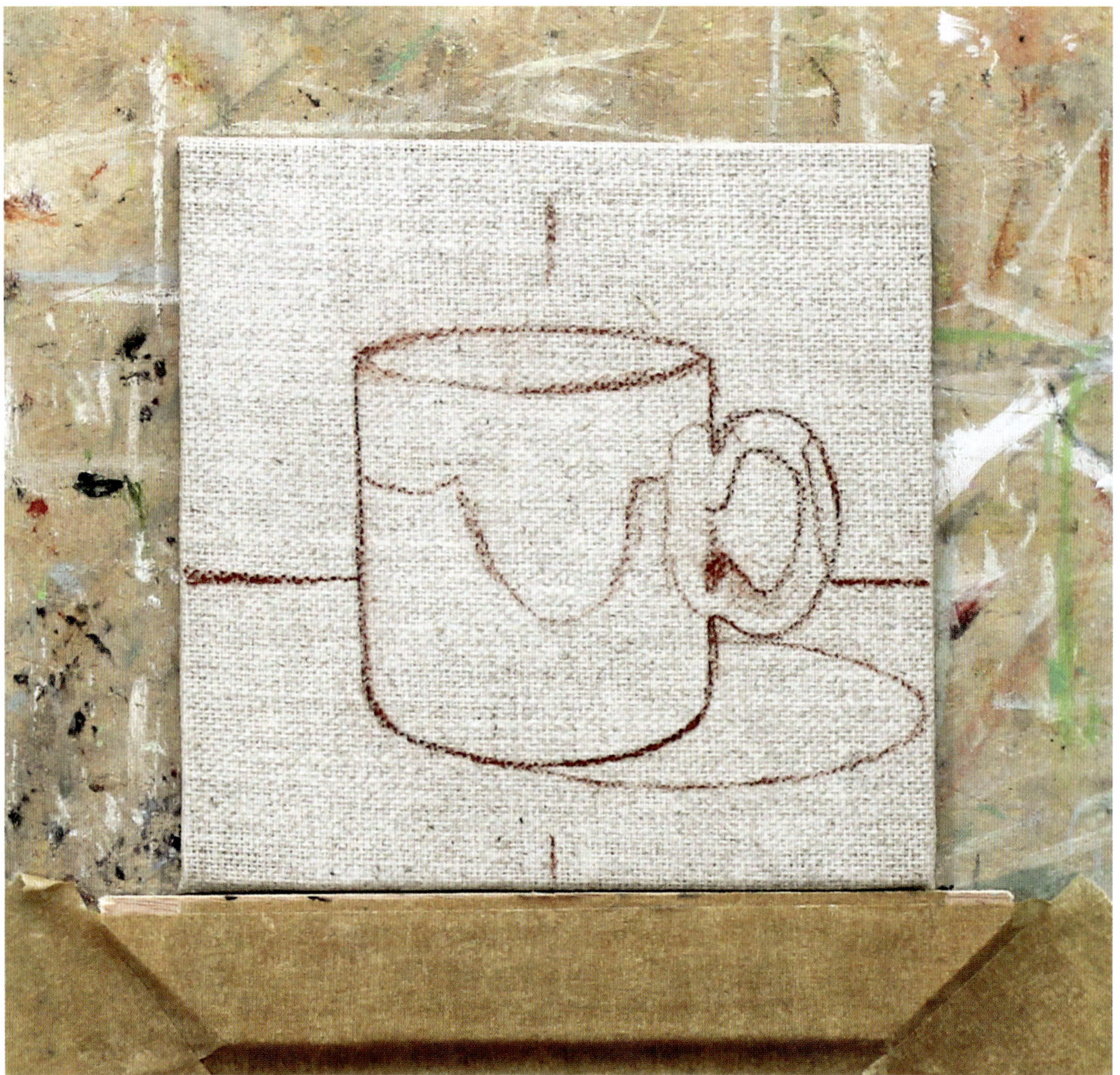

1. UNDERDRAWING

Draw out the espresso cup centred on the canvas, using a pastel
or graphite pencil. Translate the monochrome colours into areas of
light, mid- and dark tones, marking the shadows and the reflections
on the cup and the surface. Fix your drawing and, if you wish, apply
a coat of transparent primer. Allow to dry.

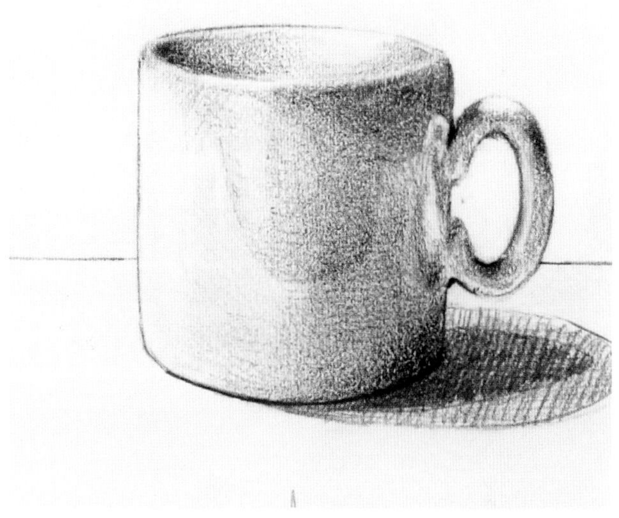

2. LOCAL COLOUR

The first step is to work out the local colour of the espresso cup. Take some Titanium White and mix it with a small amount of Raw Umber, then compare the mix against the cup, using either your palette knife or a strip of prepared paper.

TIP

Remember to mix your paints on your palette using your palette knife (not your brush), as this is the best way to achieve smooth, streak-free mixes.

3. TONAL VALUES

Once you have a close match to the local colour, you can begin to mix a range of values using only Raw Umber, Titanium White and a very limited amount of Ivory Black. To evaluate the tones, I squinted my eyes while looking at the cup as this helped me to see the whole picture in shapes of light and shade, and I was less distracted by little details. Create four base mixes from light to dark to match what you see.

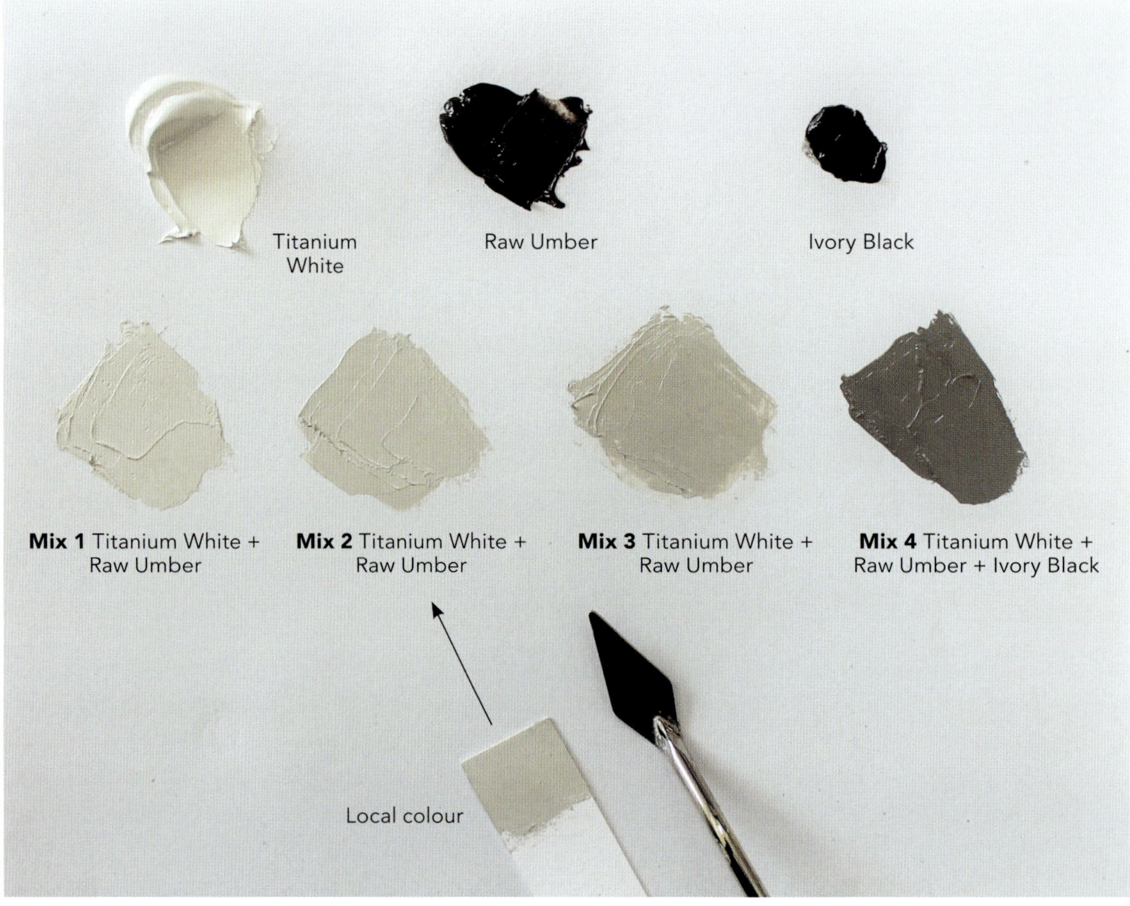

4. DARKEST VALUES

I started with the darkest value that I could see, which is the occlusion shadow. Apply a thin line of Ivory Black using a Size 0 round brush. Next, look for the darkest values on the cup itself, which are around the handle and, still using the round brush, apply some Mix 4.

Thin the Ivory Black with a tiny amount of diluent, to help with the flow of the paint.

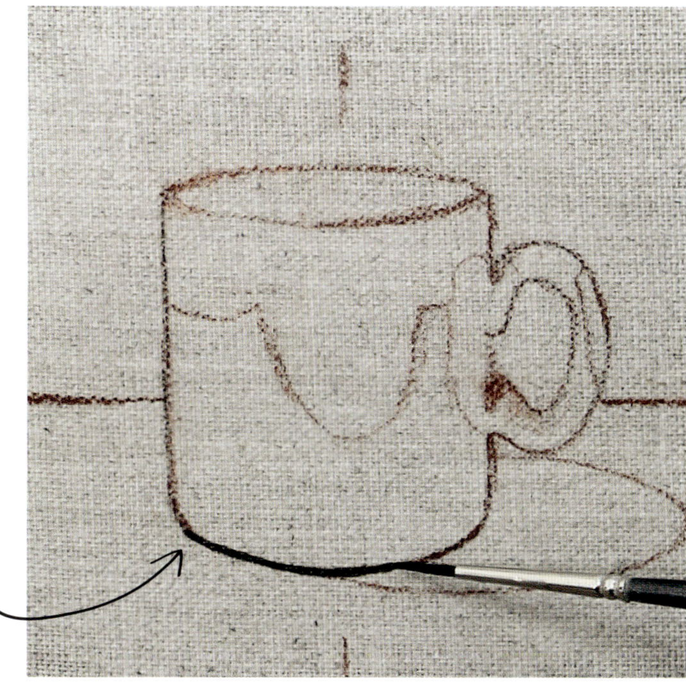

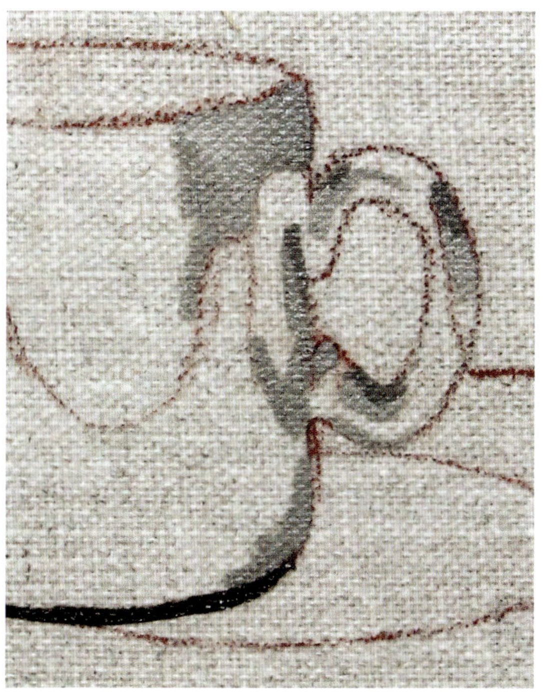

5. SHADOW SIDE

Squinting at the right side of the cup, where it is in shadow, I noticed that the value is slightly lighter than the darkest areas on the handle. Block in these shadow shapes using some of Mix 3 and the round brush.

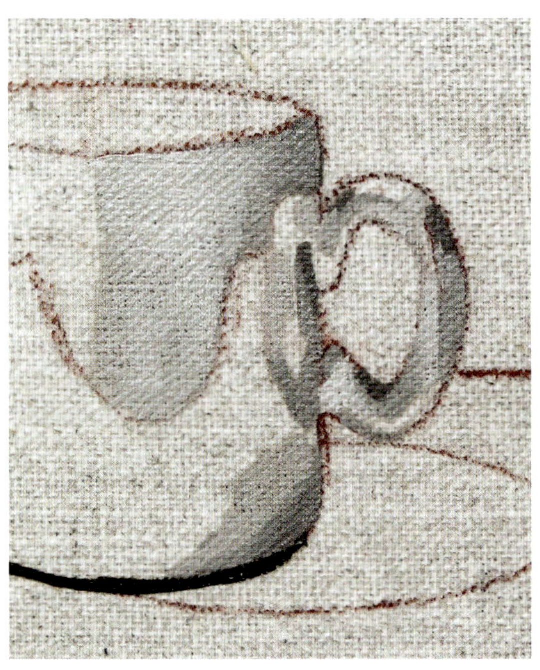

6. BLOCK IN

By observing the cup through half-closed eyes, you can constantly compare all the tonal values and work out where they sit on a dark to light scale. Switching to a Size 0 filbert brush, continue to block in the handle and the shadowy side of the cup, using the lighter Mix 3.

7. GAUGING VALUES

Now turn your attention to the left side of the cup and begin to compare the values. Looking at the cup's ellipse, I noticed that the left corner is in shadow and has the same value as the darkest areas on the handle (step 4), so I painted a little Mix 4 in this area, with the round brush.

Directly below this dark area of the ellipse, still on the left side of the cup, the values are much lighter. This part of the cup has the most light hitting it and is therefore the lightest plane. Switch to the filbert brush and apply Mix 2. Where the white surface is reflected in the cup, I decided I need a lighter value still – wipe the brush and, using Mix 1, continue to paint down the left side.

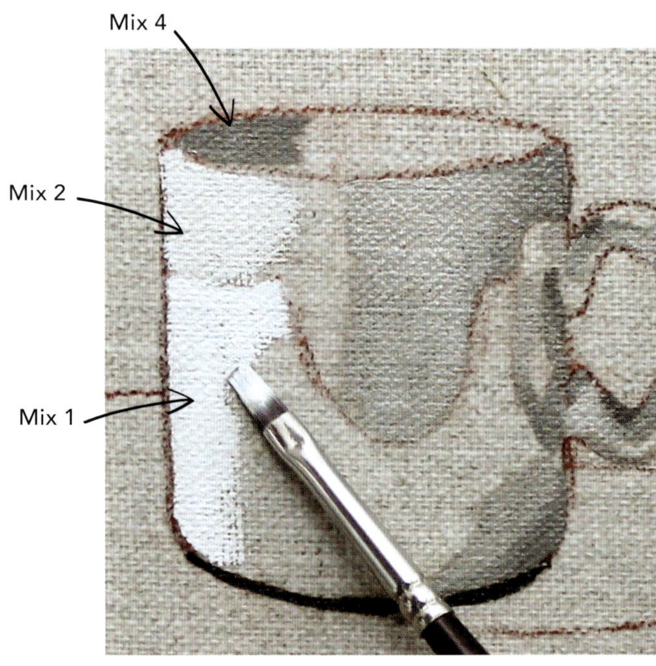

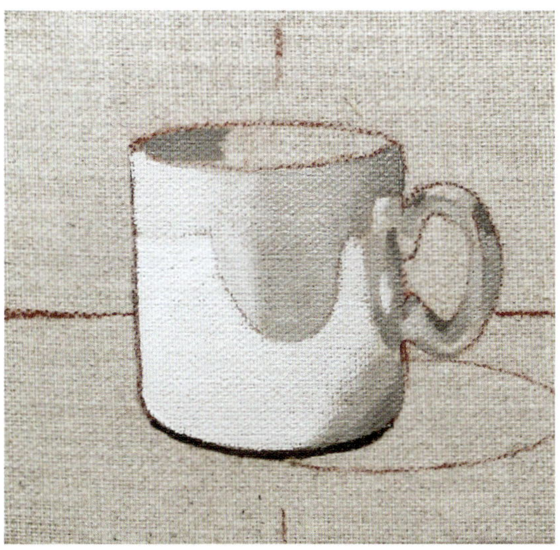

8. REFLECTED SURFACE

Continue to block in the lightest value of the reflected surface with Mix 1, using the filbert brush. Wipe the brush and roughly block in the last area just above using Mix 2, which is a slightly darker value.

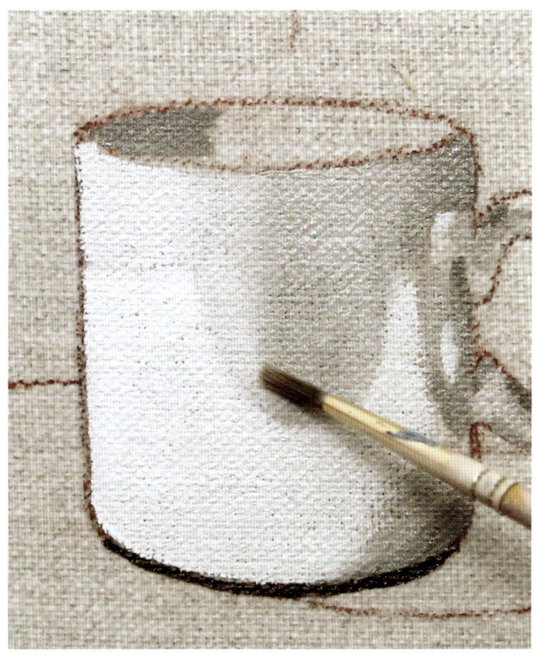

9. BLEND

Using a soft, dry and clean brush, carefully begin to blend the tones together where they meet, softening any hard edges between the values.

10. INNER EDGE

If you look closely (and squint), the inside of the cup can be split into three values. The darkest value is on the left, which we already painted back in step 7 using Mix 4. The middle area is lighter, so use the round brush to paint in some Mix 3. For the lightest value on the right, use Mix 2. Blend the three values carefully, using a soft, clean brush. Remember not to overdo the blending – we want to blend just enough to achieve a gradual transition in tone (and not a muddy mess!).

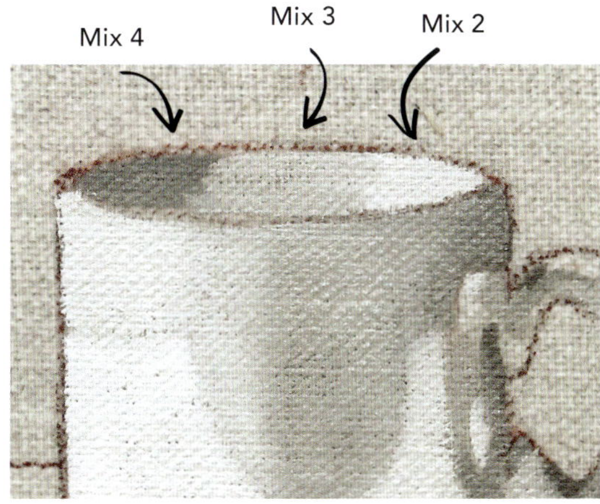

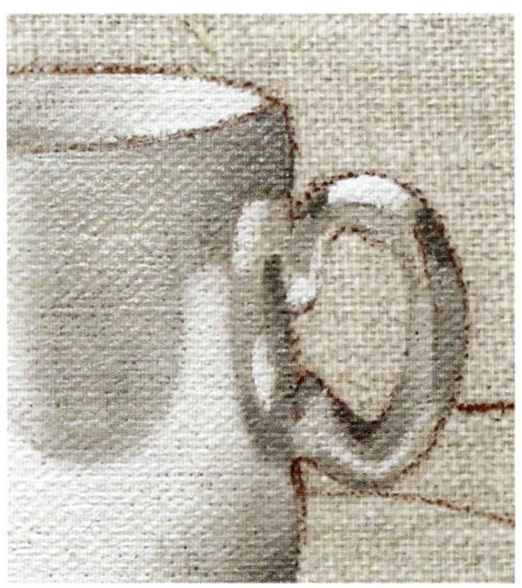

11. HANDLE

Still using Mix 2 and the round brush, turn your attention back to the handle and finish blocking in the lighter areas. Blend the handle softly.

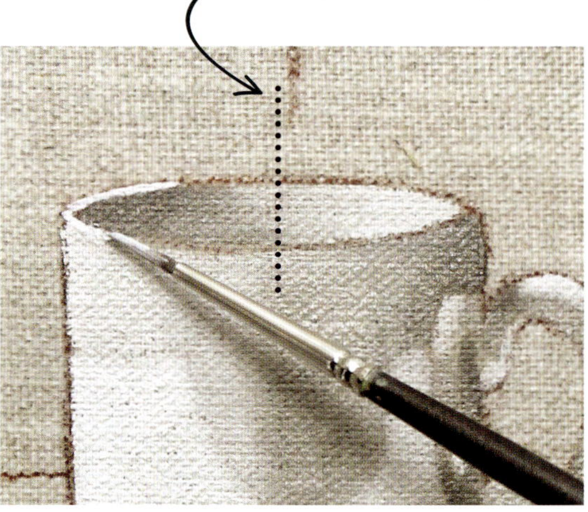

12. RIM

By looking through half-closed eyes and comparing different parts of the cup, I established that the left side of the rim had the same value as the reflected surface that we painted in step 7. Use the small round brush and Mix 1 to fill in the left-hand side, then wipe the brush and add the slightly darker right-hand rim in Mix 2.

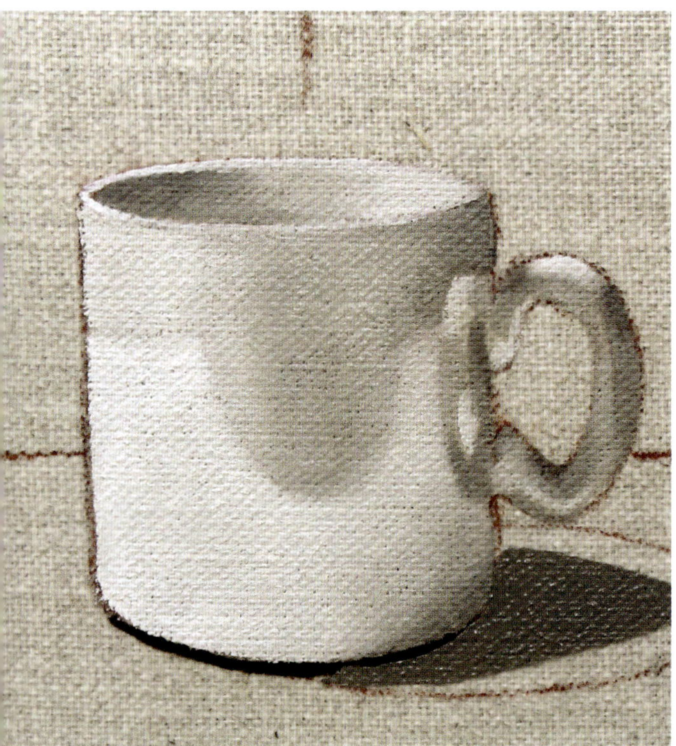

13. CAST SHADOW

The value of the cast shadow is the darkest of the mixes. Use the filbert brush to block in the core of the shadow with Mix 4, but leave the outer edges (penumbra) for now.

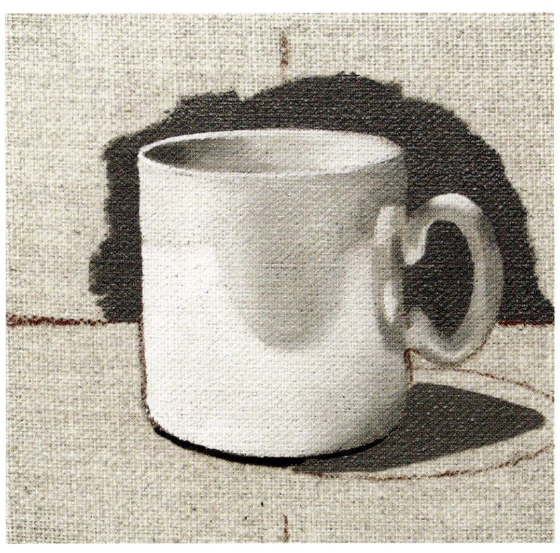

14. BACKGROUND

Conveniently, the background colour has the same value as the cast shadow, so you can continue painting with a filbert brush and Mix 4 to block in the whole area. Switch to a small round brush for the fiddly bits around the handle.

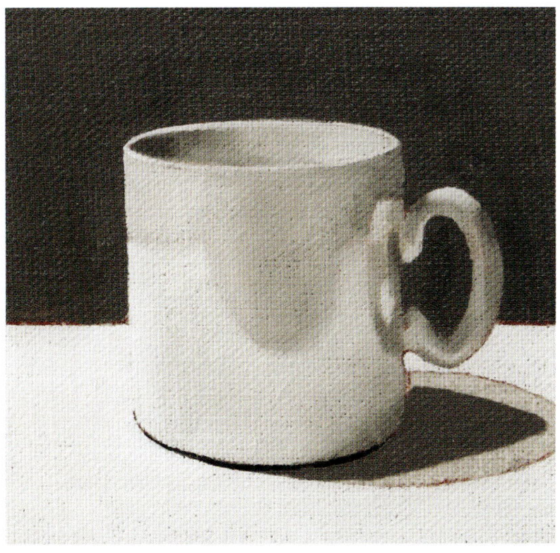

15. FOREGROUND

The white surface is very bright, reflecting the most light, and requires the lightest value on our palette, Titanium White. Wipe the filbert brush and block in the whole area, still avoiding the penumbra of the cast shadow.

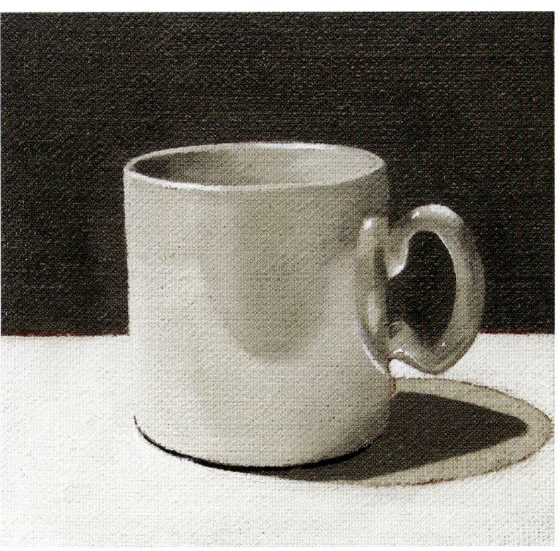

16. HIGHLIGHTS

Dip a clean Size 0 round brush in Titanium White and add the sparkly highlights to the rim and handle. Wipe the brush to leave only a little paint, then gently add the highlights that are reflected from the handle onto the side of the cup.

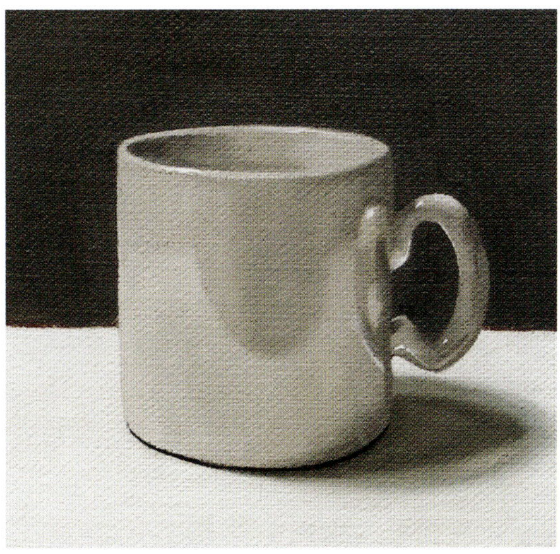

17. PENUMBRA

For the outer edge of the cast shadow you need a blend of existing colours, so mix a little of Mix 4 with some Mix 3 to create this transitional tone. Apply with the filbert brush and blend the edges with the dry, soft round brush.

LEMON

Lemons have long featured in still-life painting and have come to symbolize many things, including purity, wealth and hope. I have lost count of how many lemons I have painted over the years – I never tire of painting these cheerfully bright, yellow fruits with their unusual shape and dimply skin! This project will help build your skills with painting texture.

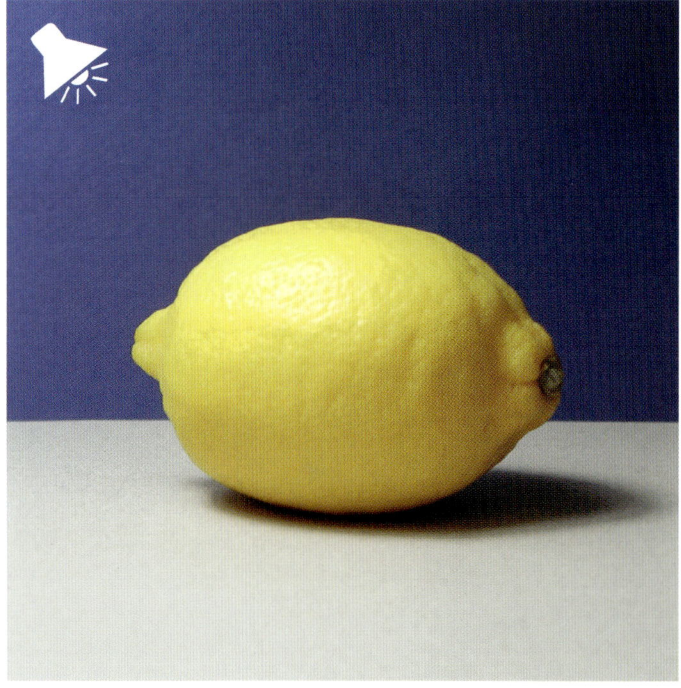

PAINT COLOURS

- Burnt Umber
- Titanium White
- Ultramarine Blue
- Cadmium Yellow

TOOLS AND MATERIALS

- Linen board (10 x 10cm/ 4 x 4in.), primed with transparent gesso (see page 12)
- Graphite or pastel pencil
- Putty eraser
- Ruler
- Fixative spray
- Transparent primer
- Primed white card strips, for colour matching (optional)
- Small palette knife, for mixing
- Rag or paper towel
- Size 0 filbert brush
- Size 0 round brush
- Size 2/0 round brush
- Size 3/16 flat brush
- Soft brush, for blending and softening

SET-UP

I positioned my lemon on some light, neutral grey paper which helped to accentuate the lovely cast shadow. After trying out several background colours, I finally settled on quite a vibrant blue – the lemon really stands out against this colour and complements it nicely.

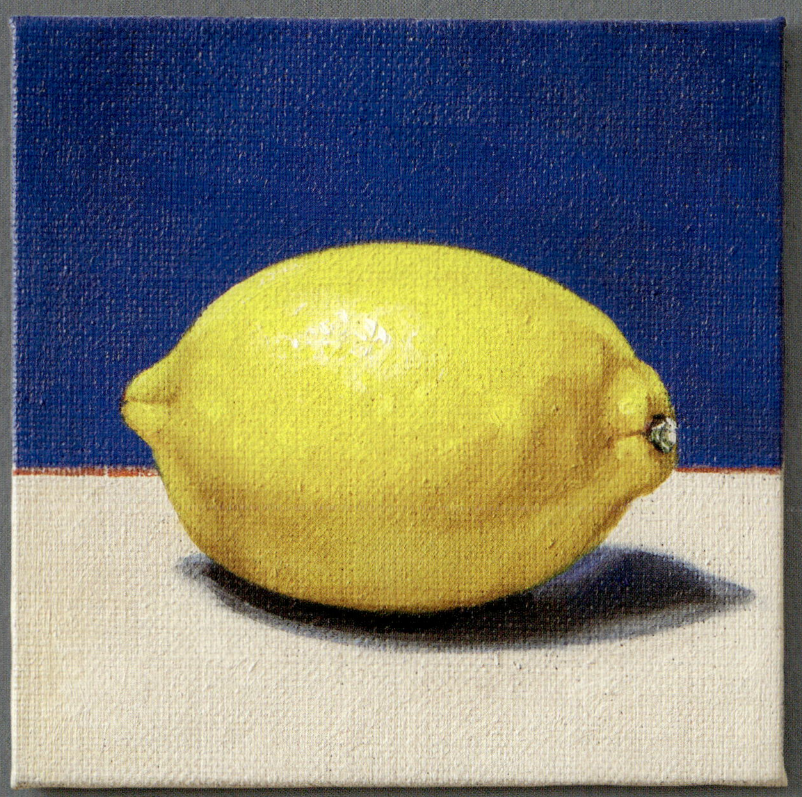

For dramatic effect, exploit how colours affect each other when they are placed together (see page 50).

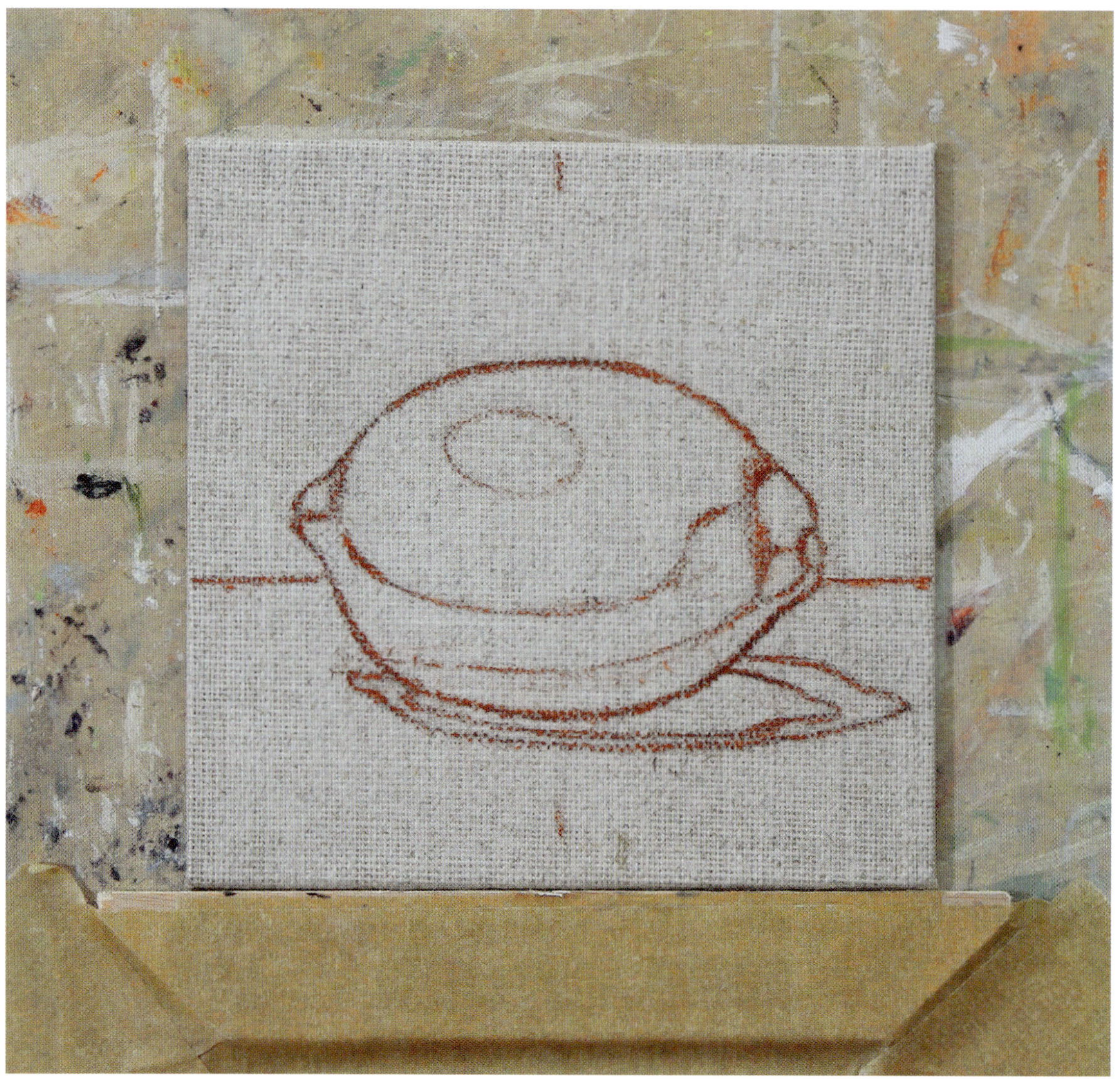

1. UNDERDRAWING

Before you do anything, take some time to really observe and familiarize yourself with your lemon. Draw it out, with either a graphite or pastel pencil, marking out the lemon's core shadow, highlights and the cast shadow, including the penumbra. Fix your drawing and, if you wish, apply a coat of transparent primer. Allow to dry.

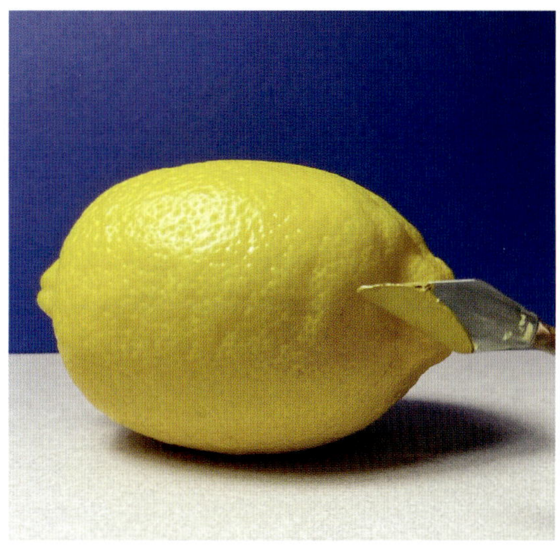

2. MIX DARKEST VALUE

Squint at your lemon and study its different values. Start by mixing together some Cadmium Yellow with Burnt Umber to create the darkest value. Check the accuracy of your colour – this can be done using one of your prepared test strips or simply by loading some of your paint mix onto your brush or knife.

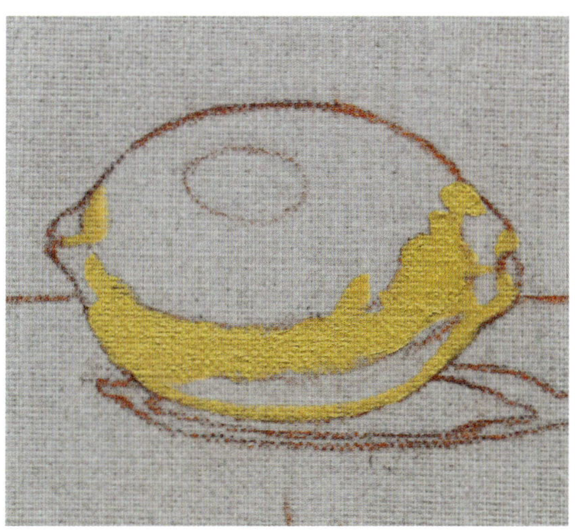

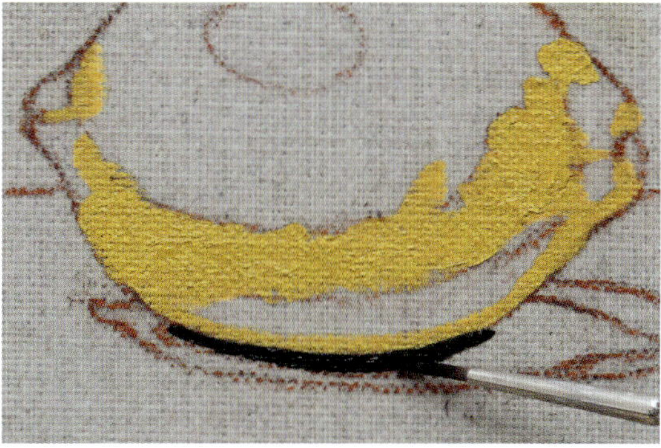

3. BLOCK IN DARKEST AREAS

Begin to block in the darker areas of your lemon – for example, the core shadow – using a Size 0 filbert brush. Don't be too precious at this stage, as we can adjust as we go along – the important thing for now is to get some paint down.

4. ADD OCCLUSION SHADOW

Next, look for the darkest part of your still life, which is the occlusion shadow, right underneath the lemon. Instead of using black straight from the tube, mix some Burnt Umber with Ultramarine Blue to create a more natural shade of black, then paint the occlusion shadow using a fine Size 0 round brush.

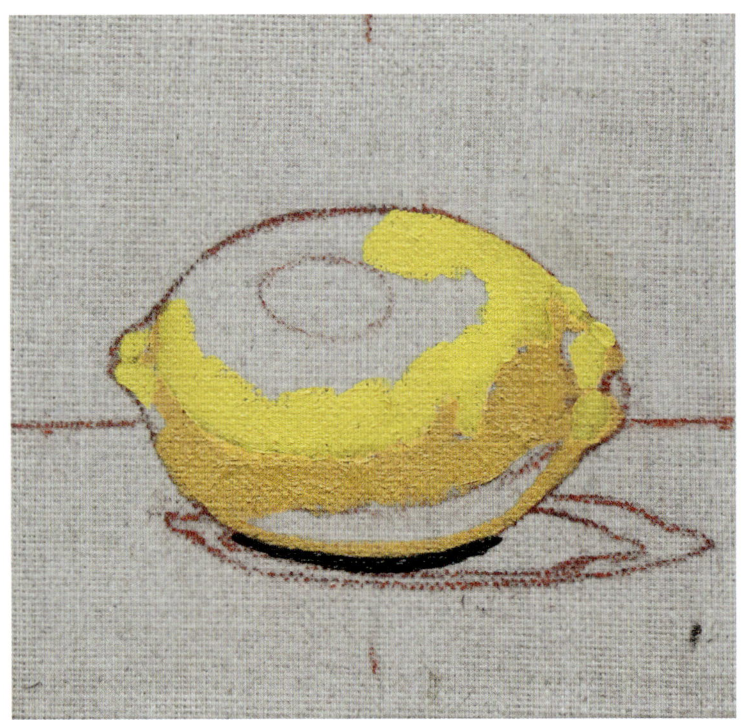

5. MID-TONE

With the darkest areas of the lemon blocked in you can now bring your attention to the mid-tone colour. Mix Cadmium Yellow with Burnt Umber, using much less Burnt Umber for this mix than you used in step 3. Wipe the filbert brush and begin to block in the area above the core shadow and any other areas with this lighter value.

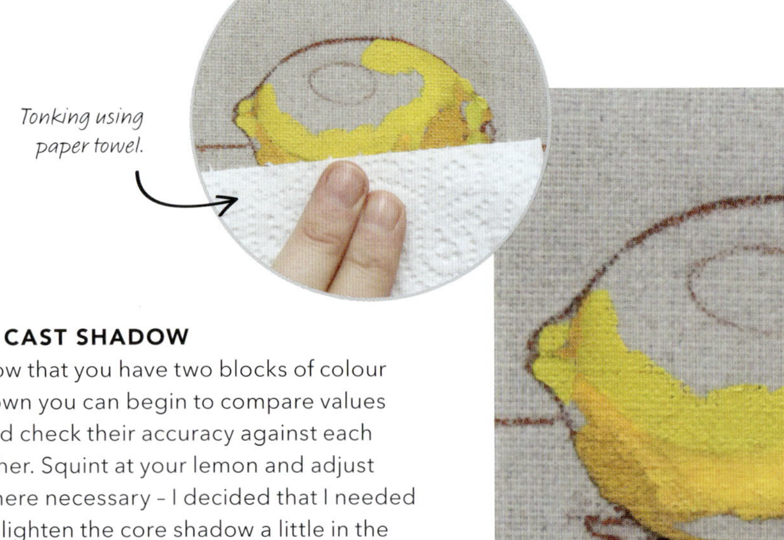

6. CAST SHADOW

Now that you have two blocks of colour down you can begin to compare values and check their accuracy against each other. Squint at your lemon and adjust where necessary – I decided that I needed to lighten the core shadow a little in the middle. Before doing this, I needed to remove some of the paint by 'tonking' that area with some paper towel. To lighten the core shadow, I added a little mid-tone mix and blended it in.

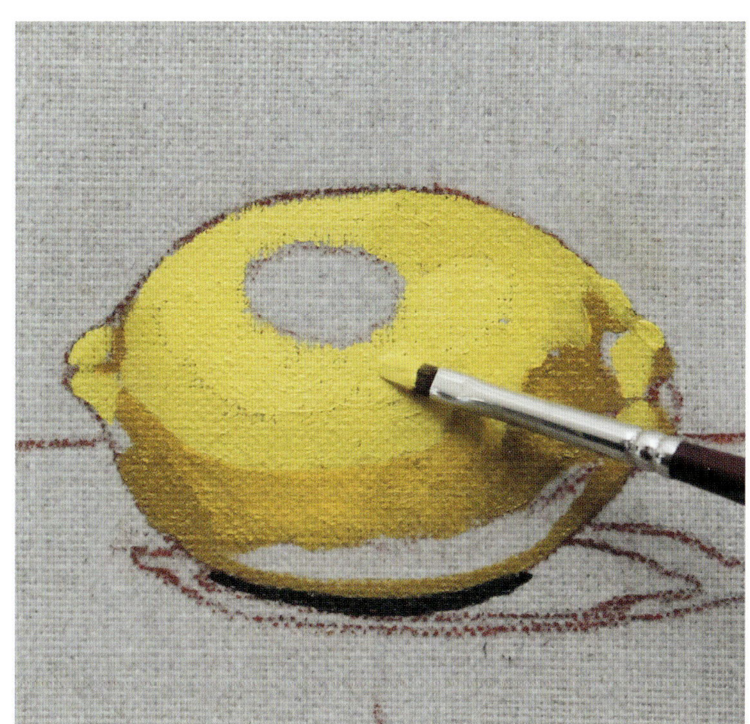

7. LIGHTER VALUE

We are working our way up into the light-facing plane of our lemon and so now need to create an even lighter value mix, still using only Cadmium Yellow and Burnt Umber. I didn't use any Titanium White to lighten my mix, just less Burnt Umber and more Cadmium Yellow.

Apply paint using the Size 0 filbert brush.

8. SHADOW

Next, block in the shadowy area beneath the core shadow, on the underside of the lemon. Although this part of the fruit is in shadow, reflected light from the surface is bouncing back onto it, making the value in this area slightly lighter than the core shadow itself. At this point, don't focus on the detail, just aim to block in the area with as accurate a value as possible. Your mix should be lighter than the core shadow but not as light as the mid-tone above it. Paint the shadowy areas using the filbert brush.

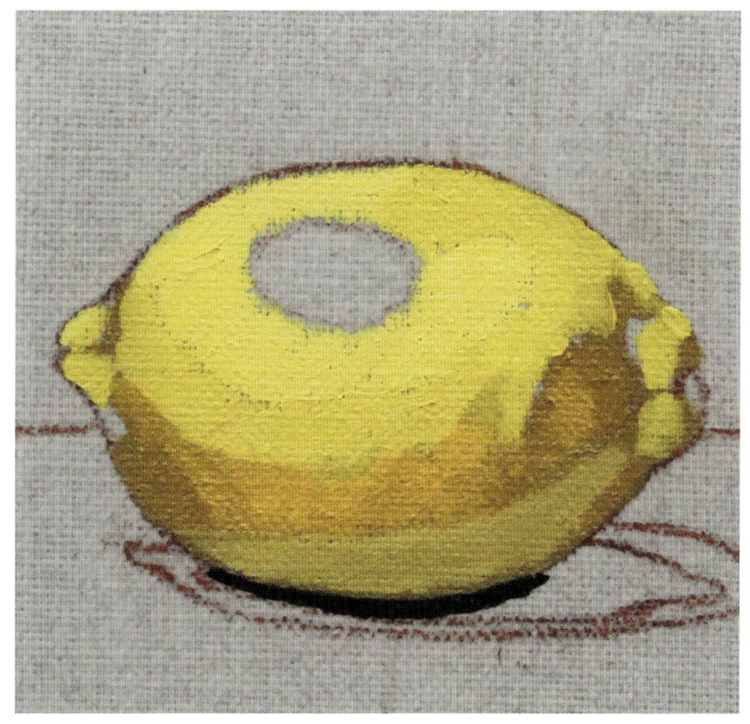

9. HIGHLIGHT

If you look closely at the highlight on your lemon, you'll see that it isn't pure white but rather a very light shade of yellow, broken up by little specks of bright white. Mix the overall colour of the highlight using Cadmium Yellow and Titanium White and apply it to the area with the filbert brush. Look for highlights on the ends of the lemon, dabbing a little of the highlight mix in these areas, too.

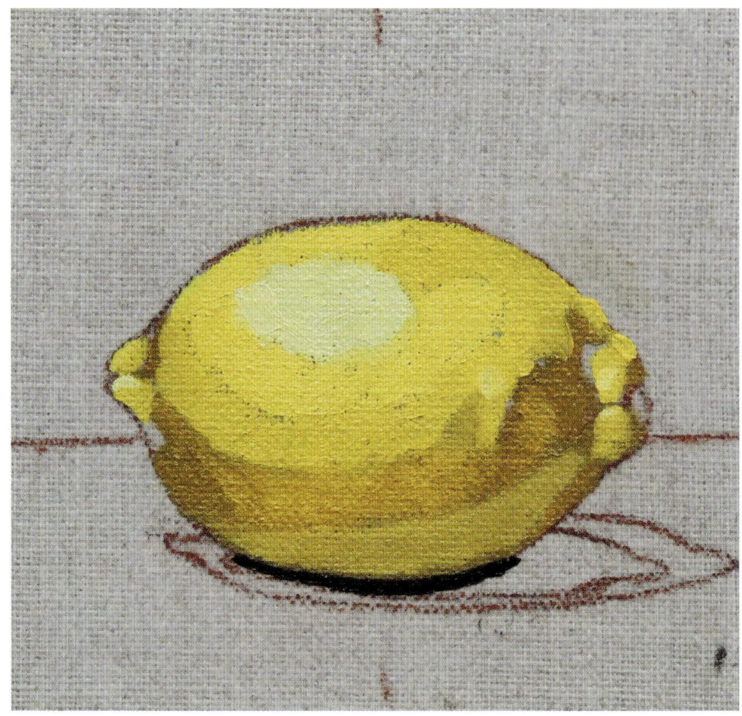

10. BLENDING

Start to soften and blend the inner edges of your lemon using a clean, dry brush – I used an old, soft Size 0 round brush. Blend small areas at a time, remembering to wipe your brush on a rag or paper towel at regular intervals, so that you don't end up smudging your hard work!

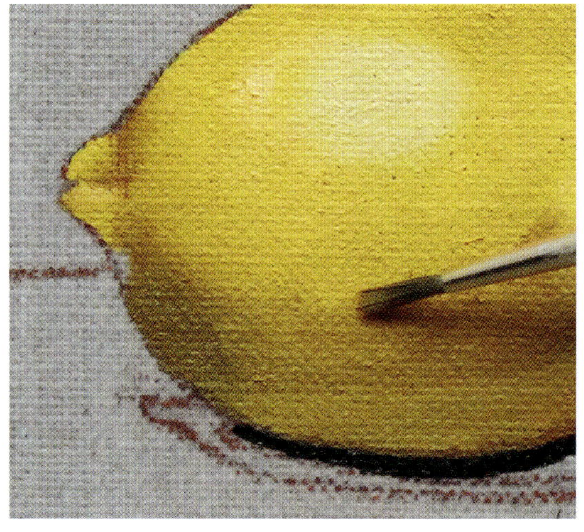

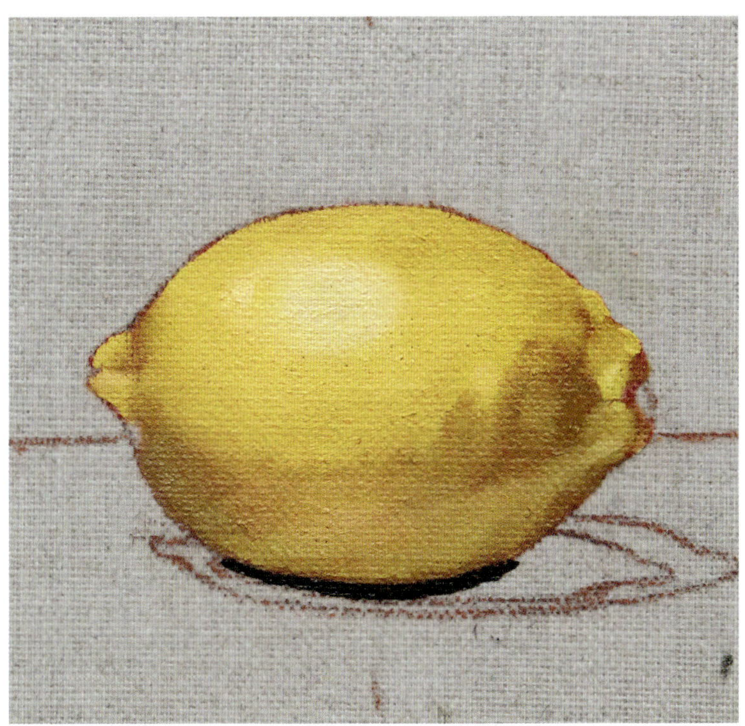

11. REFLECTED LIGHT

Revisit the shadowy part of the lemon, focusing in more detail on the reflected light. Taking a tiny amount of the lightest mix (from step 9), add in a minuscule amount of Ultramarine Blue. Tonking the area first, begin to add a little more detail to the curved reflection of the surface on the lemon, keeping it subtle and being careful not to overwork the paint.

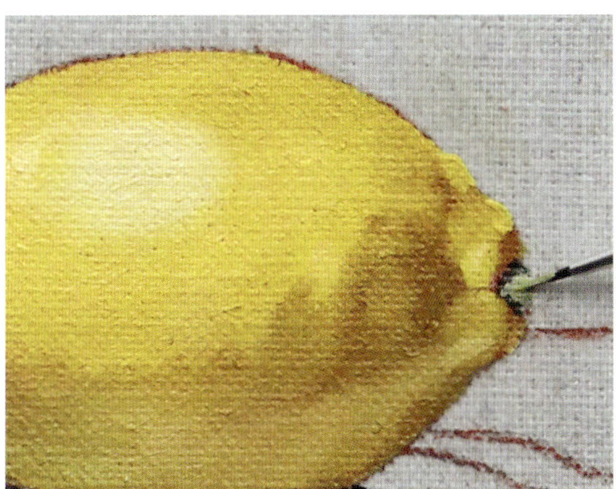

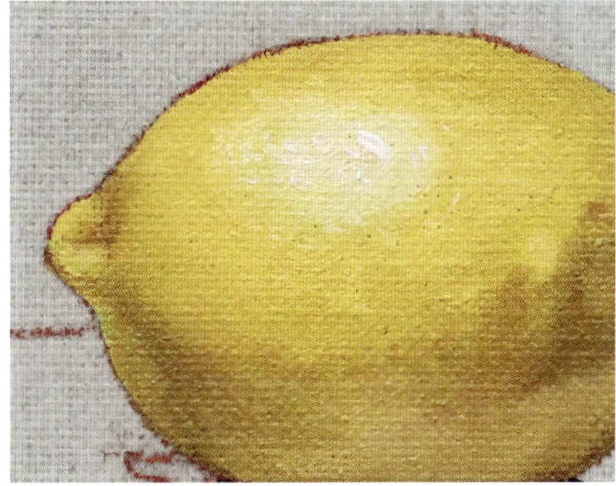

12. TEXTURAL DETAIL

Look more closely at the details on your lemon and in particular at the gnarled end where the stalk would have been (the pedicel). Use existing mixes on your palette for this tiny area, including the black mix from step 4 and the core shadow mix from step 3, adjusting as necessary. Apply with a fine Size 2/0 round brush.

13. TWINKLY HIGHLIGHTS

Wipe your fine round brush and apply tiny amounts of pure Titanium White to the brightest little highlights. At this point, check for any areas that might need attention – for example, the left end of the lemon – and continue to work over the surface with a little more gentle blending.

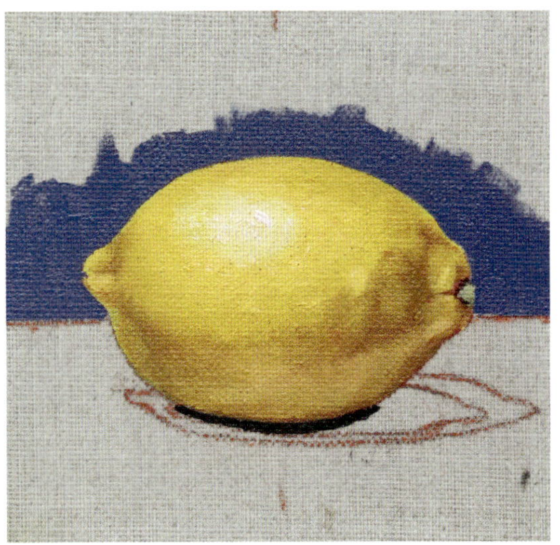

14. BACKGROUND

Using a mix of Ultramarine Blue, Burnt Umber and a little Titanium White, begin to block in the background with a Size ³⁄₁₆ flat brush. The addition of Burnt Umber helps to tone down the blue, otherwise it would be a little too saturated.

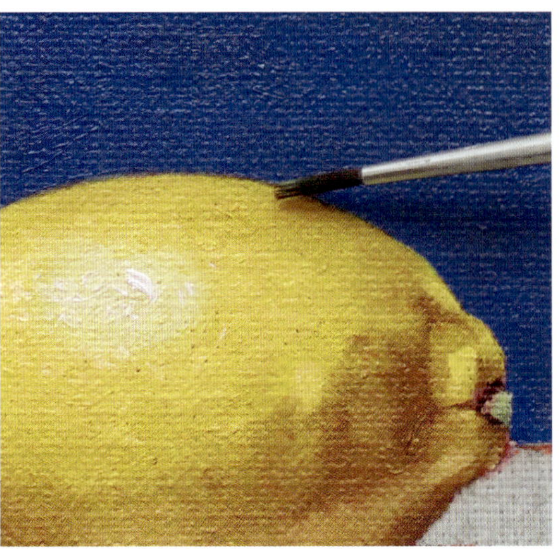

15. SOFTEN EDGES

To help unite the lemon with the background, use a dry, soft round brush to soften and blur the outer edges of your lemon.

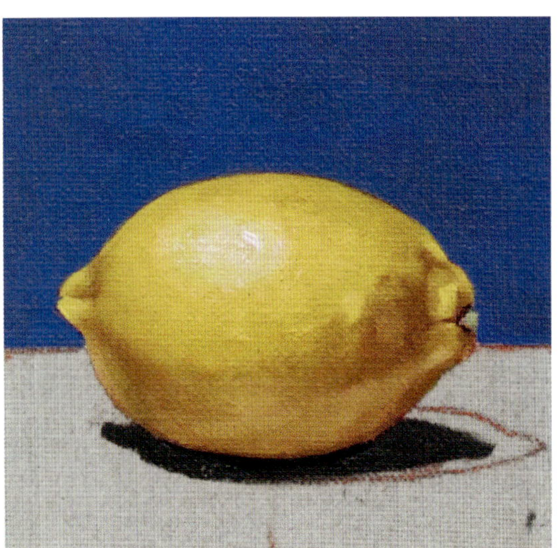

16. CAST SHADOW

Use your mix from step 14, adding in more Burnt Umber to darken it. Paint the darkest parts of the cast shadow beneath the lemon, using your Size 0 filbert brush.

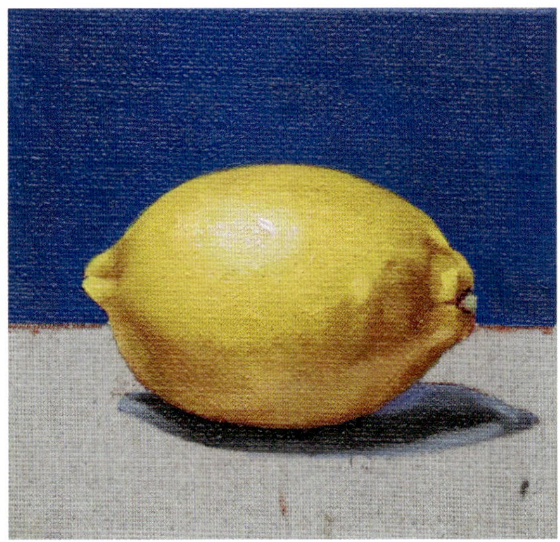

17. PENUMBRA

The outer edge of the cast shadow (the penumbra) begins to lighten and has a blue tint to it. Mix a little Ultramarine Blue and Titanium White and fill the penumbra shapes on the edge of the shadow.

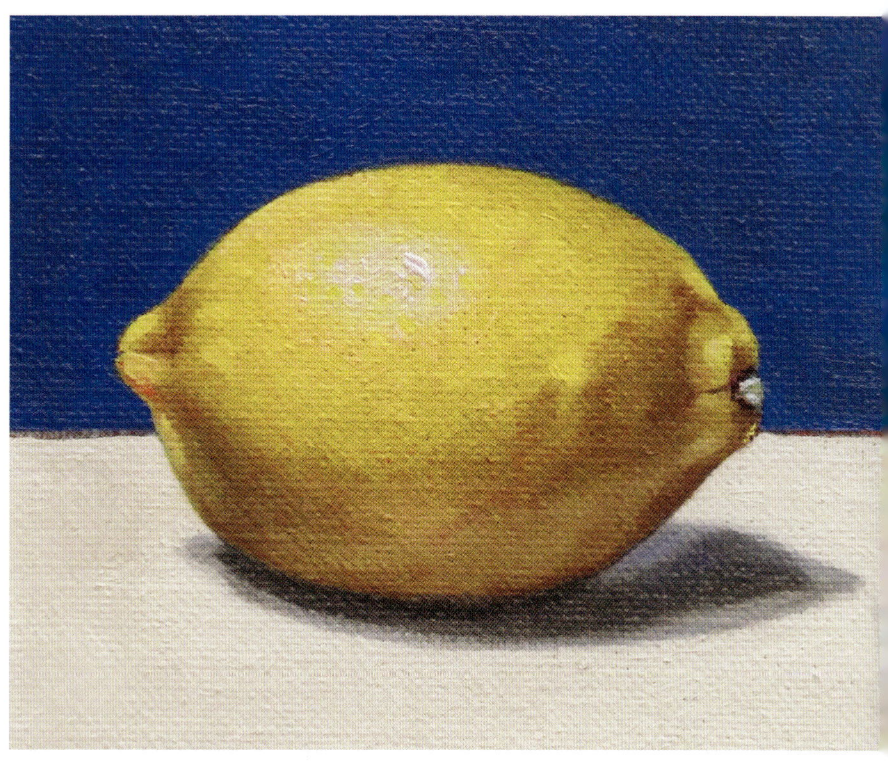

18. FOREGROUND

Mix Titanium White with a little Burnt Umber and paint the foreground with your Size 3/16 flat brush. Using the clean, dry round brush, blend the outer edges of the penumbra gently into the foreground.

19. FINAL TWEAKS

Using up the existing mixes on your palette, add details to the skin by dabbing on a few little pock marks using the fine round brush. Be careful, though, as it is easy to get carried away with the details and end up overworking the painting! Our aim is to give an impression of the skin's texture – keep stepping away regularly to assess your progress and decide when it is time to stop!

APPLE

An apple may not seem all that exciting as a subject, but it is ideal for building your confidence with texture, shadows and reflections. Try to do this painting in a single session. Or, if you're just starting out with oil paints, take it slowly, allowing the paint to dry between sessions.

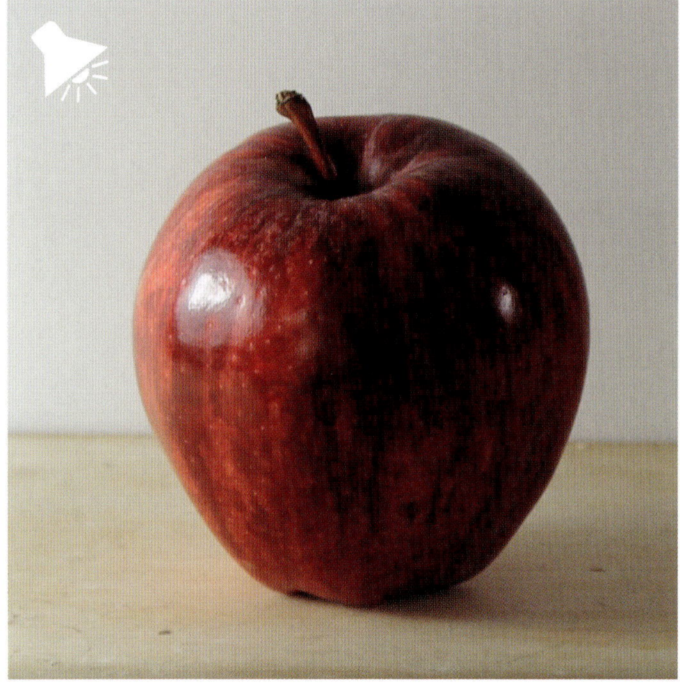

PAINT COLOURS

- ■ Raw Umber
- ■ Ivory Black
- ■ Permanent Magenta
- ■ Cadmium Red
- ☐ Titanium White
- ■ Kings Blue Deep
- ■ Brown Ochre
- ■ Burnt Umber
- ■ Cadmium Yellow
- ▦ Yellow Ochre

TOOLS AND MATERIALS

- ☐ Linen board (10 x 10cm/ 4 x 4in.), primed with transparent gesso (see page 12)
- ☐ Graphite or pastel pencil
- ☐ Putty eraser
- ☐ Ruler
- ☐ Fixative spray
- ☐ Transparent primer
- ☐ Primed white card strips, for colour matching (optional)
- ☐ Small palette knife, for mixing
- ☐ Rag or paper towel
- ☐ Diluent
- ☐ Size 0 filbert brush
- ☐ Size 0 round brush
- ☐ ¼in. flat brush
- ☐ Soft brush, for blending and softening

SET-UP

Here, the apple is positioned so that it is not quite at eye level but slightly lower, enabling its top to be seen as it tilts towards the light. Rotate your apple until you find the most interesting view of it. The rich colour of the apple is the dominant element of the composition, so keep the background neutral.

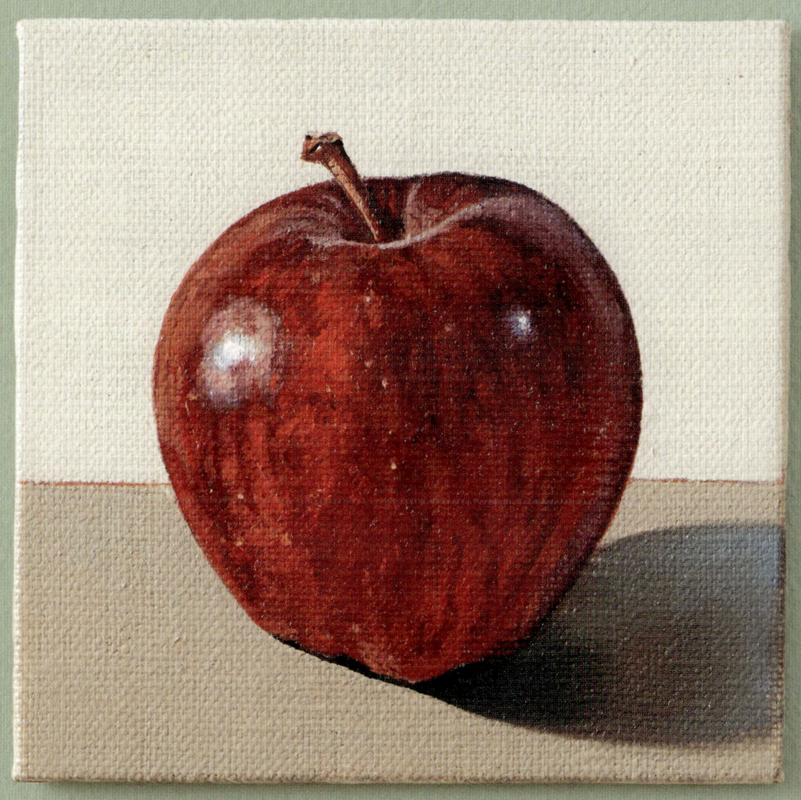

Throughout the
painting process,
remember to wipe
your brush before
changing colours.

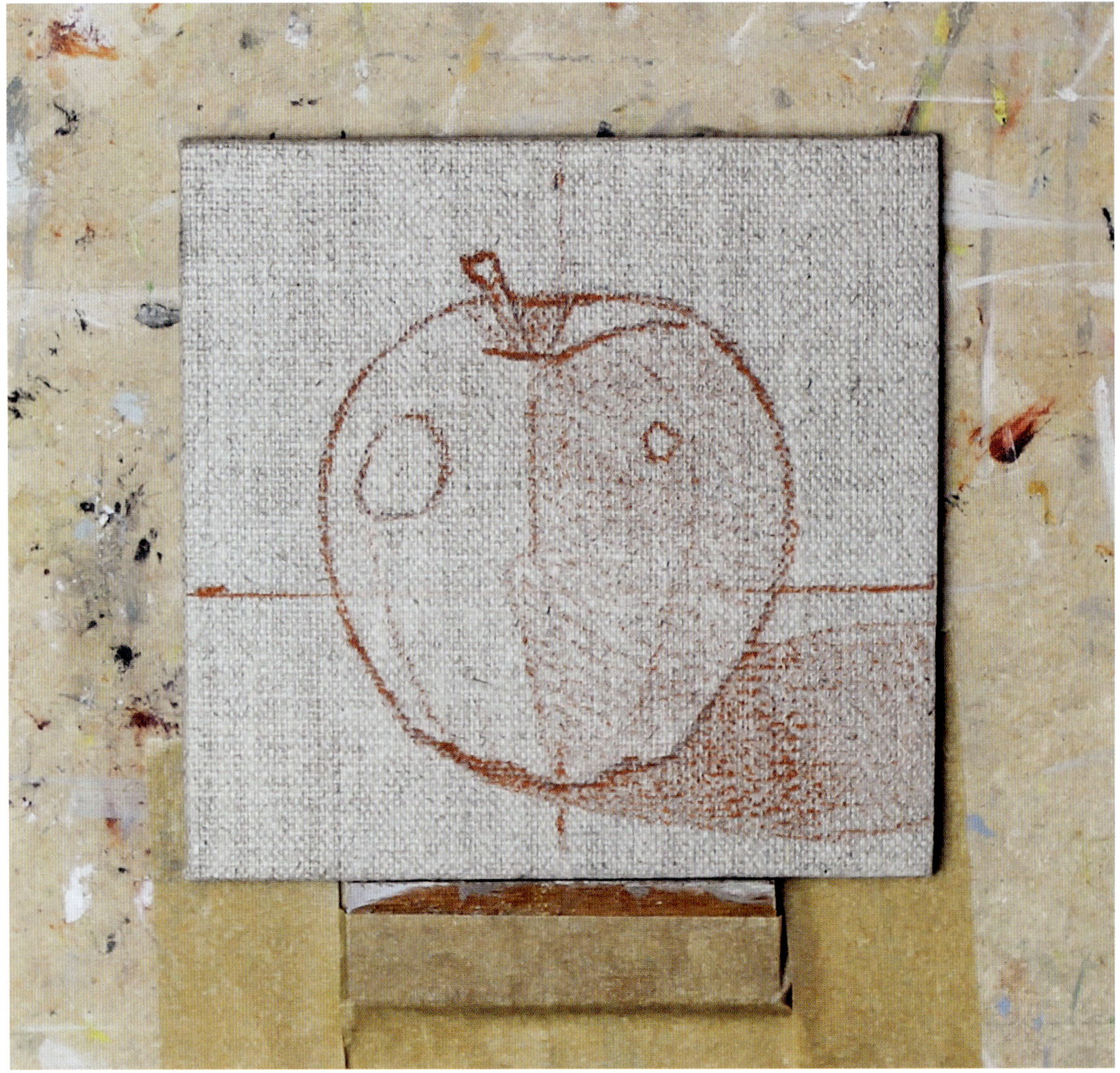

1. UNDERDRAWING

Using a pastel pencil, draw a horizontal line (approximately a third of the way up) and outline the shape of the apple, the shadows and the main highlight, making sure the drawing is positioned in the middle of the board (see tip). Loosely shade in areas of different values as a guide. Fix your drawing and, if you wish, apply a coat of transparent primer. Allow to dry.

TIP

Use a ruler and draw a faint line down the centre of your board to guide you when positioning your subject on the canvas.

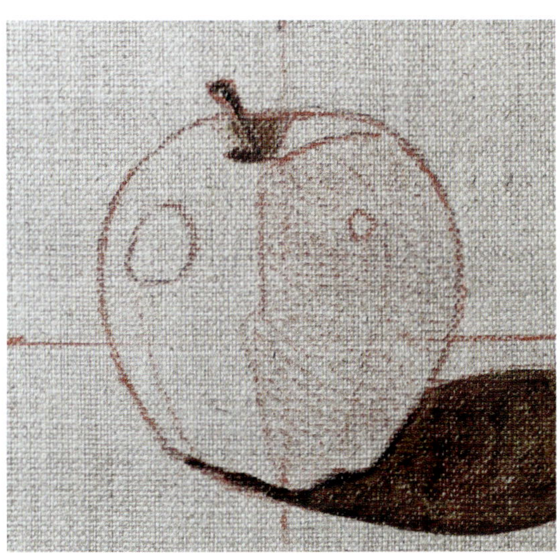

2. START WITH SHADOW

Start painting the shadow cast by the apple and the darkest side of the stalk. For this step, use Raw Umber, thinned out with a little diluent and applied to the surface using a Size 0 filbert brush.

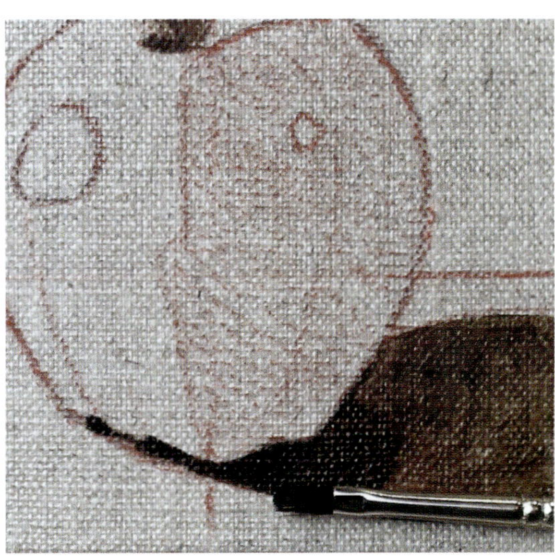

3. DEEPEN THE SHADOW

Add a little Ivory Black to your Raw Umber for the deepest, darkest shadows nearest the base of the apple. You have now established the darkest value in the painting and you know that no other areas in this painting will be as dark as this.

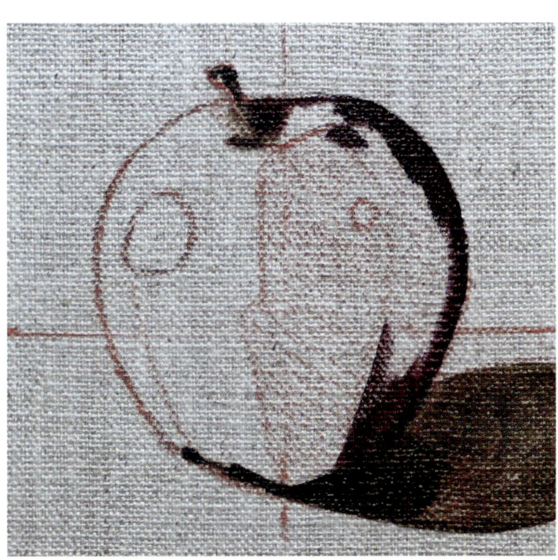

4. DEEPEST COLOURS OF THE APPLE

Use Permanent Magenta mixed with Raw Umber to begin painting the right side of the apple where the colours are the darkest.

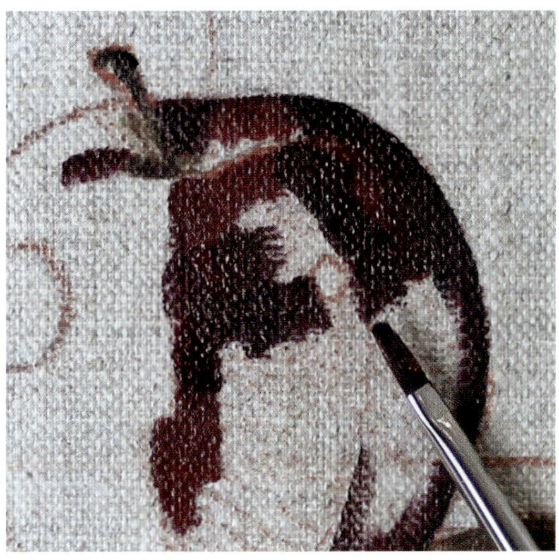

5. BUILDING UP

Continue slowly to build up the darkest side of the apple, adding a little Cadmium Red to the mix and blocking in the main areas.

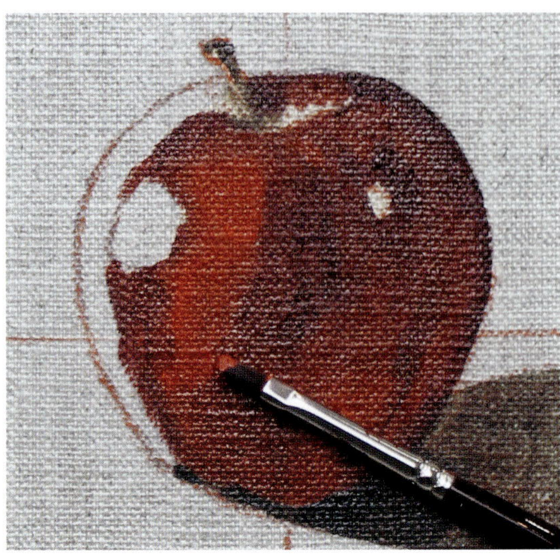

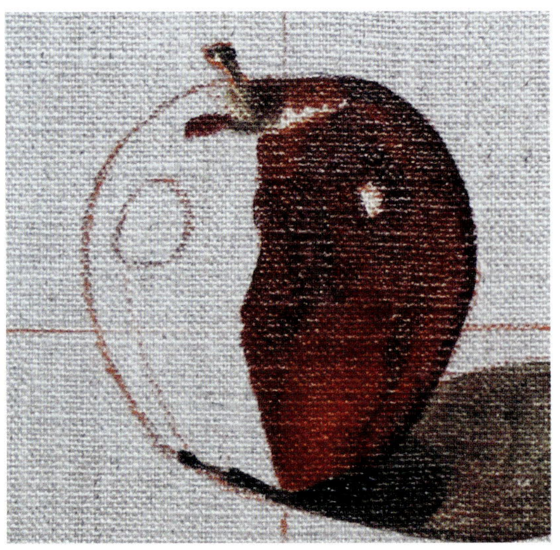

6. ADD CADMIUM RED
The colours in the apple become richer towards the middle, so begin adding small amounts of pure Cadmium Red to the subject.

7. WORK DARK TO LIGHT
Continue to work across from right to the left (dark side to light side), observing any subtle changes in value and colour. At this stage, I used less and less Raw Umber and more pure Cadmium Red.

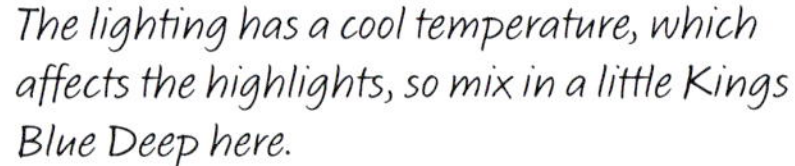

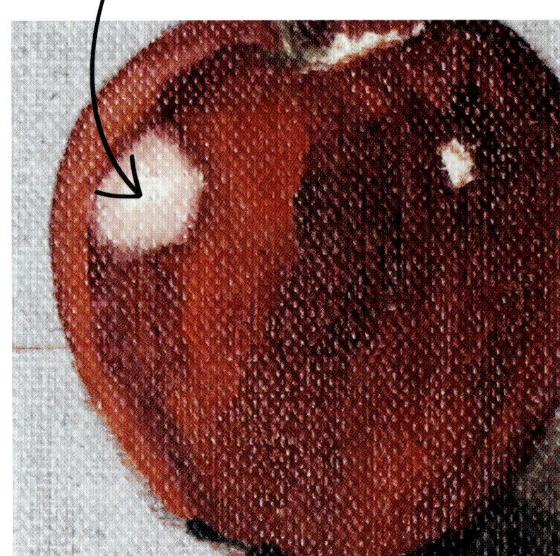

8. HIGHLIGHTS
Having painted the first layer, mix tiny amounts of Titanium White, Raw Umber and Magenta and paint the outer portion of the brightest highlight on the apple. If you look carefully at the highlight, you'll see that it is not just an area of pure white; there are various subtle colours depending on the object's colour (the local colour) and it is also affected by the temperature of the lighting too, which is cooler. For the central part of the highlight, use a little Kings Blue Deep mixed with Titanium White, then a tiny little blob of pure Titanium White to make the highlight sparkle.

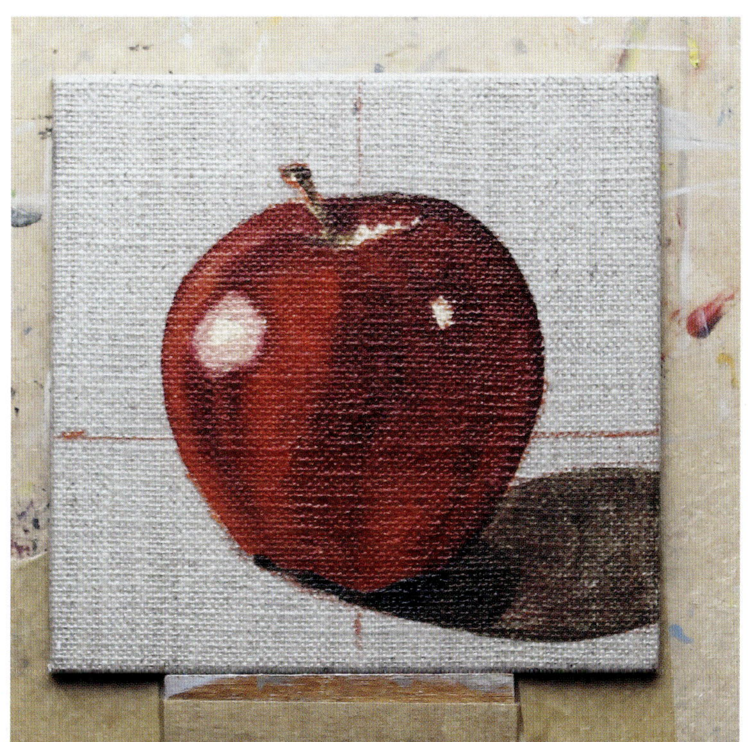

9. BLENDING

Using a soft, dry filbert brush, gently blend areas of the painting, softening the appearance of the apple, but be careful not to overwork it as it can muddy your paint.

TIP

Step back from your easel and check your work, comparing it with the actual apple. I find that squinting slightly can help to eliminate the tiny details and this allows you to focus on the larger details and the values.

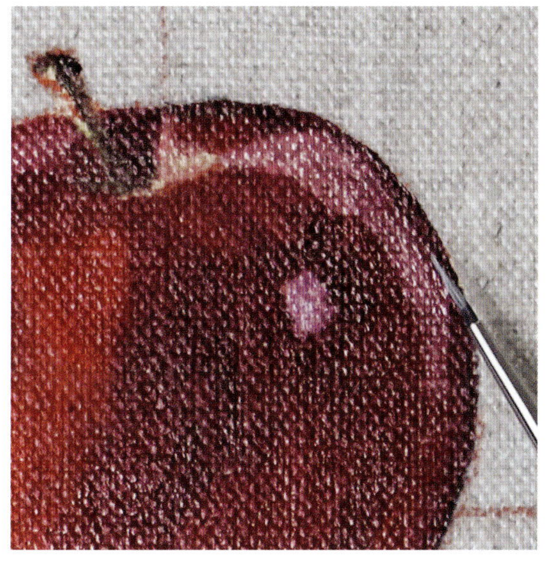

10. DIMPLE

Study the top part of the apple where the stalk emerges. With the fine Size 0 round brush, apply Yellow Ochre and Raw Umber, adding a little white to the mix for the lightest parts in this area. Leading down from the top right, there is a faint highlight (which is coming from a window on the right of the set-up). It is not nearly as bright as the main highlight and is painted with Kings Blue Deep, slightly diluted and applied sparingly.

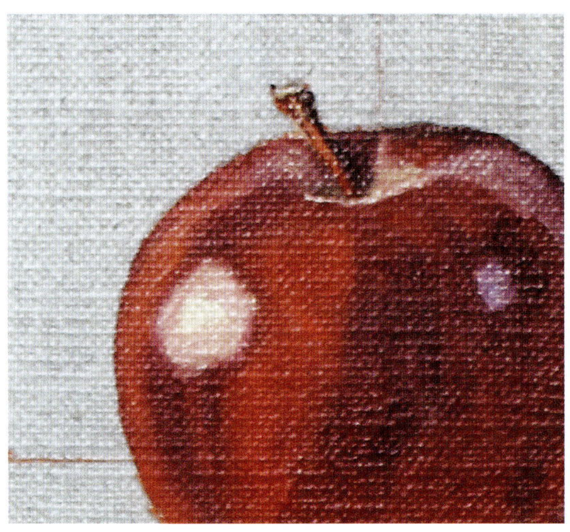

11. STALK

For the stalk, use Cadmium Red and the Yellow Ochre and Raw Umber mix from the last step, adding a little Titanium White to the mix for the stalk's highlight. Also use this combination of colours for the highlight running across the top of the apple (at the base of the stalk).

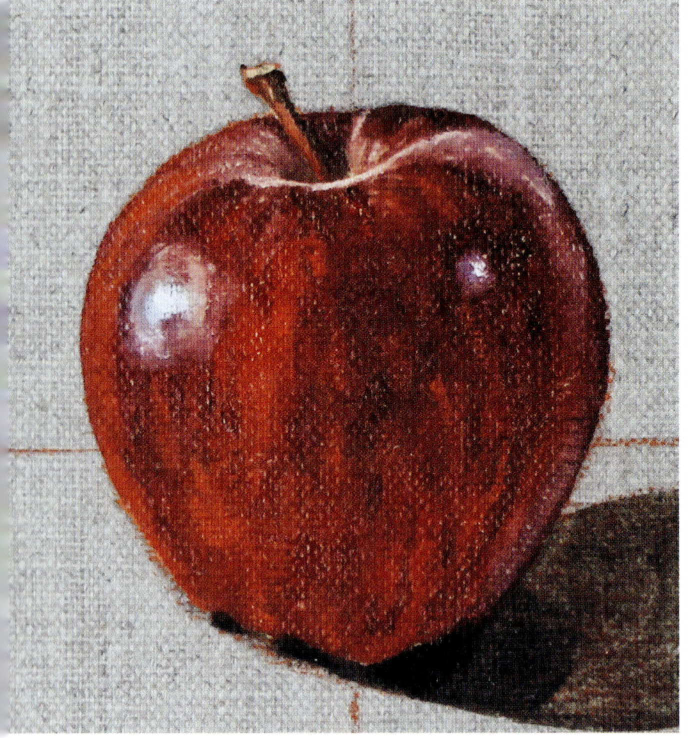

12. SPECKLES

Now look more closely at the details on the apple – for example, the little speckles. Aim to use whatever colours you have on your palette. However, in this instance a little Cadmium Yellow was added for the little patches and patterns on the skin. The apple is starting to look more three-dimensional and 'real'.

13. BUILD DETAILS

Continue adding details to your apple, dabbing or 'tonking' any excess paint if necessary, and remember to step back to check your work.

TIP

Occasionally, leave your painting and take a little break to give your eyes a rest. I find that when I return, I am able to 'see' things more clearly and I can spot anything that needs correcting/adding.

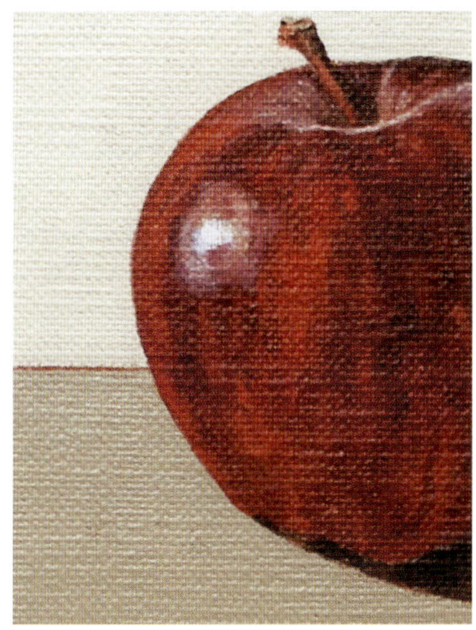

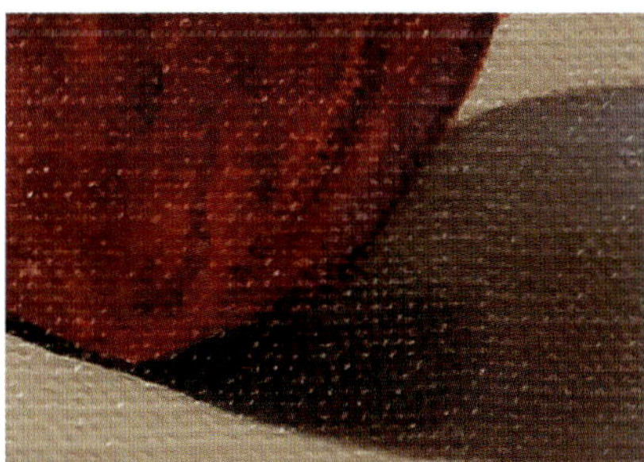

14. UPPER BACKGROUND

I never use pure white for my background colour as I find it too cold and harsh. For this painting, use a mix of Titanium White, Burnt Umber and Kings Blue Deep (all colours that are already on the palette – I always try to use up any paint that is already mixed on my palette when possible, to avoid wastage). Use the ¼in. flat brush for blocking in and switch to a fine brush to soften the edges between the apple and the background, carefully dabbing away any excess paint to avoid a ridge.

15. LOWER BACKGROUND

For the lower background, go a few shades darker simply by adding more Burnt Umber to the mix from the previous step. Avoid the shadow area for now and use your fine brush to soften the edges.

16. SHADOW DETAILS

Now return to the apple's shadow. As with the highlight, if you look closely at the shadow you will see other subtle colours. Go over the original painted shadow from the start of the exercise and darken any areas with Raw Umber and a little Ivory Black, and add a little Kings Blue Deep for the outer parts of the shadow. Use your soft brush to soften and blend.

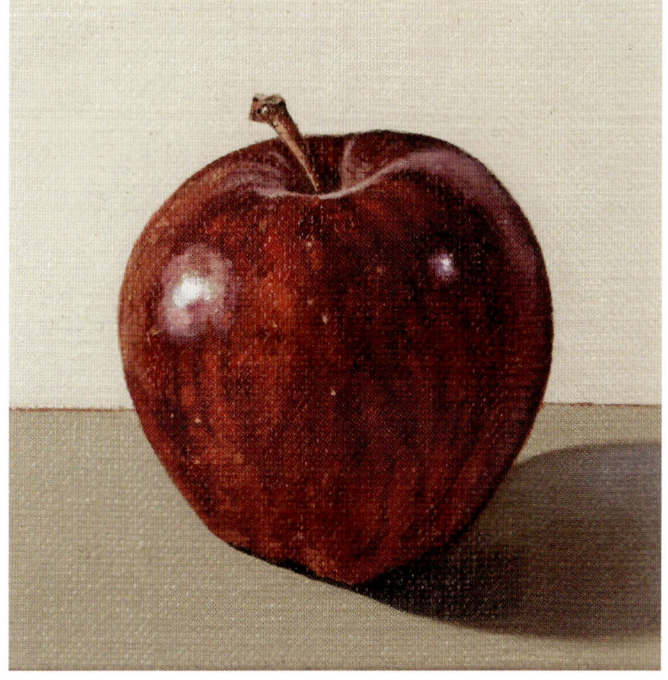

17. FINISHING TOUCHES

Step back from your work and walk away for a little while, to refresh your eyes. When you are ready, check for any minor changes that you need to make – I use this opportunity to tidy edges and add any final little details.

SILVER JUG

I am intrigued by the way reflections in shiny, metallic objects appear distorted and how, with the right lighting, these objects come to life with eye-catching highlights and interesting shadows. A reflective object may seem difficult to paint, but if the process is broken down, and you paint what you see (and not what you think you see), then it is definitely achievable.

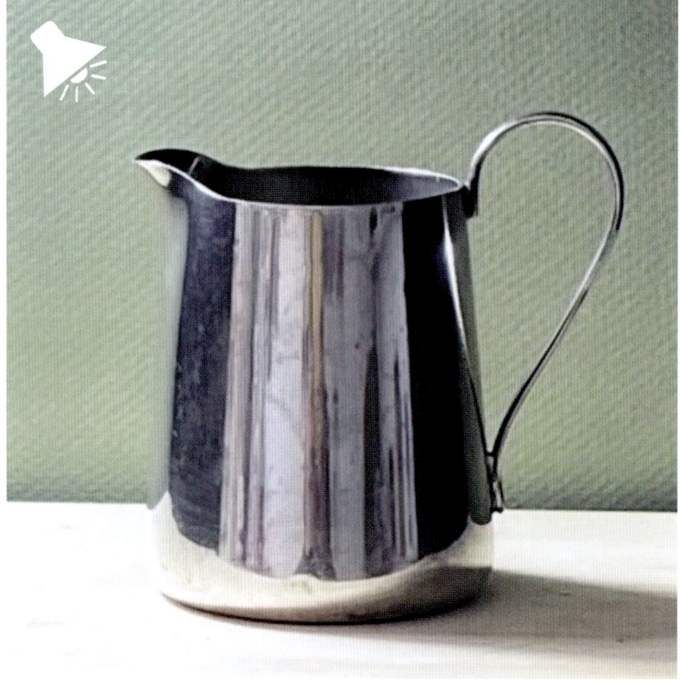

PAINT COLOURS

- Raw Umber
- Ivory Black
- Cadmium Red
- Titanium White
- Kings Blue Deep
- Cobalt Blue
- Permanent Green Light
- Burnt Umber
- Cadmium Yellow
- Yellow Ochre

TOOLS AND MATERIALS

- Linen board (10 x 10cm/ 4 x 4in.), primed with transparent gesso (see page 12)
- Graphite or pastel pencil
- Putty eraser
- Ruler
- Fixative spray
- Transparent primer
- Diluent
- Primed white card strips, for colour matching (optional)
- Small palette knife, for mixing
- Rag or paper towel
- Size 0 filbert brush
- Size 0 round brush
- Size 15/0 round brush
- Soft brush, for blending and softening

SET-UP

For this exercise I positioned a small, plain silver milk jug on top of a couple of wooden boxes, in front of the table easel. Because the jug has muted tones, I have chosen to place some green card behind it, in order to add some colour to the scene. Place your silver object so that you can see interesting reflections, highlights and shadows.

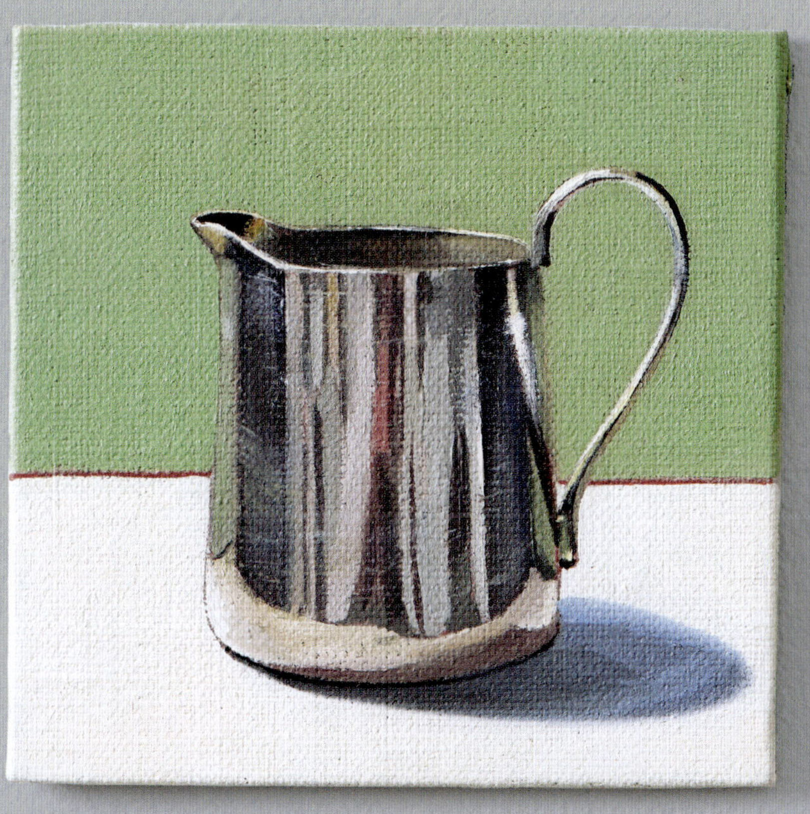

Your colour palette
will be determined
by the lighting and your
surroundings, which are
reflected in the surface
of the object.

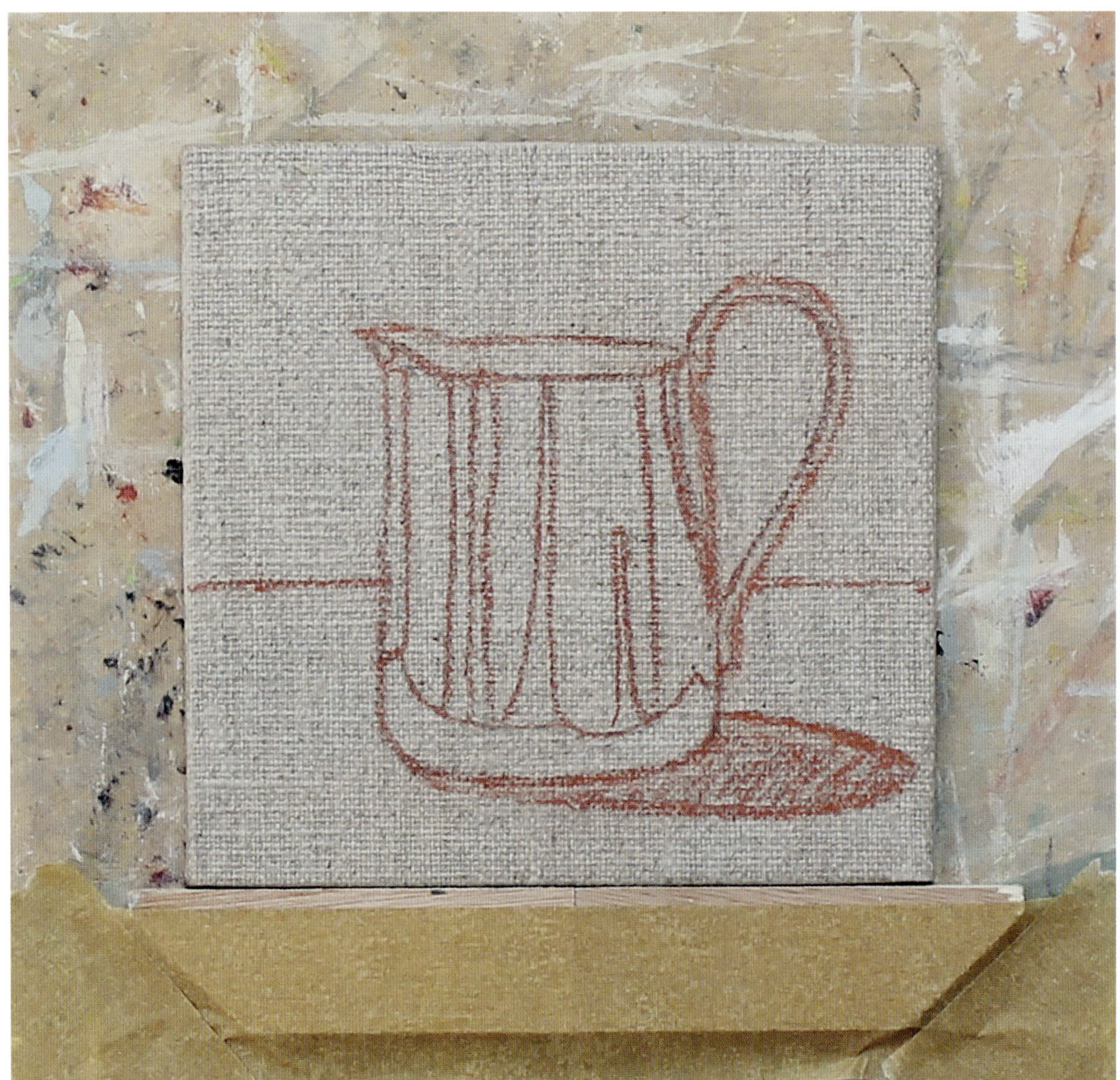

1. UNDERDRAWING

Using either a graphite or pastel pencil, draw the outline of your silver object and its cast shadow. Look carefully at the larger, most obvious reflected shapes in your silver object – in this case, I can see vertical stripes and a horizontal strip running across the base, which curves along with the shape of the jug. Fix your drawing and, if you wish, apply a coat of transparent primer. Allow to dry.

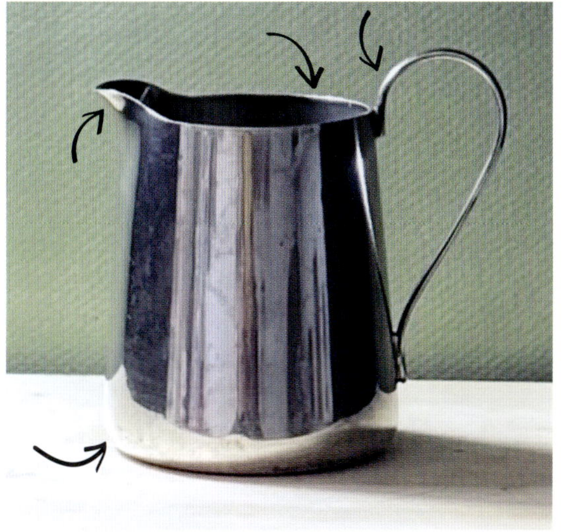

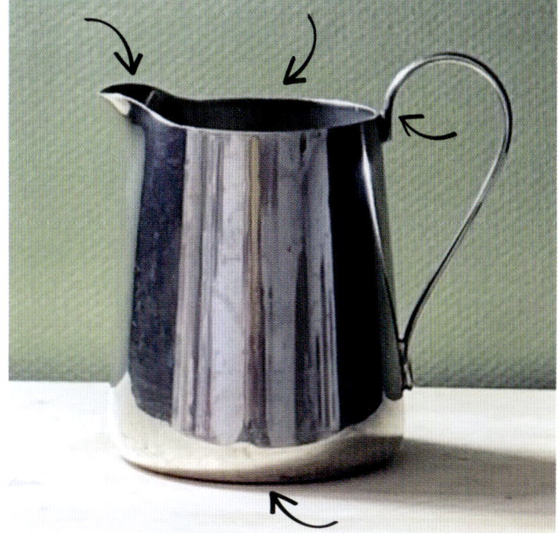

2. HIGHLIGHTS

Look for the brightest highlights on your object – the brightest highlights on the jug are found under the spout, the upper edges around the rim, on top of the handle and on the bottom left side. There is also light reflecting off the inside of the handle and onto the side of the jug.

3. DARKEST AREAS

Look for the darkest areas of your object – the darkest areas on the jug are inside the spout and in a couple of areas on the handle. Where the jug sits on the surface, there is a thin, dark shadow.

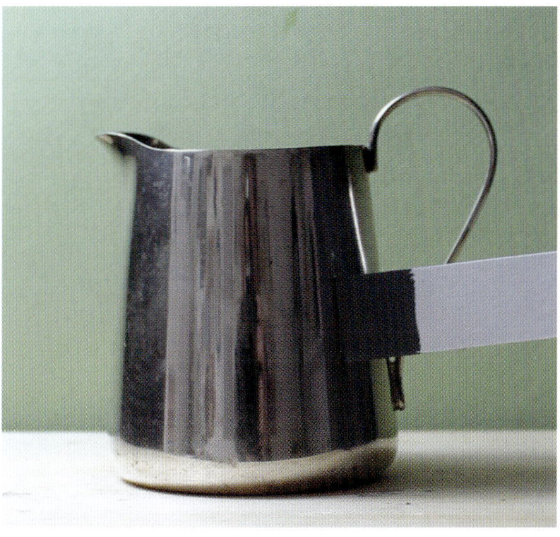

4. MIXING COLOURS

Once you have made a mental note of the lightest and darkest values, you can think about selecting and mixing all the colours for your palette. The jug as a whole is not simply grey (that is, mixes of black and white paint). On close inspection, it contains various colours, including browns, blues, beige, green and, because I am seated directly in front of the jug, it has hints of colour reflected from my face and sweater.

Based on these careful observations, use mixes of Burnt Umber, Raw Umber, Kings Blue Deep, Cobalt Blue, Permanent Green Light, Cadmium Yellow, Yellow Ochre and Titanium White to match the reflections.

TIP

If you are unsure whether any of the colours you have mixed are accurate enough, try painting a little colour onto the tip of a strip of white card and hold the strip close to your object. This will help you to ascertain if the colour needs adjusting.

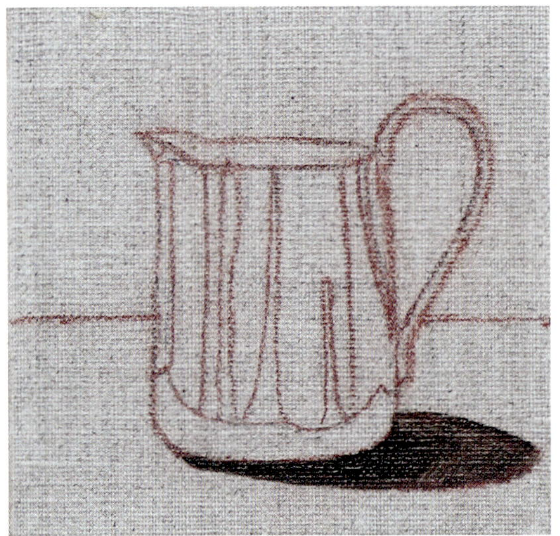

5. CAST SHADOW

Now you're ready to begin painting! Using a Size 0 filbert brush, start with the cast shadow, applying a layer of diluted Raw Umber to the whole shape, with a darker application nearer to the base of the jug.

6. DARKEST AREAS

Using a Size 0 round brush, paint the darkest areas of the jug with a mix of Cobalt Blue and Burnt Umber to create a chromatic black. Try not to reach for your tube of black paint when mixing your darkest shades, but if you do, remember to use it very sparingly (see tip below).

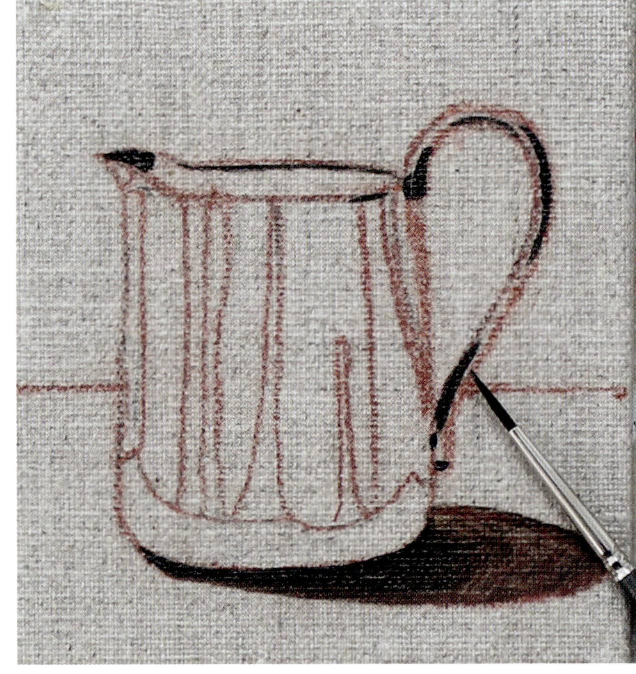

TIP

Many artists don't use black straight from a tube at all and prefer to mix their own chromatic blacks using, for example, Ultramarine Blue and Raw Umber. Adding these chromatic blacks to your colour mixes will darken them without overpowering them completely.

7. BUILD DARKER SHAPES

Begin painting the larger reflected shapes, starting with the darker values first using mixes of Raw Umber, Cobalt Blue and a little Titanium White. Don't worry about smaller details for now, just focus on the biggest, most obvious shapes and try to get the overall colours as close as possible. The most important thing is to get some paint down because it is only once you've done this, that you'll be able to gauge whether your colours are accurate in value and tone or whether adjustments are required.

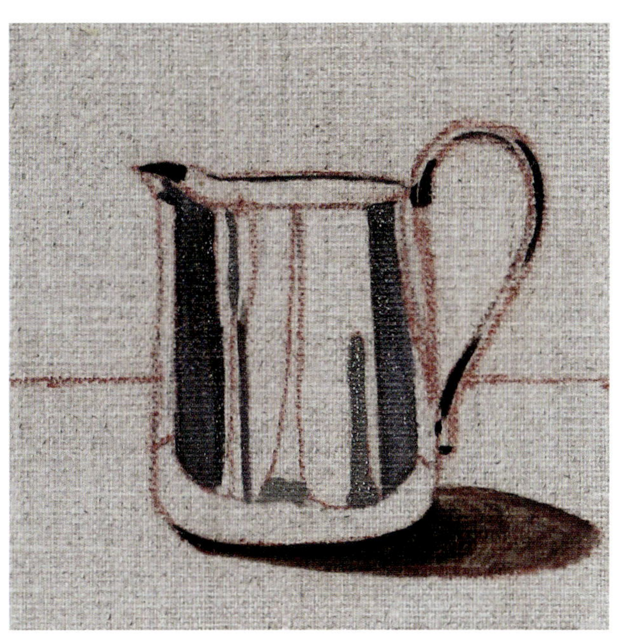

8. BUILD UP COLOURS IN REFLECTED SHAPES

Continue building on the reflected shapes by carefully selecting the colours from your premixed palette, checking that the values and tones are correct. I have noticed a couple of areas in my painting that are too light and which need darkening; for example, the green reflected edge to the right.

Use a mix of Raw Umber with a little Yellow Ochre for the warm reflections.

9. ADD MORE DETAIL

As you continue to develop the reflected shapes and adjust your values, start to look at the smaller details. Here, the finer reflections (in the form of thinner stripes) are added and a start is made on the horizontal reflection on the base of the jug, from a mix of Titanium White with Yellow Ochre and a little Raw Umber.

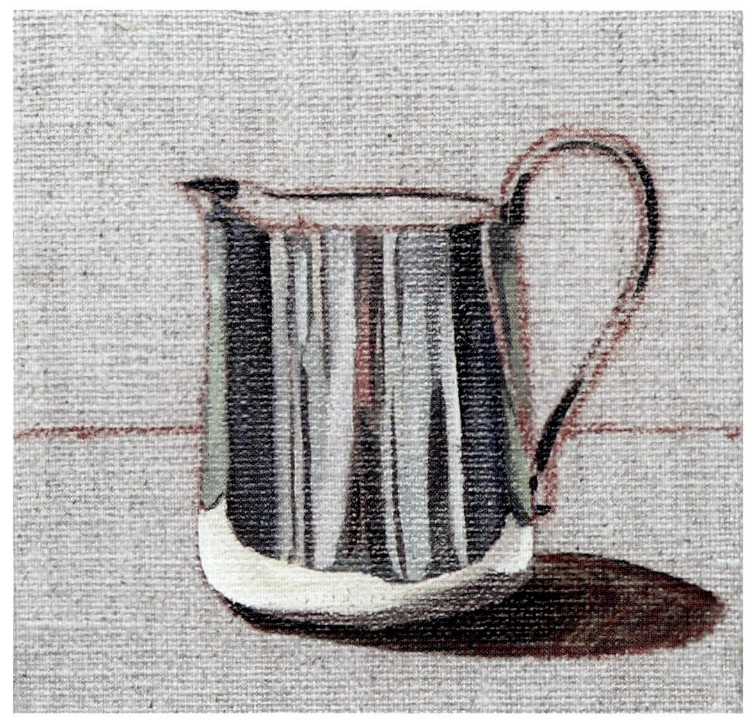

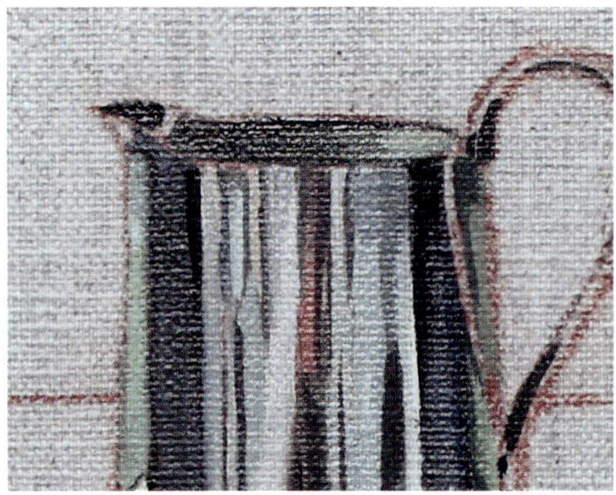

10. THE OPENING

The opening to the silver jug is quite dark but not as dark as the areas painted in step 6. Gauge colour mixes against these darkest parts. The opening is darker to the left and lighter to the right. Mix Burnt Umber with Cobalt Blue for the darker part of the opening. For the lighter area of the opening, add a little Kings Blue Deep and a tiny amount of Cadmium Yellow and Titanium White. The very light reflection on the inside of the spout is left for now.

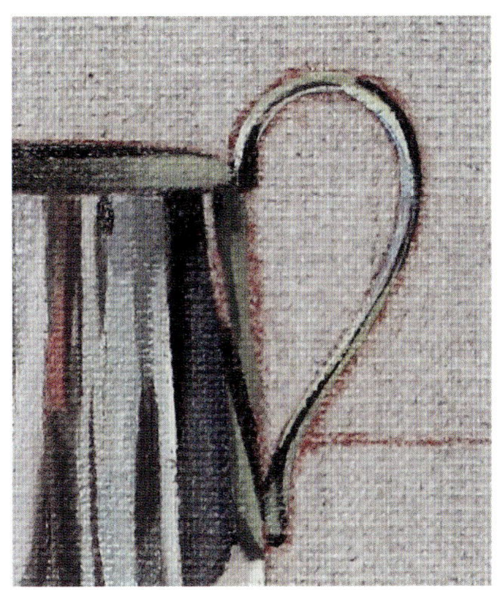

11. THE HANDLE

Using paint from the previous step, plus a lighter mix of Cadmium Yellow, Yellow Ochre and Titanium White, begin work on the handle, using the Size 0 round brush.

For the subtle touches of green, which are reflected from the background, add a little Permanent Green Light to the mix. Continue to block in any other areas at this point, using the colour mixes on your palette.

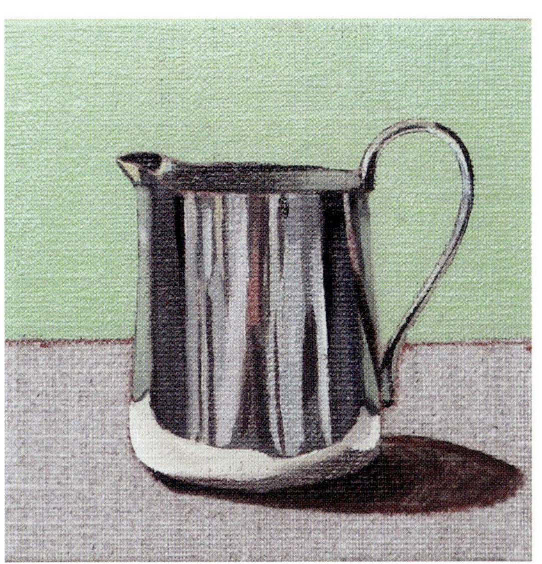

12. BACKGROUND

Begin to work on the background with the filbert brush and a mix of Permanent Green Light, Yellow Ochre and a tiny amount of Titanium White.

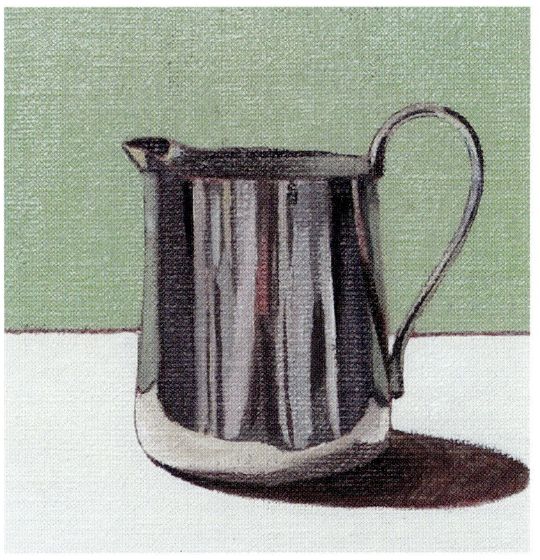

13. FOREGROUND

The silver jug is sitting on a pale wooden surface, which is reflected in the jug. Block this in with the same mix from step 9 that you used for the horizontal reflection of the surface. Lighten the mix a little with a small amount of Titanium White (the reflected surface is slightly darker than the actual surface).

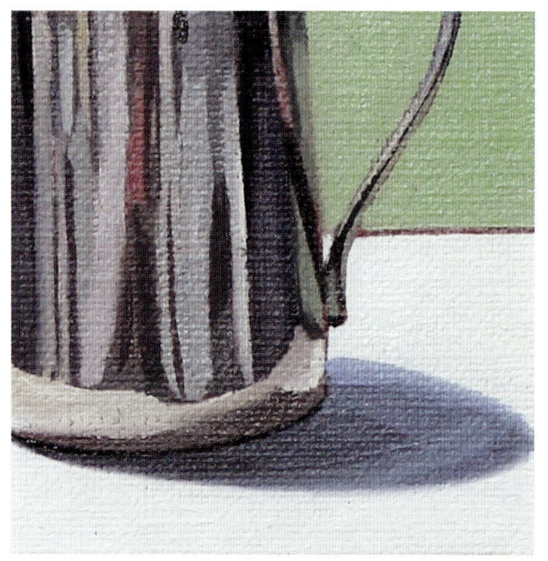

14. CAST SHADOW

Return to the cast shadow, looking carefully at the colours and, using a filbert brush, deepen the shadows with a mixture of Raw Umber and Cobalt Blue. For the lighter, outer edges of the shadow, add some Kings Blue Deep. To enhance the darkest shadow, where the jug is in direct contact with the surface, carefully paint a thin black line using a small amount of Ivory Black applied with a very fine Size 15/0 round brush.

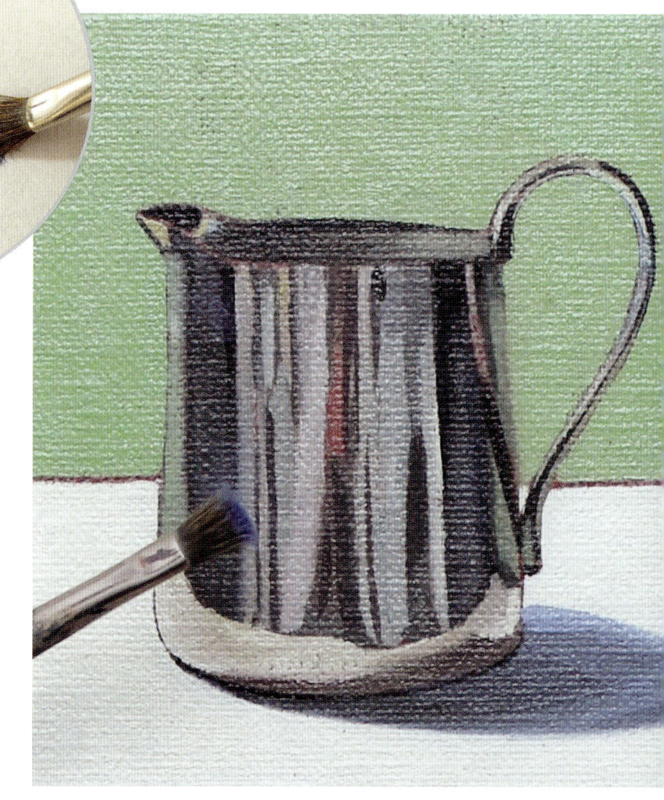

15. REFLECTION DETAILS

Upon closer inspection, I noticed that the silver jug is covered in tiny scratches and little blemishes, giving the surface an almost hazy, pale blue appearance. To achieve this effect, select an old filbert brush with worn, soft bristles – and very importantly, keep the brush dry – and gently tap it in a small amount of Kings Blue Deep, applying a really tiny amount of the paint to the tips of the bristles. Using a piece of clean paper, brush any excess paint off and, once your brush is leaving only a faint amount of paint on the paper, begin to work on the hazy areas on the painting.

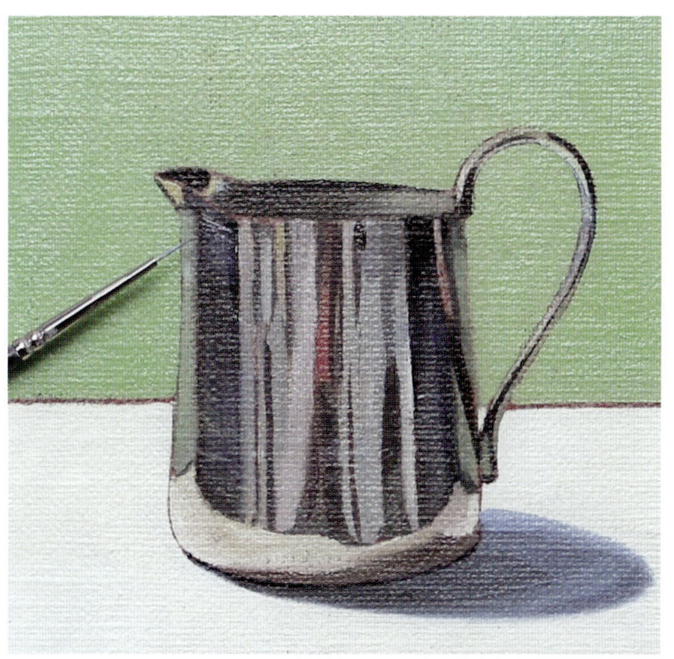

16. TINY SCRATCHES

Next, paint some of the really tiny scratches, which give the jug character and an appearance of age. Using the very fine round brush, carefully paint the little marks, making use of the lighter mixtures already on your palette. If you wish, you can wait for your painting to dry and use the dry brushing technique (see page 32) to achieve the scratch marks on the silver surface.

TIP

Don't get too hung up on the details in the reflections. Squint your eyes when looking at your silver object – this helps to make the details become less distracting.

17. SPARKLY HIGHLIGHTS

The pure Titanium White has been saved for the very brightest highlights. Add these highlights, on the rim and handle of the jug, to make your silver object really sparkle and come to life.

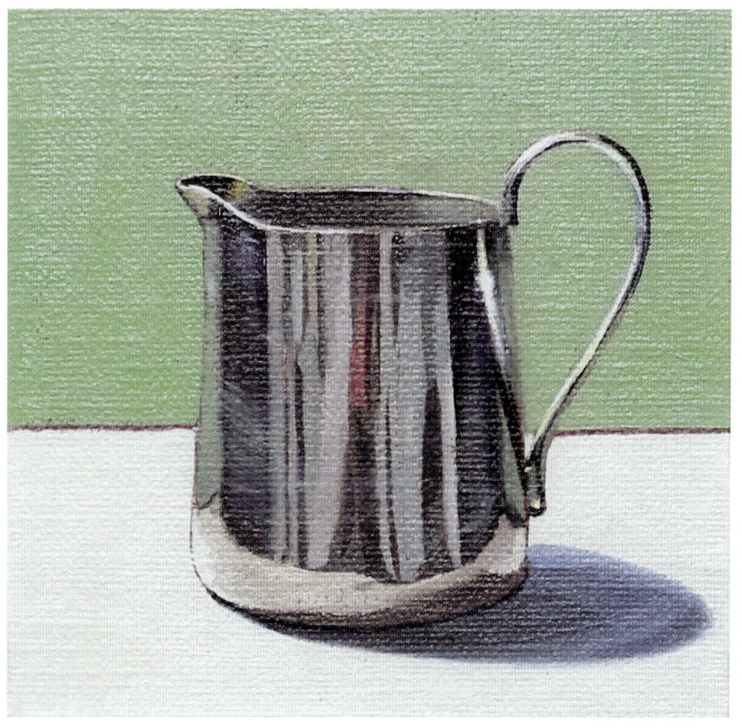

RED ONION

Onions are really quite beautiful, in particular red onions with their deep, purple-red colours. Their papery skins, luscious layers and solid, bulbous shape make them perfect for stretching yourself and your new painting skills. The rich colour of the onion works well against a neutral background, or try something bolder with a complementary colour.

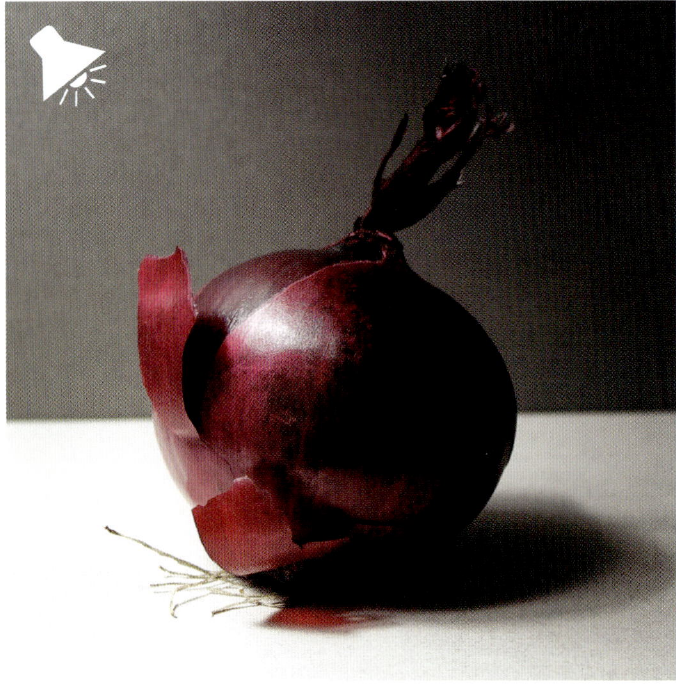

PAINT COLOURS

- ■ Raw Umber
- ■ Ivory Black
- ■ Permanent Magenta
- ■ Cadmium Red
- ☐ Titanium White
- ■ Kings Blue Deep

TOOLS AND MATERIALS

- ☐ Linen board (10 x 10cm/ 4 x 4in.), primed with transparent gesso (see page 12)
- ☐ Graphite or pastel pencil
- ☐ Putty eraser
- ☐ Ruler
- ☐ Fixative spray
- ☐ Transparent primer
- ☐ Primed white card strips, for colour matching (optional)
- ☐ Small palette knife, for mixing
- ☐ Rag or paper towel
- ☐ Size 0 filbert brush
- ☐ Size 0 round brush
- ☐ Size 1 round brush
- ☐ Soft brush, for blending and softening

SET-UP

I have placed my red onion on some light grey paper with a darker grey card for the background. I raised the lamp up a little higher than usual until I was happy with the highlight and the cast shadow. The peeling skin creates lovely shapes and shadows, including a soft red glow on the surface where the light is shining through it.

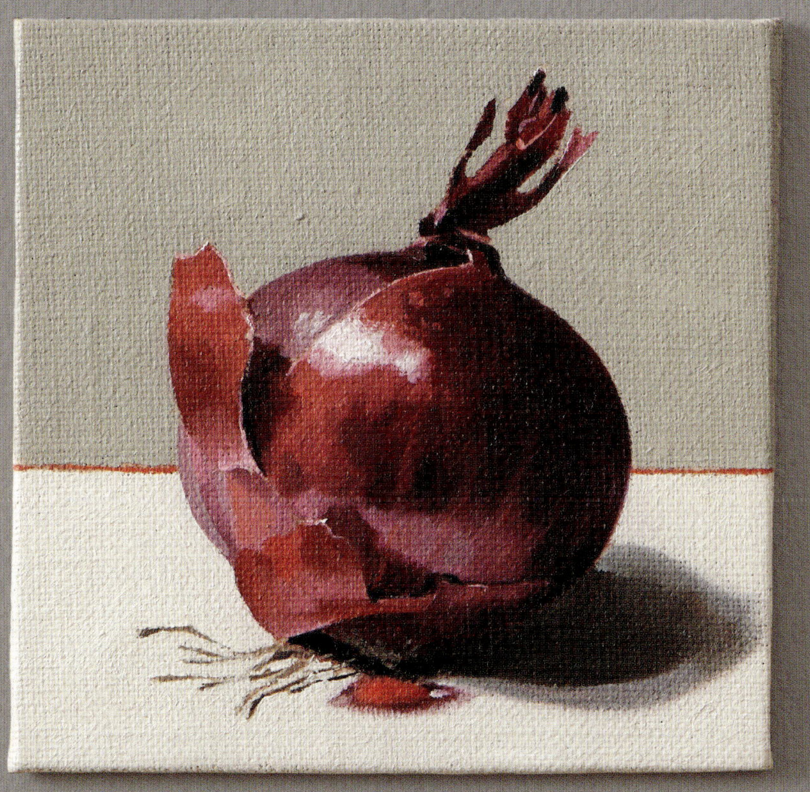

What looks like a complex subject can be broken down into just three main paint mixes from dark to light.

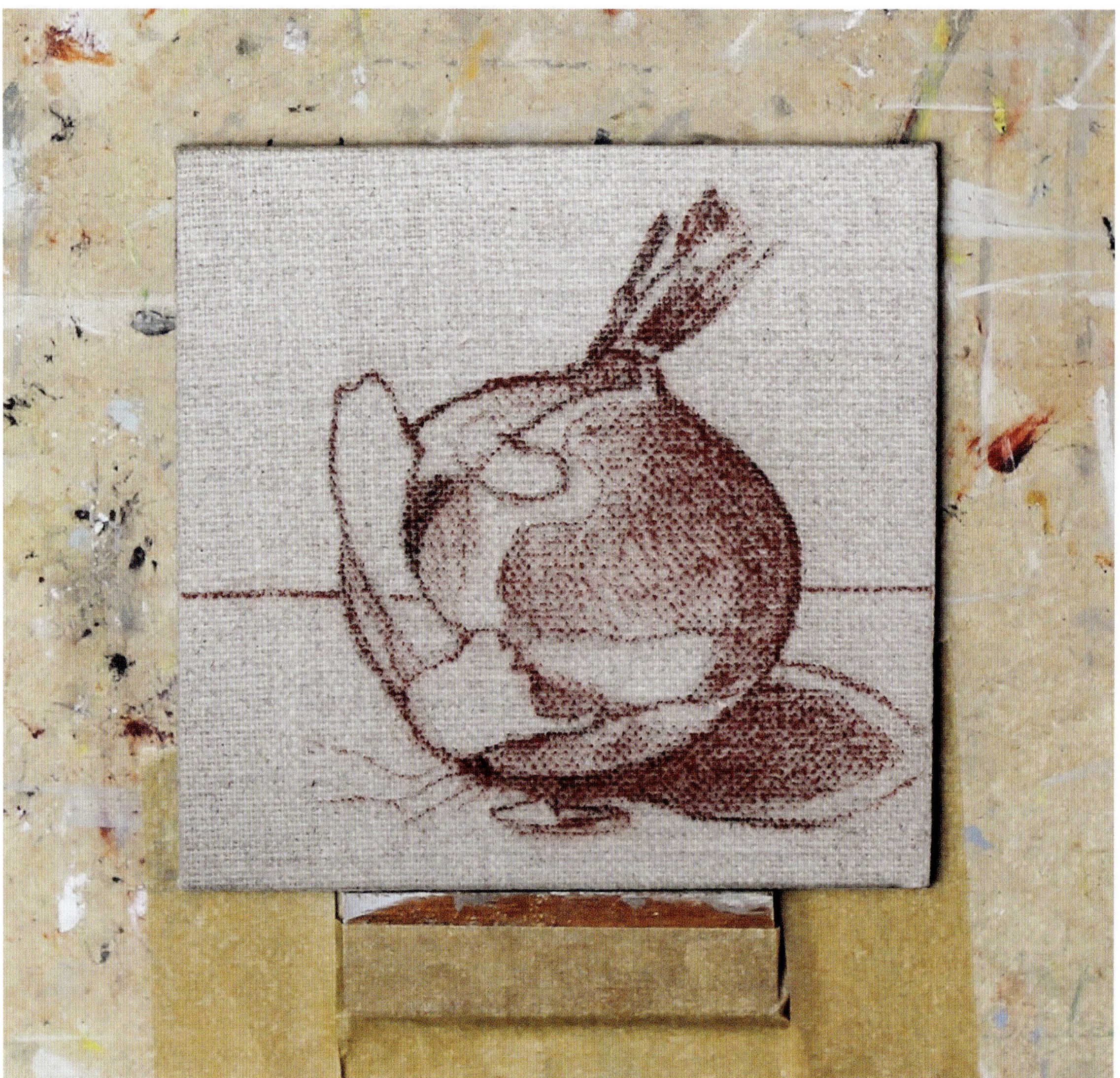

1. UNDERDRAWING

I've drawn my red onion, marking out where the highlights and shadows
are and shading in the tonal areas to help assess the mixes. Fix your
drawing and, if you wish, apply a coat of transparent primer. Allow to dry.

TIP

*Take some time to observe your red onion – look for the darkest areas and
the lightest areas. Remember to squint! How many values do you see?*

2. ASSESS VALUES

Excluding the highlights and the reflected light, I can break my red onion down into three main values. I premixed these colours as follows from a limited palette of just five paints:

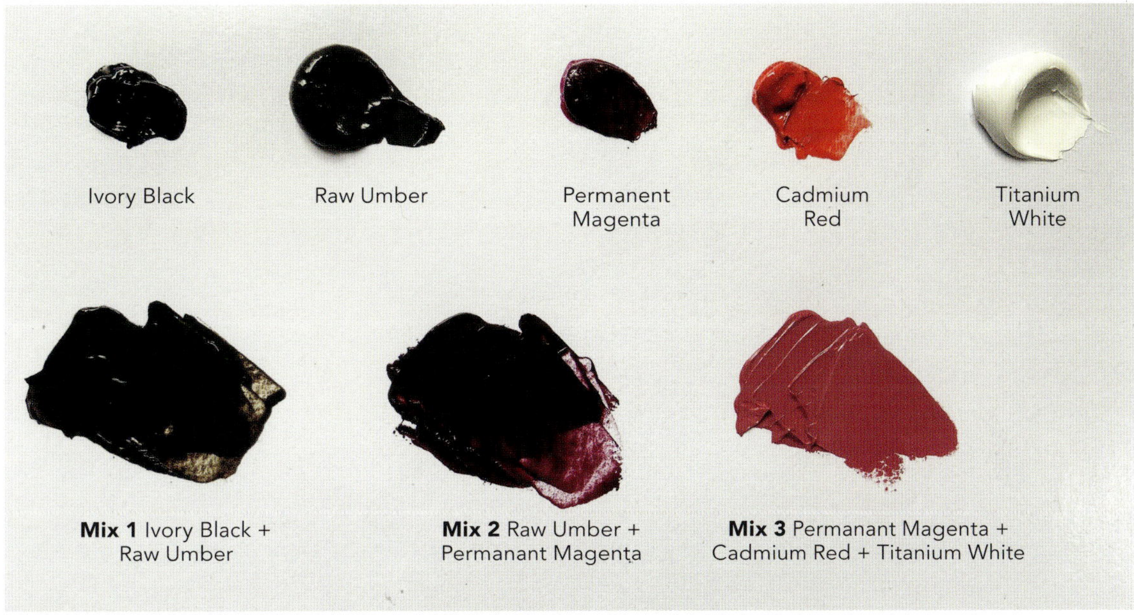

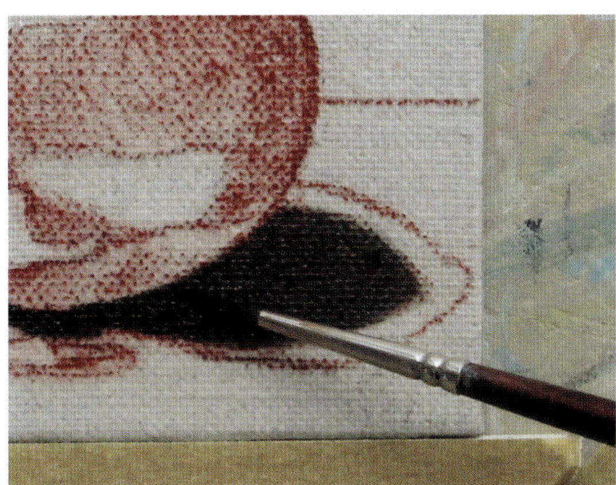

3. CAST SHADOW

Using Mix 1, the darkest colour mix of Ivory Black and Raw Umber, block in the cast shadow with a Size 0 filbert brush, leaving the outer shadow, the penumbra, blank for now. Don't worry about being too neat at this stage; you are just blocking in and establishing the values.

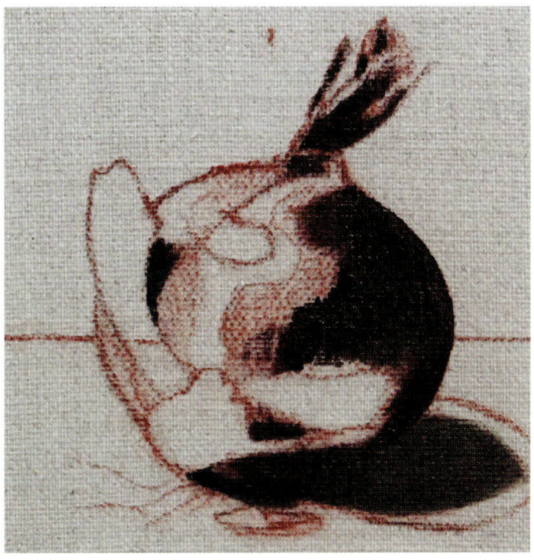

4. DARKEST PARTS

Next, wipe the brush and begin to roughly block in the darker parts of the onion using Mix 2 of Raw Umber and Permanent Magenta.

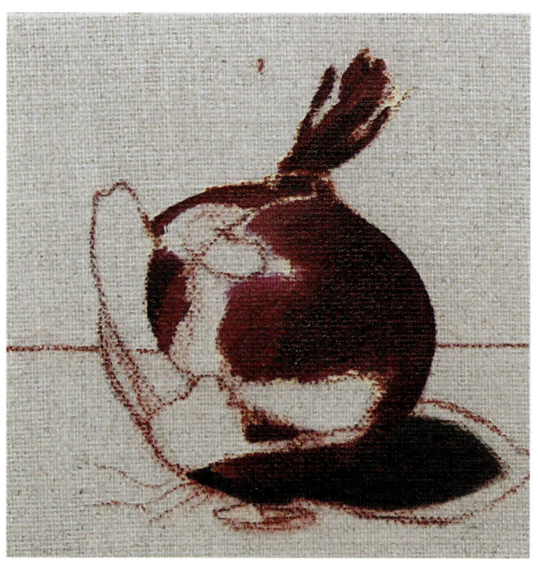

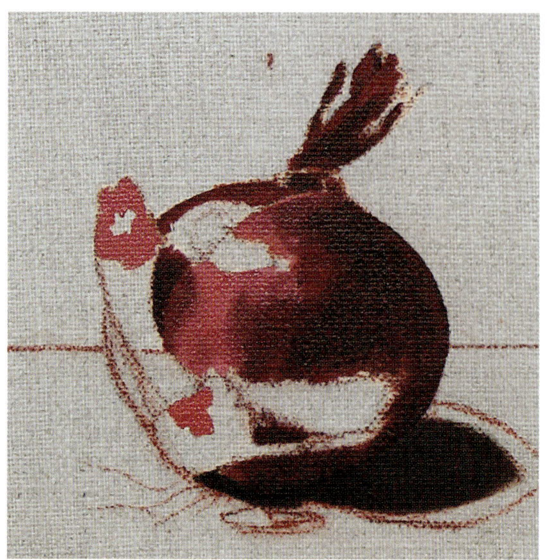

5. BLOCK IN BASE COLOUR

Work your way into the light-facing plane of the onion. At this stage you're not quite ready to use the lightest mix. Instead, continue to block in some more shapes using only Permanent Magenta with the filbert brush.

6. LIGHTEST VALUE

Wipe the brush and begin to paint the lighter parts of the red onion with the lightest Mix 3 (Permanent Magenta, Cadmium Red and Titanium White). Use your fine round brush for the more fiddly areas.

7. BUILD DARKER VALUE

Using Mix 1 and the fine Size 0 round brush, continue to block in the darker areas, including the shadowy parts where the skin is peeling away.

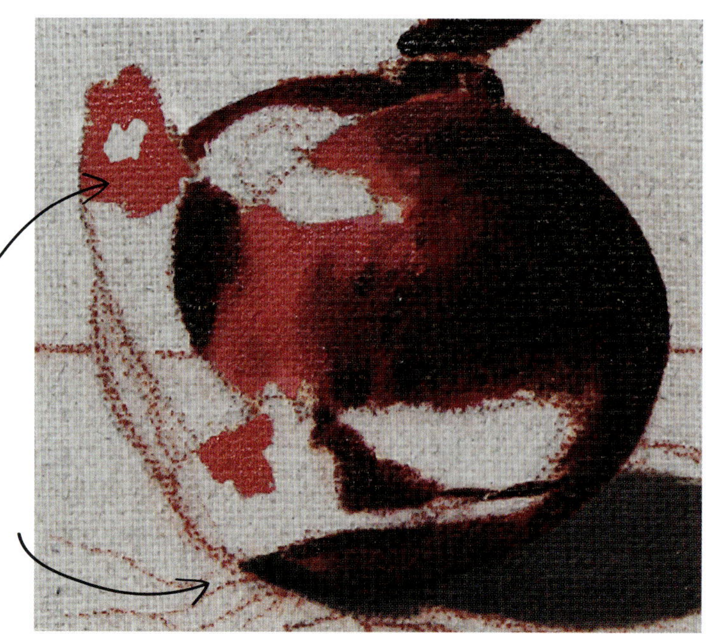

Building layers of colour will intensify the darker areas of shadow.

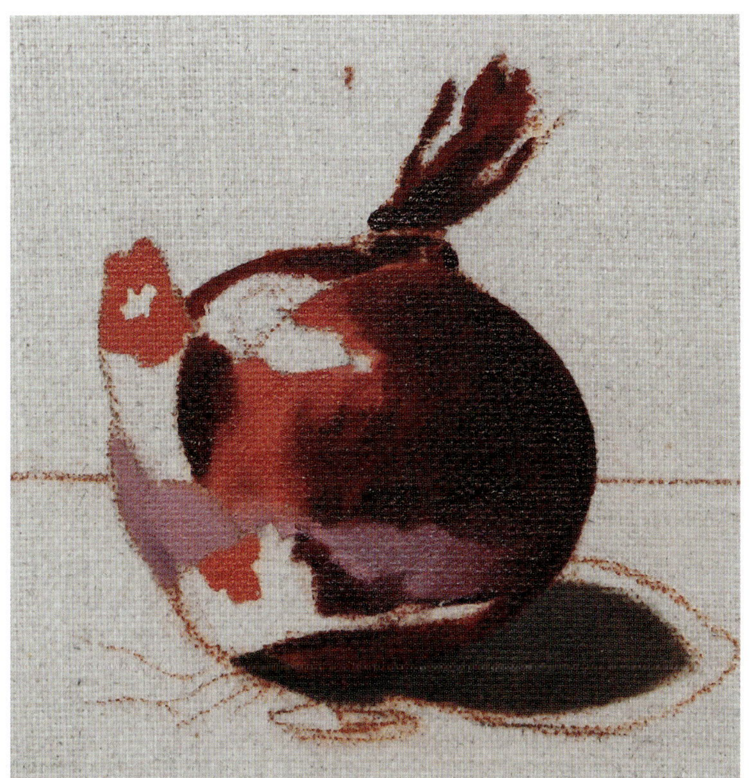

8. REFLECTED LIGHT

Now bring your attention to the area of reflected light – this is where light is bouncing off the surface back onto the underside of the red onion. Squint at the red onion to work out the correct value – I decided to lighten some of Mix 2 with a tiny amount of Titanium White. Now roughly block in this area with the filbert brush.

9. CONTINUE BLOCKING IN

Next, darken a little of Mix 3 with some Permanent Magenta and continue to block in areas on the peeled skin. I look for any other areas that have this value and use this opportunity to make any little adjustments (for example, I needed to darken a little spot near the peeling skin, directly above the reflected light).

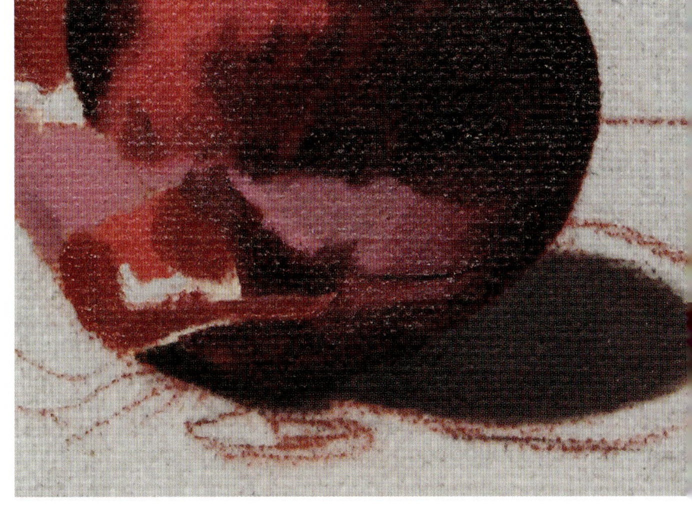

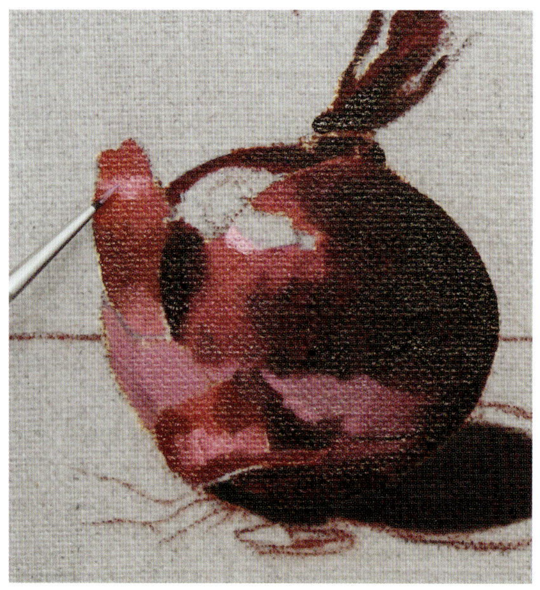

10. HIGHLIGHTS

Now use a Size 0 round brush to paint the highlights on the peeled skin using some of Mix 3 that has been lightened with a tiny amount of Titanium White.

11. BLEND

Using a clean, dry Size 1 round brush, gently soften some internal edges – for example, the border between the reflected light and the darkest part of the onion – and just slightly blend the edges of the peeled skin.

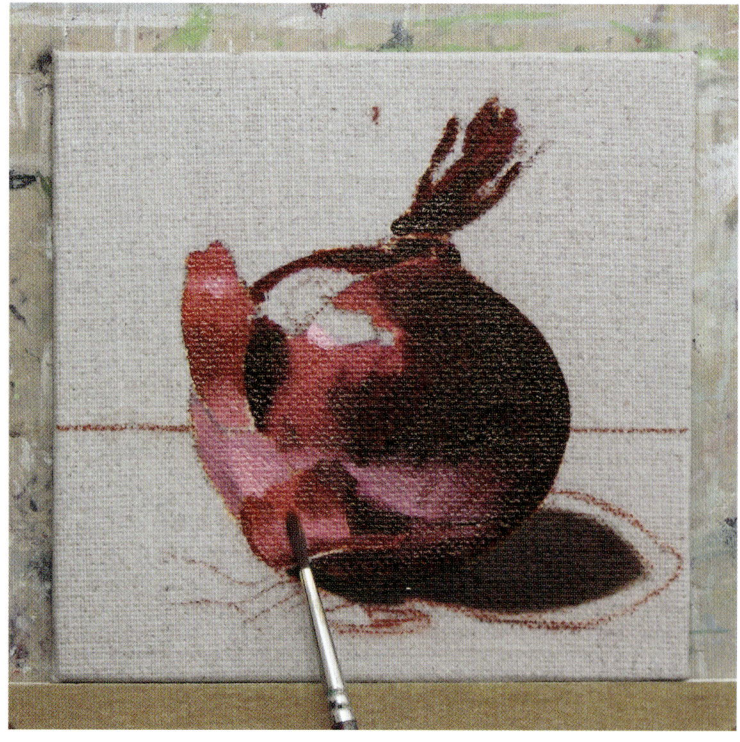

12. LIGHT EDGES

Lighten a little of Mix 3 with some Titanium White (enough to make it a little lighter than the mix from step 10) and, using the Size 0 round brush, carefully paint the edges of the peeled skin that are catching the light.

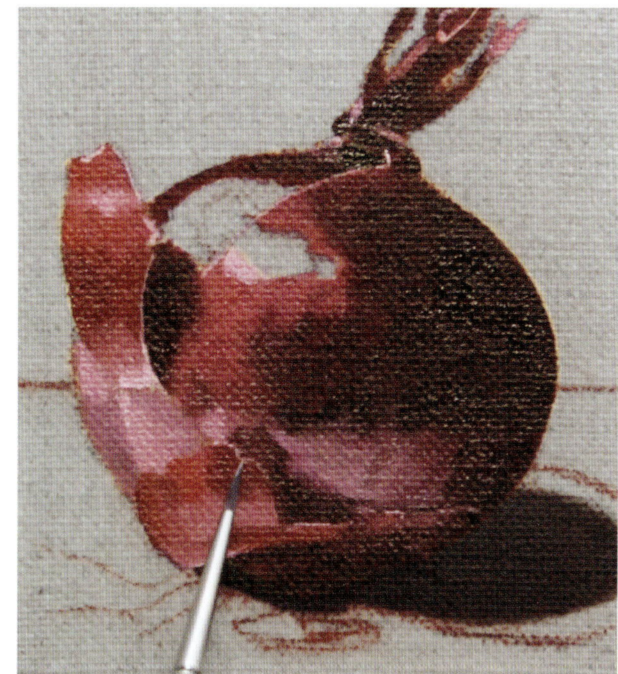

13. FINE DETAILS

The onion's main highlight is split in two halves and the light is reflecting differently on each side due to the different skin textures. The right side of the highlight is by far the brightest, so add some Titanium White to the lightest Mix 3 (a little more than in step 12) and block in this part with a Size 0 filbert. For the left side of the highlight, lighten a little of Mix 2 with some Titanium White and, with a clean brush, roughly block in this area, too.

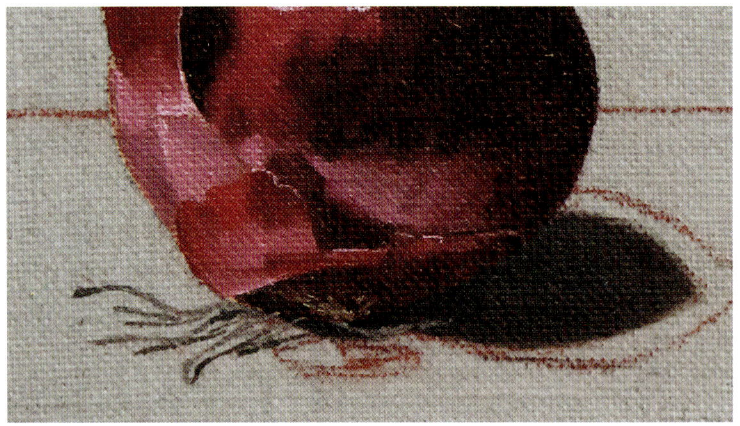

14. ROOTS

To create the colour of the roots, mix a little Raw Umber and Titanium White and paint these in with the fine round brush. Use this same mix to paint a few little marks on the bottom of the onion where the roots are coming out (you may need to 'tonk' this little area first by dabbing with a rag or paper towel).

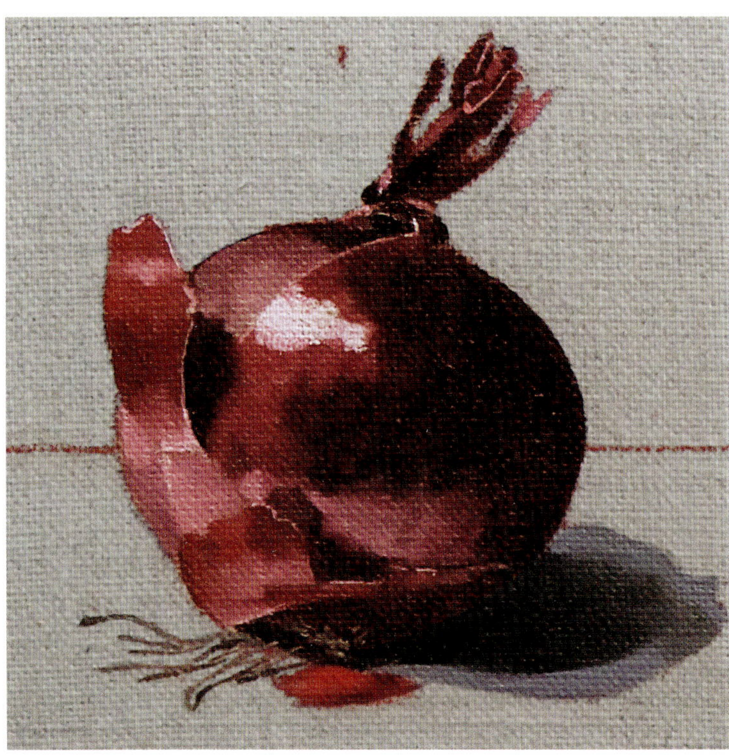

15. SHADOW COLOUR

For the cooler shadow, mix a tiny amount of Kings Blue Deep and Raw Umber and, using a dry filbert brush, roughly paint in the outer edge of the shadow. For the red glow, use a little Cadmium Red at its centre and a little Permanent Magenta around its edges.

TIP

If your paint has been applied quite thickly, you may need to 'tonk' carefully with a rag or paper towel to remove excess paint before embarking on the next step, blending colours or adding the finer details.

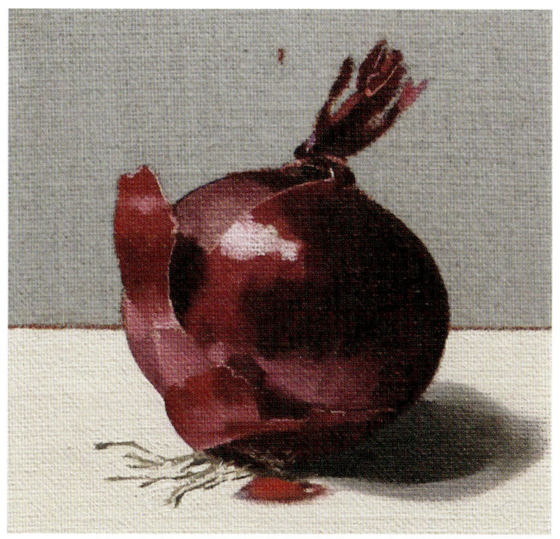

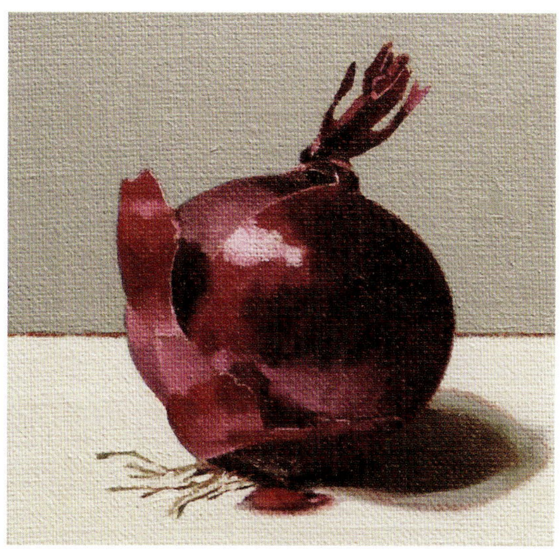

16. FOREGROUND

For the foreground, mix some Raw Umber with Titanium White. Block in the colour with the Size 0 filbert brush and use the Size 0 round brush for the fiddly bits around the roots.

17. BACKGROUND

To create harmony between the foreground and background, use the same mix of Raw Umber and Titanium White from step 16, but with less white to make the colour a shade or two darker. Block in with the filbert brush.

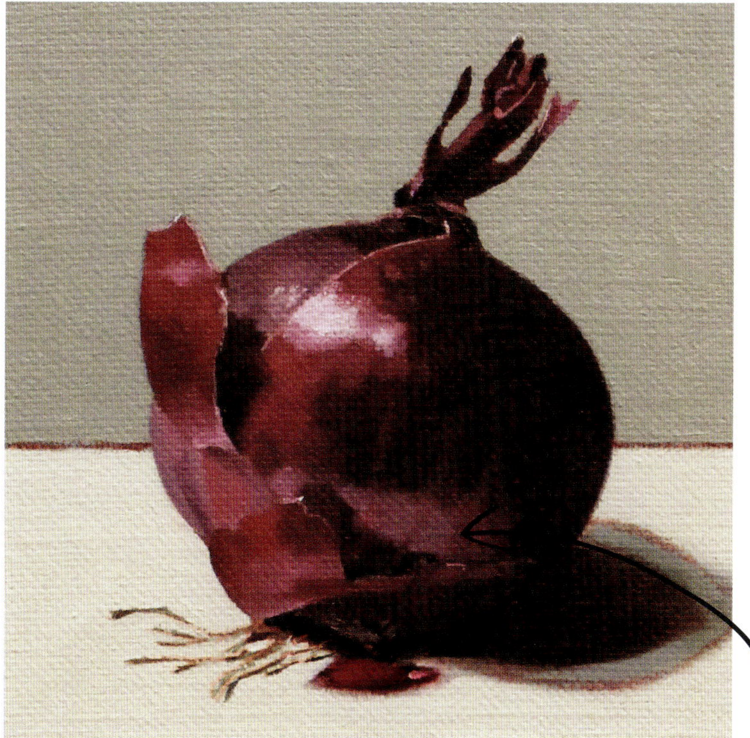

18. HIGHLIGHTS AND DETAILS

I save the brightest part of the highlight until now. Using the Size 1 round brush, dab some pure Titanium White in the centre to really make the onion shine. Use the fine round brush to add some tiny bright spots of highlight here and there; for example, on the edges of the peeled skin and also on the left side of the highlight, being careful to keep it subtle.

Using only the paint mixes already on your palette, paint a few more little details such as the very faint lines on the skin.

GLASS VASE

There is something quite magical about painting glass and I always love the challenge of making an object look transparent. It may seem like a very difficult subject to attempt but, as with our silver jug on page 92, there is less mystery in how to achieve the illusion of glass than you might think, just take it step-by-step as usual.

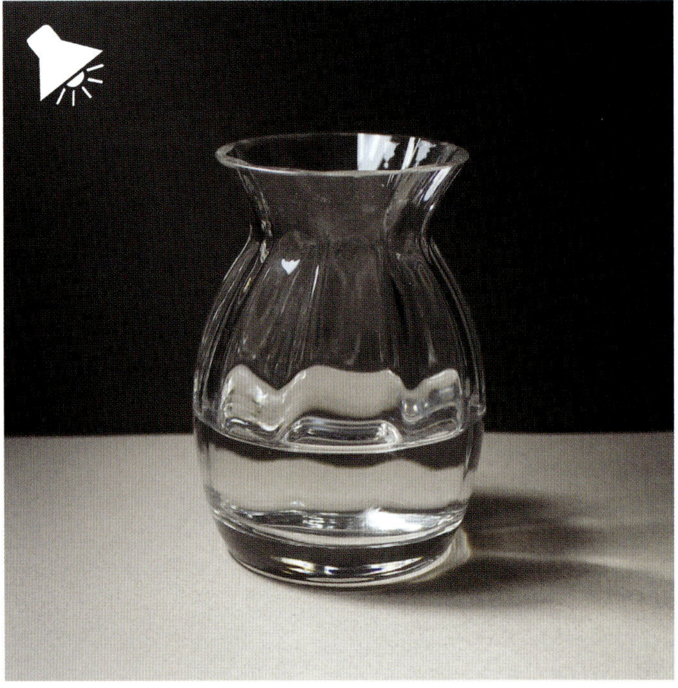

PAINT COLOURS

- Raw Umber
- Ivory Black
- Titanium White
- Kings Blue Deep
- Burnt Umber
- Cadmium Yellow

TOOLS AND MATERIALS

- Linen board (10 x 10cm/ 4 x 4in.), primed with transparent gesso (see page 12)
- Graphite or pastel pencil
- Putty eraser
- Ruler
- Fixative spray
- Transparent primer
- Primed white card strips, for colour matching (optional)
- Small palette knife, for mixing
- Rag or paper towel
- Size 0 filbert brush
- Size 0 round brush
- Size ³⁄₁₆ flat brush
- Soft brush, for blending and softening

SET-UP

I have positioned my little glass vase on a light, neutral base and chosen a contrasting, darker background. The water in the vase causes interesting distortions and reflections and adds another element to the set-up. I played around with the angle of my lamp until I was happy with the reflections and shadows.

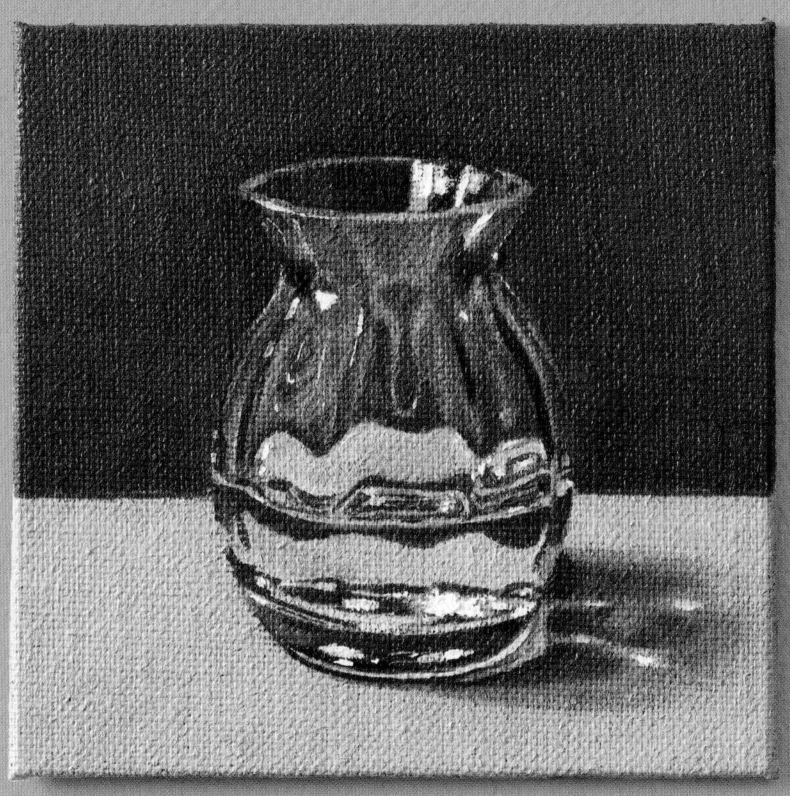

Merging the object with the background and foreground avoids a solid outline and helps to create the illusion of glass.

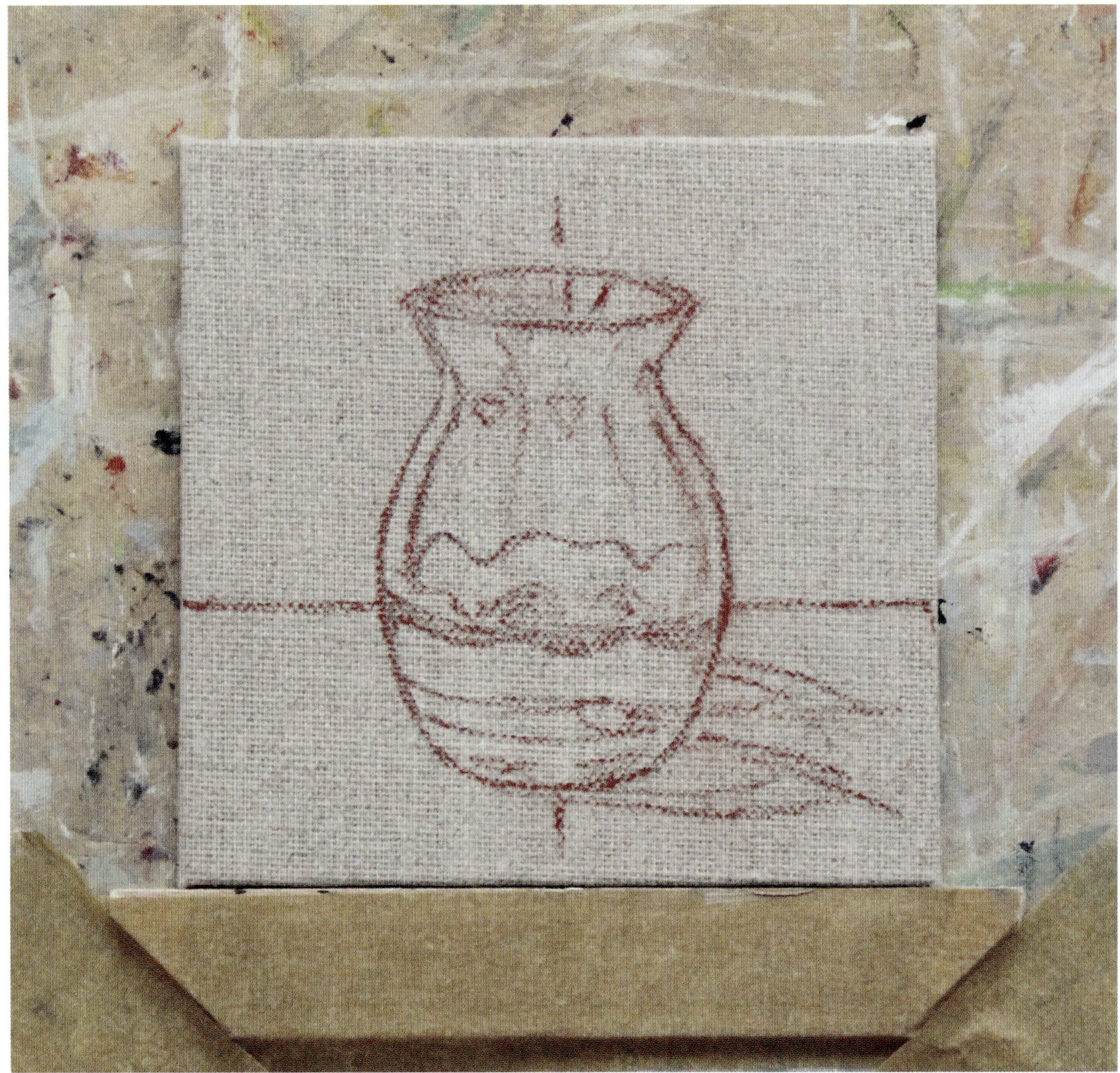

1. UNDERDRAWING

Draw your vase, roughly marking out the highlights, cast shadows and refracted light, and the main abstract shapes within the vase. See step 2 for how to use the local colour to help map out the different areas and shapes in a transparent object. Fix your drawing and, if you wish, apply a coat of transparent primer. Allow to dry.

TIP

To check if the ellipse shape at the top of the vase is symmetrical, draw a vertical line down the centre of the ellipse, use tracing paper to trace the left half of the shape, then flip the paper over to check the right half looks the same. You can use this method to check the symmetry of any shape.

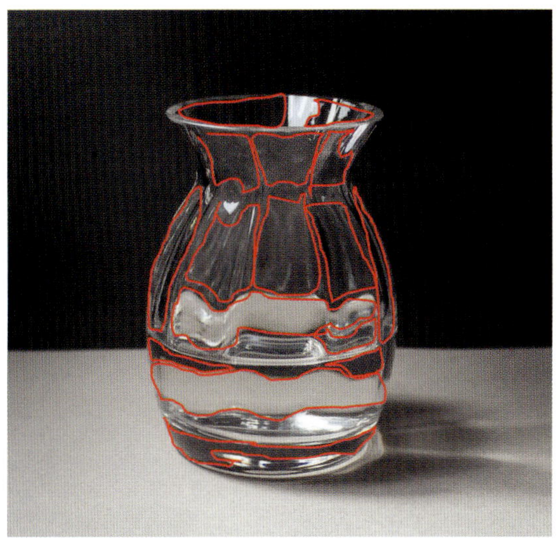

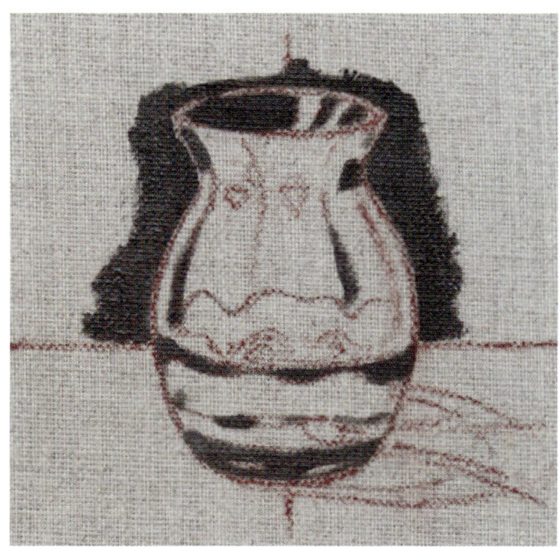

2. OBSERVING AND DRAWING

Take some time to observe your glass vase and look for any interesting abstract shapes. Look at the colour of your background and then see where this colour can be found within your vase. Do the same with the foreground colour.

3. BACKGROUND MIX

I prefer to work from dark to light when I paint, so I begin by mixing my background colour. Mix Raw Umber, Titanium White and a little Ivory Black, and use the Size 0 filbert brush to block in a small area of the background around the vase and look for the same colour within the vase.

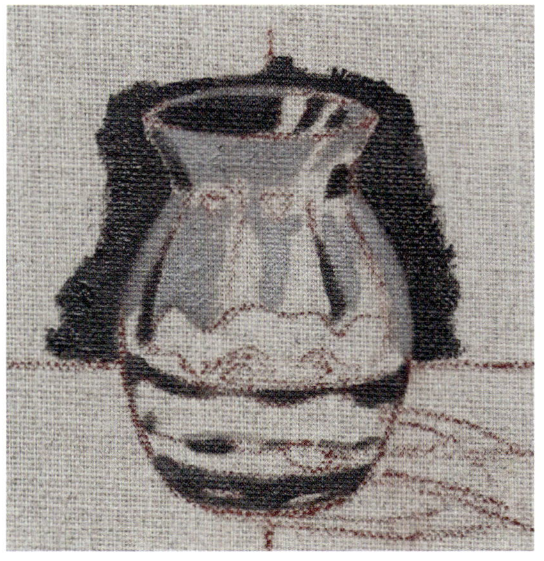

4. LIGHTER SHAPES

With a palette knife, take some of the background mix from the previous step and add a little Titanium White to create a lighter mixture. Still using the filbert brush, begin to block in some of the lighter abstract shapes above the water line.

TIP

At this early stage it is important to get some paint down so that you can start gauging values and checking your mixes against each other. By blocking in only a little of the background, you can easily adjust it later if you discover it should be darker or lighter.

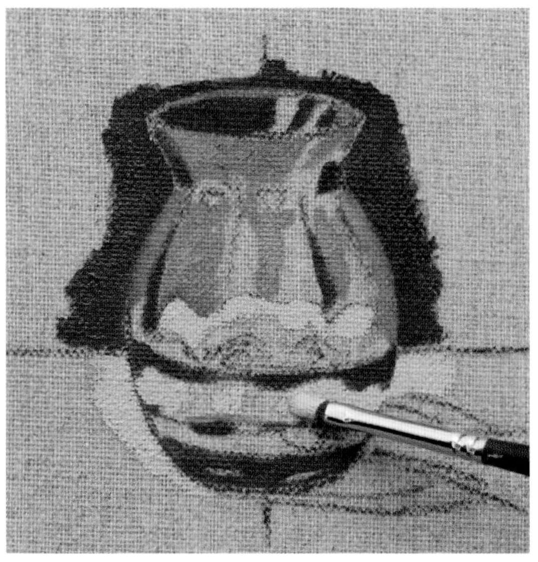

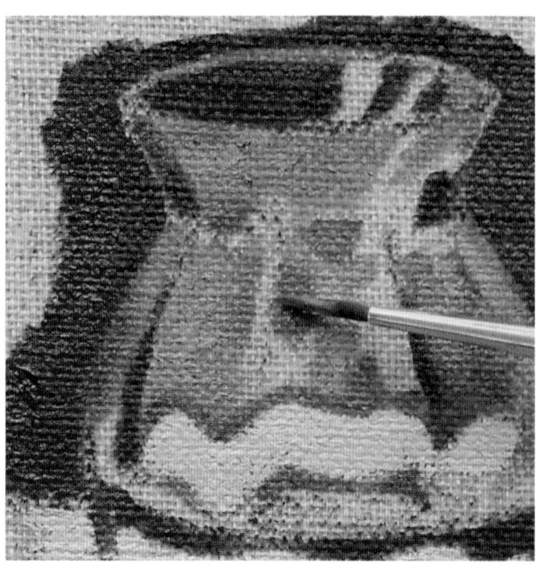

5. FOREGROUND MIX

Using Titanium White, Burnt Umber and a little
Ivory Black, mix up a colour for the foreground.
After wiping the filbert brush, begin to block in
the lighter shapes in and around the vase.

6. DEFINITION

Now bring your attention back to the area above
the waterline. Take a little background mix and
lighten it with a tiny amount of Titanium White,
taking care not to make it as light as the mix from
step 4. Use the Size 0 round brush to add a little
definition to the glass in this area.

TIP

*Remember to leave out the highlights for now,
as we will focus on the sparkly bits later!*

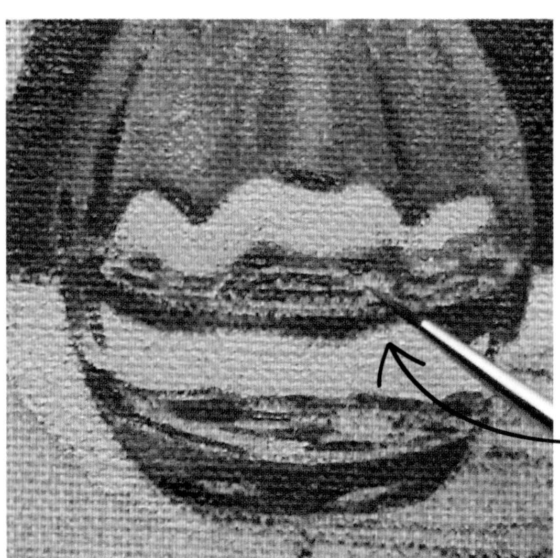

7. WATER SHAPES

Look closely at the water in the vase and notice
patterns of dark and light swirly lines. Still using
the round brush, carefully begin to paint the
darker lines using the tip of the brush to describe
the swirling shapes.

*Follow the lines with
a fluid action.*

8. LIGHT LINES

Wipe your brush and paint in the lighter lines in the water using the pale foreground mix from step 5.

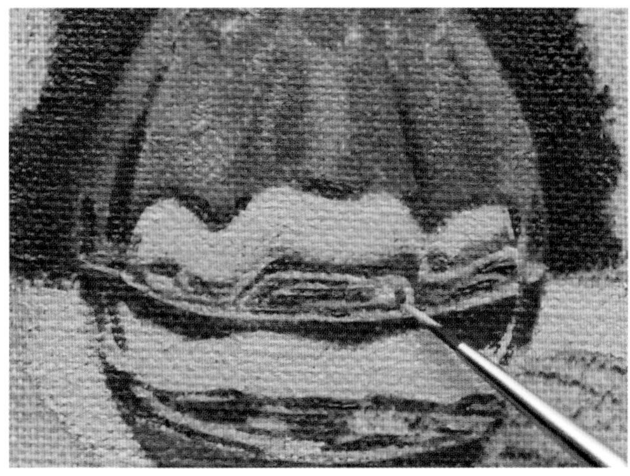

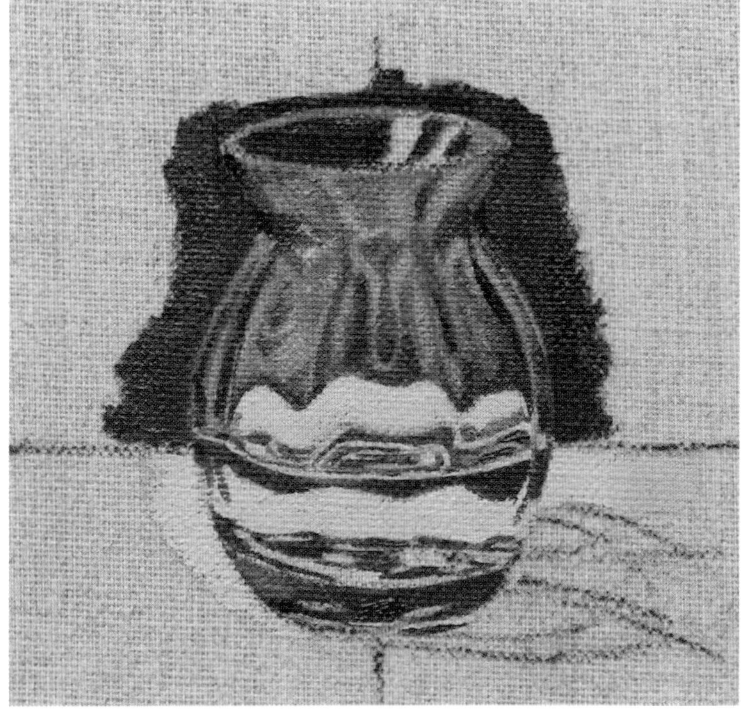

9. ADD DETAILS

Using only the mixes you already have on your palette, add a few more details and descriptive lines to the area above the water line using the fine Size 0 round brush.

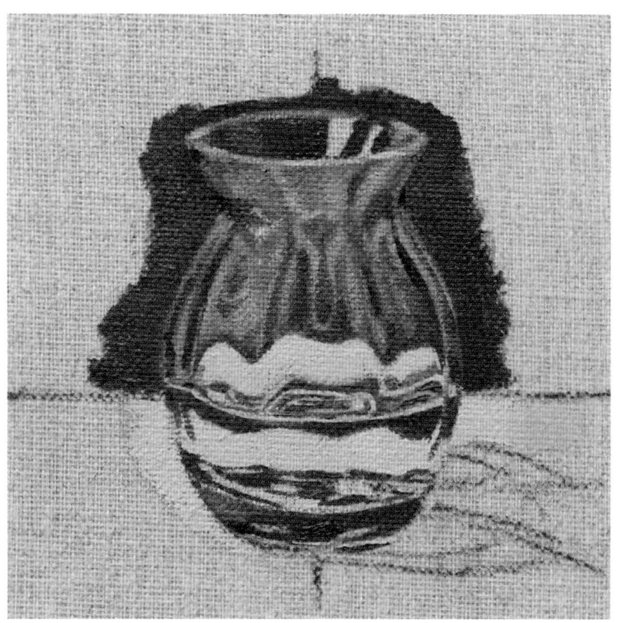

10. ELLIPSE AND OPENING

The ellipse is lighter at the front, so use some of the foreground mix here, painting with a fine round brush. The ellipse darkens slightly as it moves around the back, so choose a slightly darker mix from your palette. Squinting again at the vase, I noticed that a small area to the left of the opening needed lightening a little, too.

11. CAST SHADOW

The shapes in the cast shadow aren't a single colour but take on different values, so observe closely as you block them in. For the darker parts, closest to the vase, use some of the background mix applied with a Size 0 filbert brush. As the shadow moves away from the vase it lightens, so wipe your brush and apply a little of the mix from step 4. Add the occlusion shadow with a fine round brush and some slightly diluted Raw Umber.

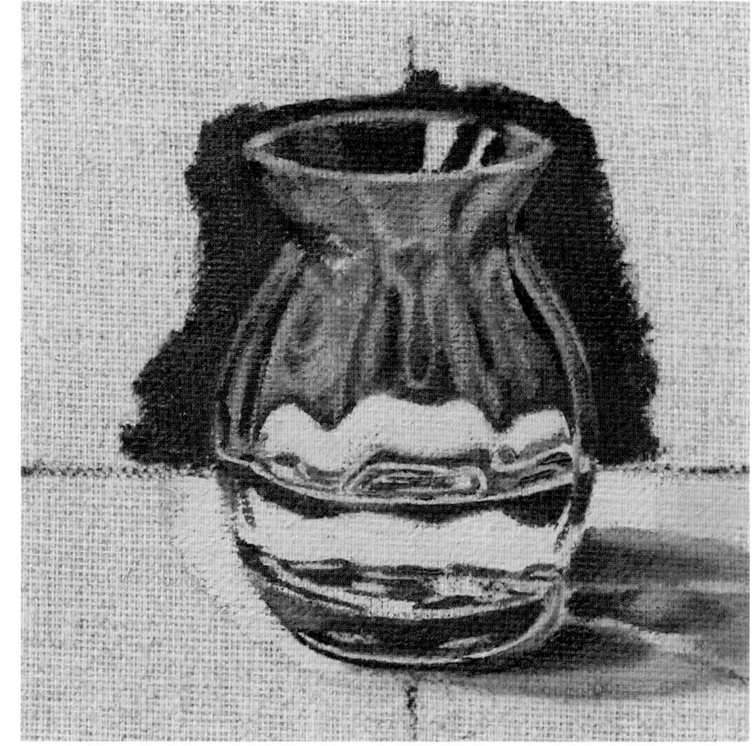

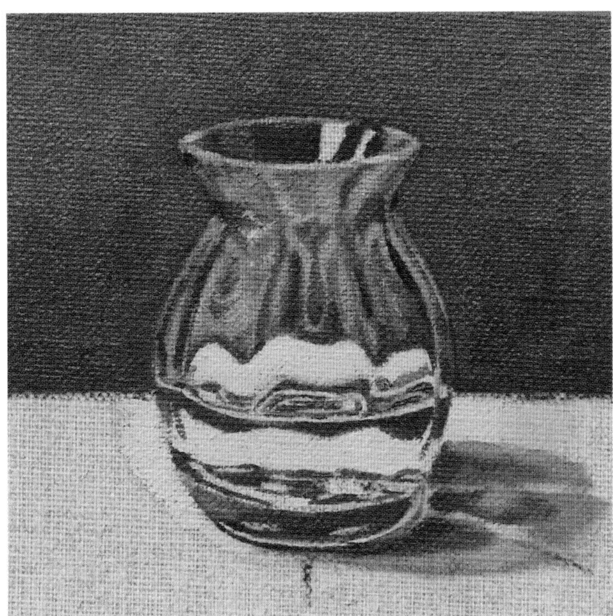

12. FINISH BACKGROUND

Block in the rest of the background using your mix from step 3, using the wider Size 3/16 flat brush to cover the area more quickly. You can make small changes to the outer shape if necessary – at this point, I adjusted the top of the ellipse which was a little too thick.

13. FINISH FOREGROUND

Wipe your brush and block in the rest of the foreground using your mix from step 5.

Rather than a solid outline, parts of the vase are almost merging with the foreground to give the illusion of glass.

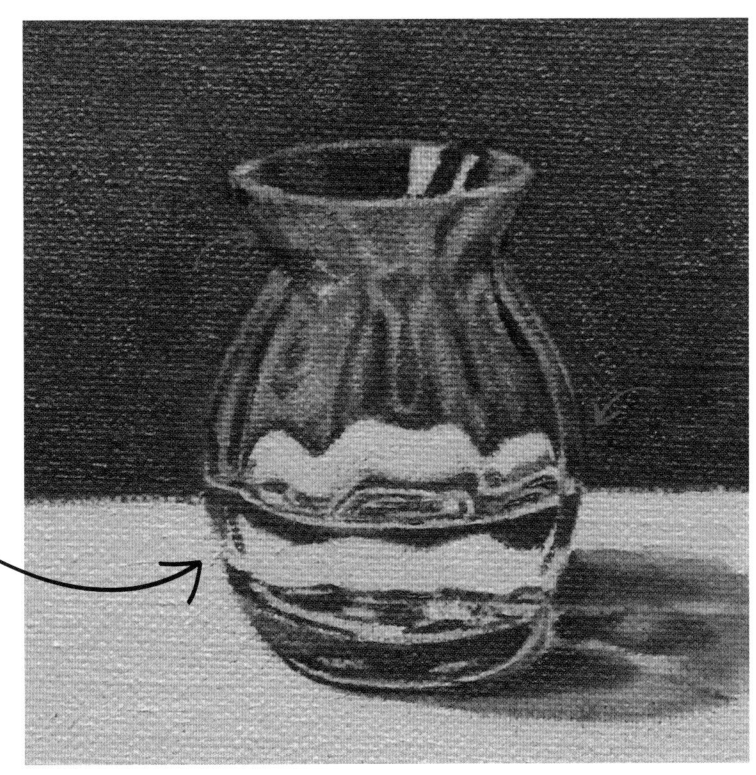

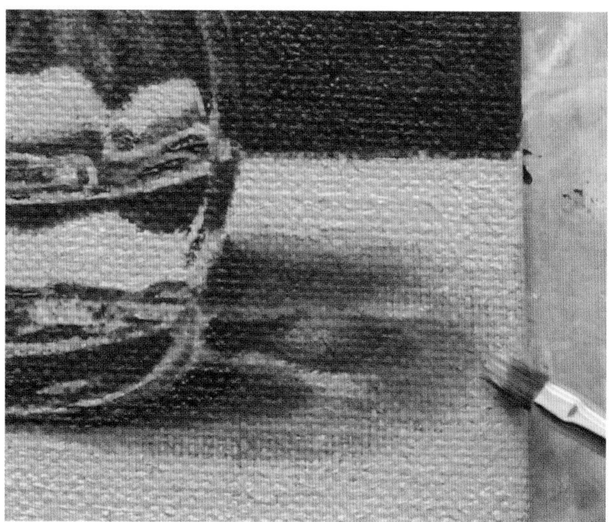

14. PENUMBRA
Dab a little Kings Blue Deep onto the filbert brush and blend the penumbra, the edge of the shadow, where it meets the foreground colour.

15. YELLOW HIGHLIGHTS
I took some time to look closely at the highlights on my vase and I could see that they were made up of three colours: yellow, light blue and white. The yellow highlights are really tiny but important to include nevertheless – they help to make our highlights look more realistic.

Dab the tiniest amount of Cadmium Yellow in a few spots on the vase with the tip of the fine round brush.

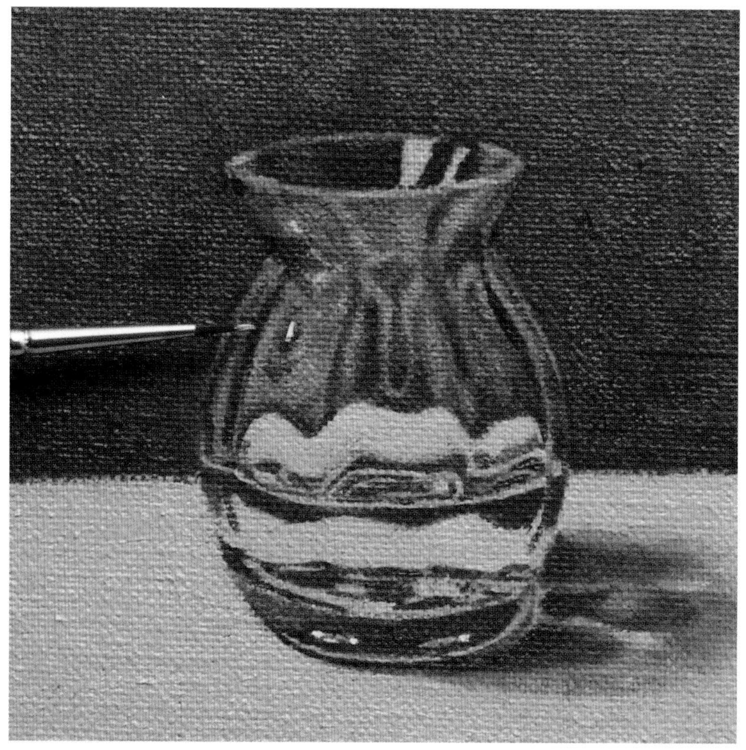

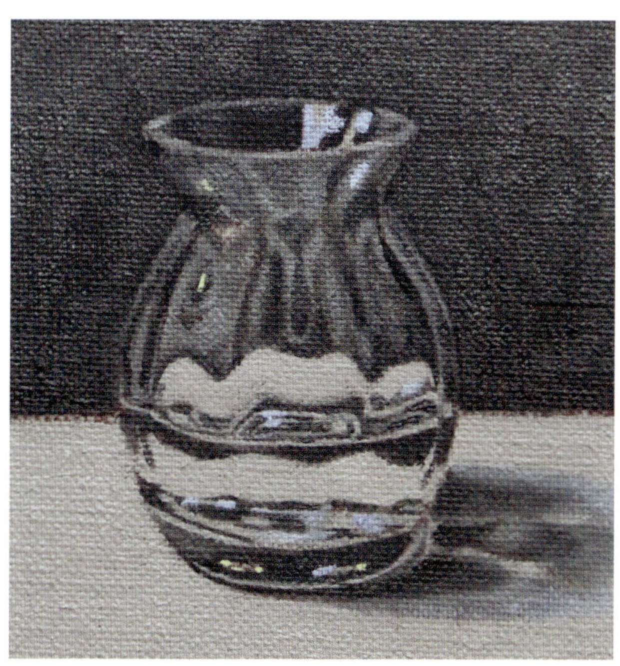

16. BLUE HIGHLIGHTS

The biggest highlight (in the opening of the vase) has blue outer edges, so mix a little Titanium White and Kings Blue Deep and paint this area with a fine round brush. I also painted some tiny dots of this blue which I could see reflected in the water.

17. WHITE HIGHLIGHTS

I have saved the brightest highlights until last. Paint these using Titanium White and a fine round brush. Add a few little spots of white in the cast shadow, where the highlights are being reflected onto the surface. After stepping back to check my work, I decided to add a few more little details here and there, using only the mixes left on my palette.

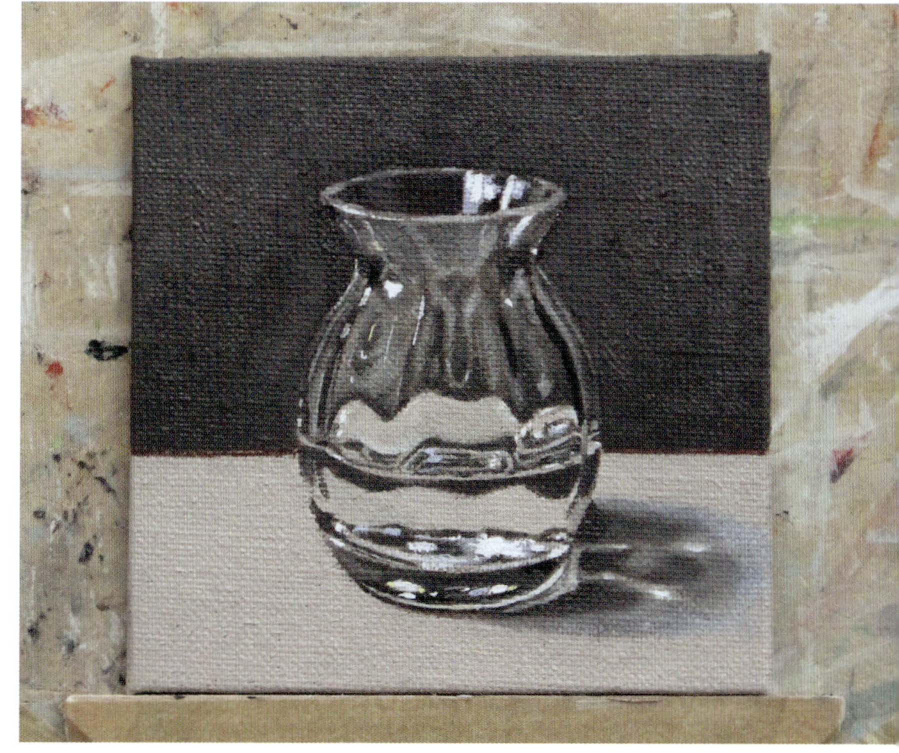

AUTUMN LEAVES

Autumn is possibly the most beautiful and striking season, with flamboyant leaves on display for a few magical weeks of the year. For this project, we will attempt to capture these fleeting colours and paint them in the form of a *trompe l'oeil*, creating the illusion of three-dimensional reality. The biggest challenge will be painting the leaves before they dry up!

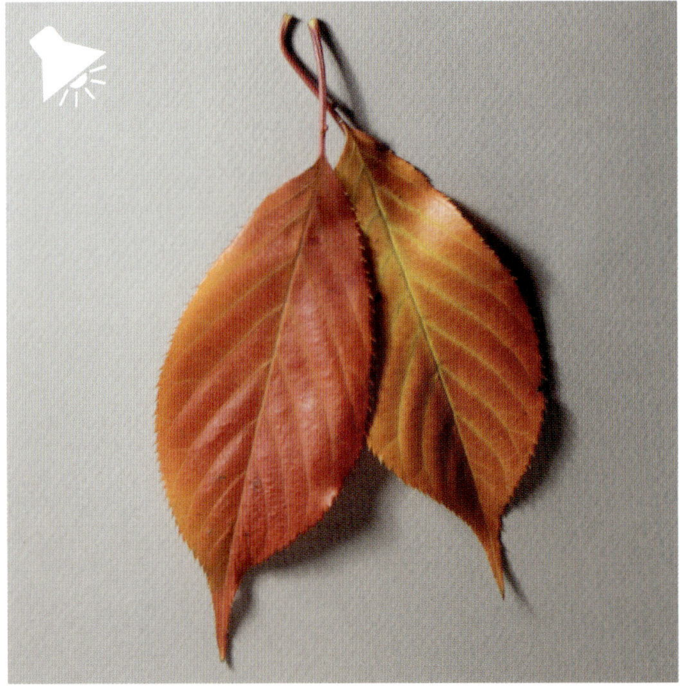

PAINT COLOURS

- ■ Ivory Black
- ■ Permanent Magenta
- ■ Cadmium Red
- ☐ Titanium White
- ■ Kings Blue Deep
- ■ Burnt Umber
- ■ Cadmium Yellow
- ■ Yellow Ochre

TOOLS AND MATERIALS

- ☐ Linen board (10 x 10cm/ 4 x 4in.), primed with transparent gesso (see page 12)
- ☐ Graphite or pastel pencil
- ☐ Putty eraser
- ☐ Ruler
- ☐ Fixative spray
- ☐ Transparent primer
- ☐ Diluent
- ☐ Primed white card strips, for colour matching (optional)
- ☐ Small palette knife, for mixing
- ☐ Rag or paper towel
- ☐ Size 0 round brush
- ☐ Size 2/0 round brush
- ☐ Size 0 filbert brush
- ☐ Soft brush, for blending and softening

SET-UP

I selected two autumn leaves from a cherry tree, one red and the other more yellow in colour. I stuck them onto some neutral grey paper inside my shadow box, using a little double-sided tape. My light is positioned at an angle that produces clear shadows on the grey paper and I moved my shadow box a little closer to my desk easel, so that I could see the leaves better.

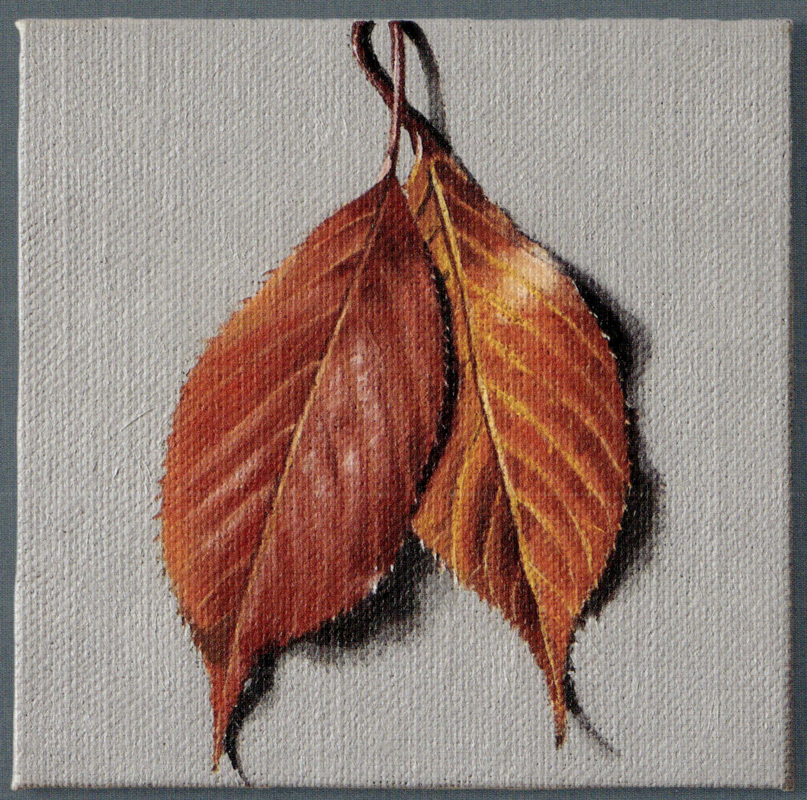

Take a good-quality
photo of your leaves to
use as a reference in case
they start to shrivel up
as you work!

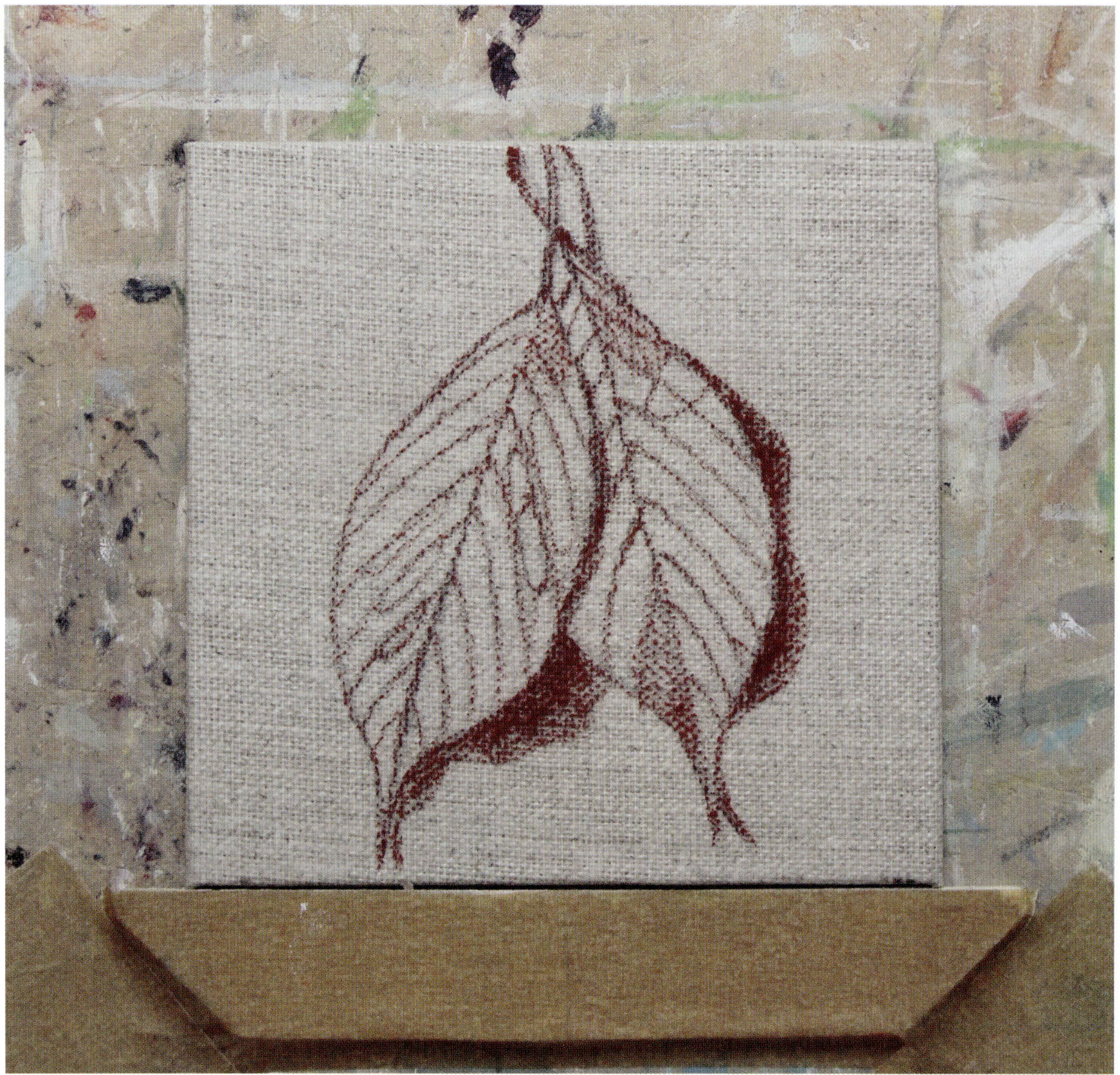

1. UNDERDRAWING

Draw out your leaves, marking where the shadows and highlights are. I also find it helpful to draw the leaf veins. Don't draw a horizon line for this painting, as this would spoil the *trompe l'oeil* effect – we want the leaves to look as if they are hanging in space, not lying on a surface. Fix your drawing and, if you wish, apply a coat of transparent primer. Allow to dry.

TIP

To keep it simple, try drawing and painting just one leaf, building up a collection of different studies as you master the style.

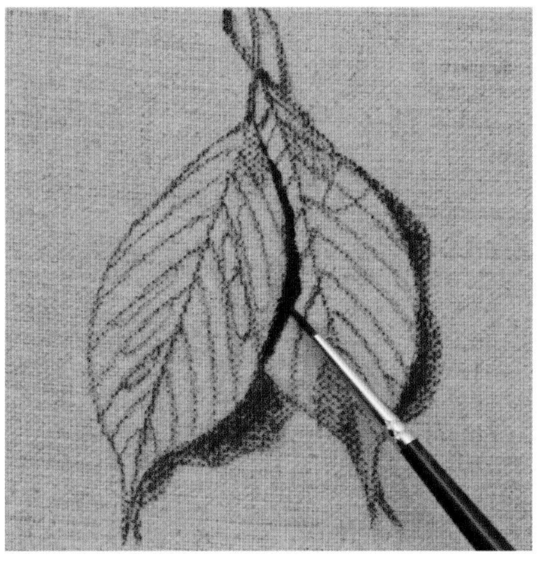

2. DARKEST SHADOW

Look for the darkest shadow, which in my case is in between the two leaves. Rather than using pure Ivory Black, which would be too harsh, mix a warmer dark using Burnt Umber, Permanent Magenta and a little Cadmium Red. Paint in the shadow using a Size 0 round brush.

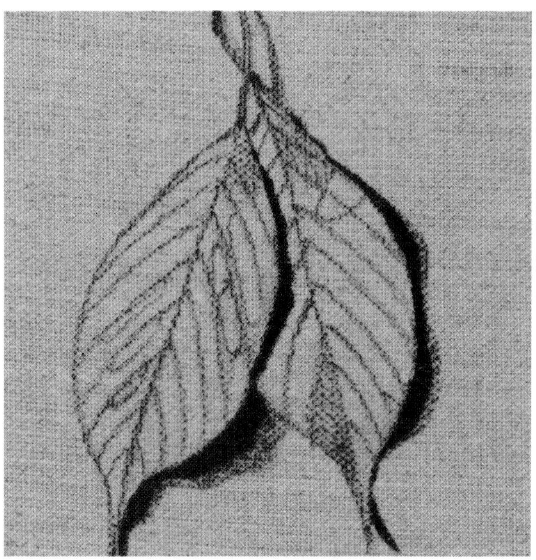

3. DARKEST PARTS OF CAST SHADOWS

Next, paint the darkest areas of the cast shadows, which differ in colour to the shadow from the previous step (less red, more grey in tone). For this tone, mix a little Burnt Umber and Ivory Black. Leave the penumbras at this point.

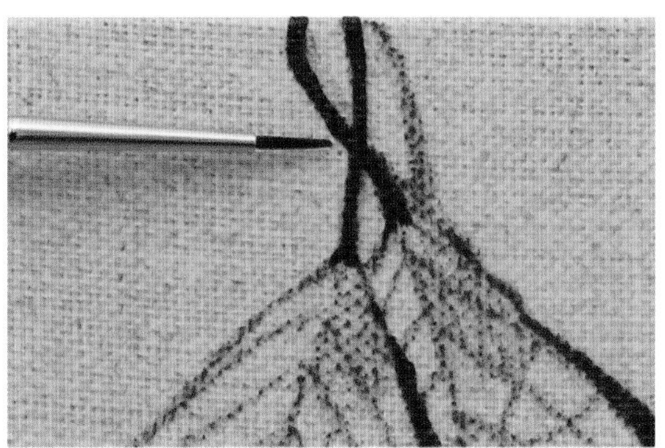

4. STALKS

Use some of the dark shadow mix from step 2 to paint the stalks with a Size 2/0 round brush. You will add the highlights to these stalks at a later point, so just follow the solid shape at this stage.

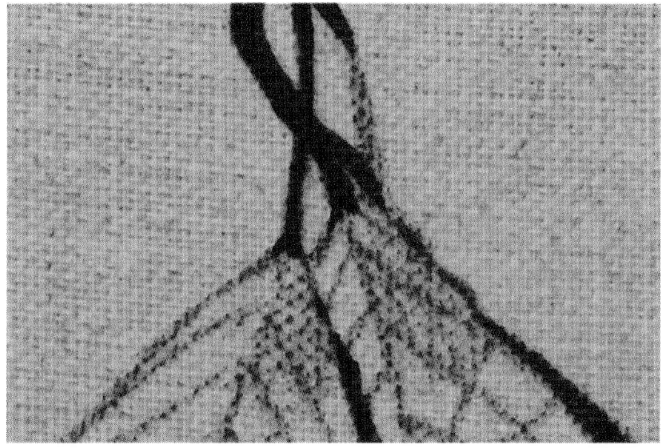

5. STALK SHADOWS

Now focus on the darker part of the stalks' shadows first and, using some of the Burnt Umber and Ivory Black mix from step 3, begin to paint these areas with the Size 2/0 brush. For now, leave out the parts where the stalk shadows lighten; you will return to these later.

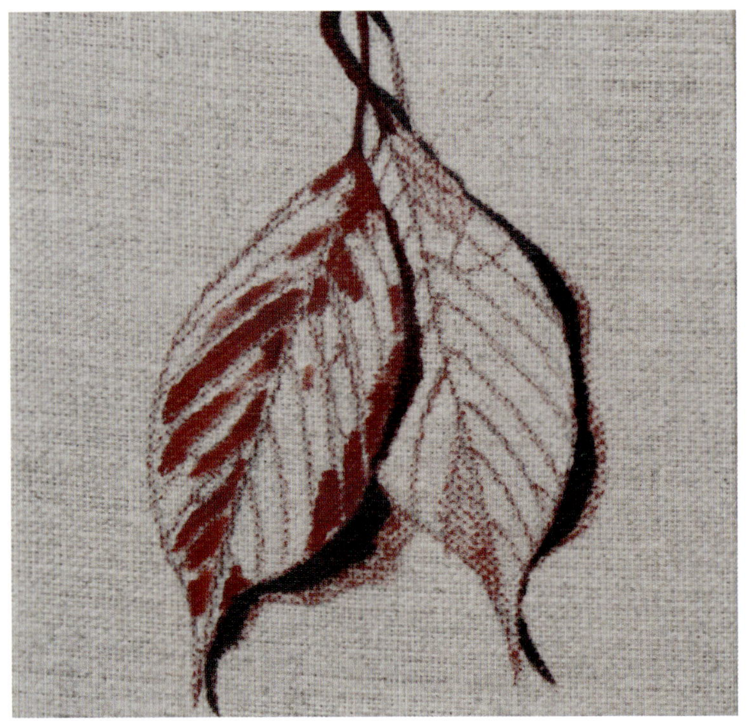

6. MID-TONE ON RED LEAF

Now look closely at the leaves themselves and identify the darker parts to establish the mid-tone. Starting with the red leaf, mix some Cadmium Red with a little Burnt Umber and roughly block in these darker areas using the Size 0 round brush.

7. YELLOW PARTS OF RED LEAF

The left-hand side of the red leaf is more yellow in colour; roughly brush on a mix of Cadmium Yellow, Yellow Ochre and a tiny amount of Cadmium Red, still using the round Size 0 brush. Switch to the finer Size 2/0 brush and paint the yellow veins on the left-hand side of the leaf.

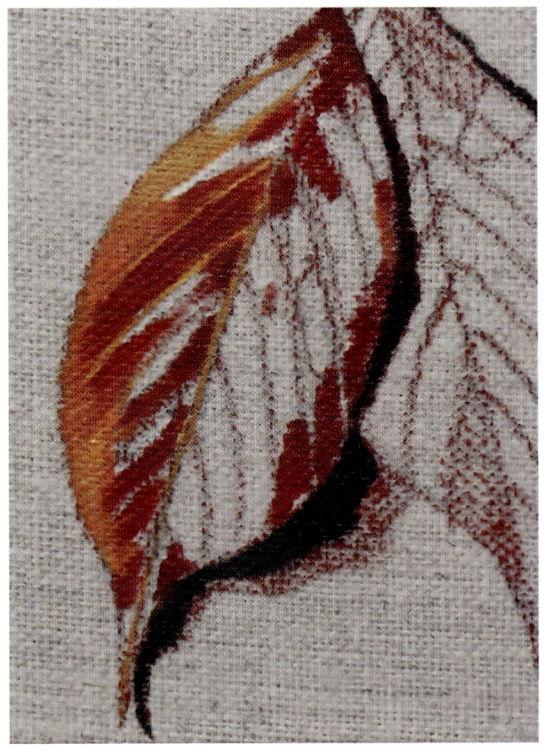

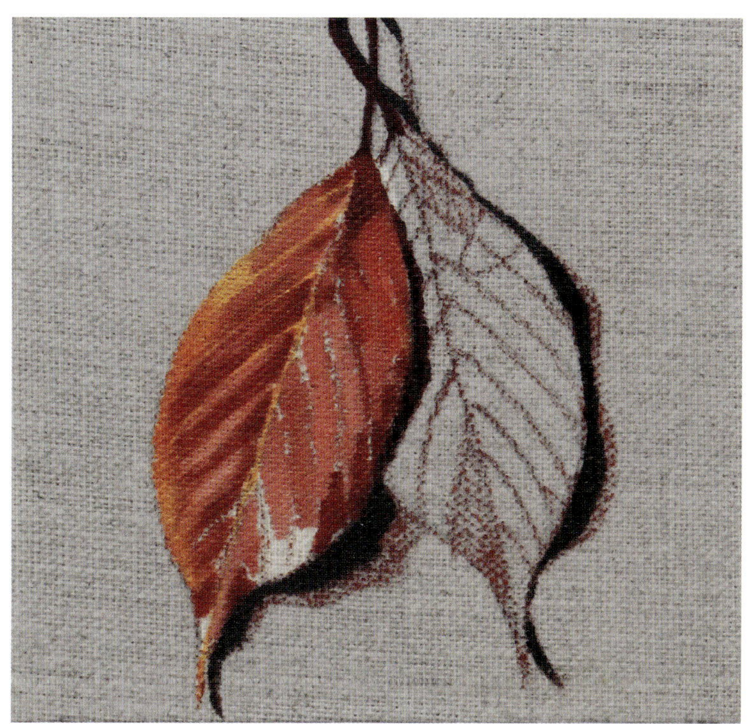

8. LIGHT TONES ON RED LEAF

Take some of the mid-tone of Cadmium Red and Burnt Umber mix from step 6 and lighten it with a little Titanium White, then continue to block in the slightly lighter parts of the red leaf, following the bands of colour between the fine leaf veins.

9. FINISH RED LEAF

Block in the remainder of the red leaf using the Size 0 round brush and the mix of Cadmium Red and Burnt Umber from step 6.

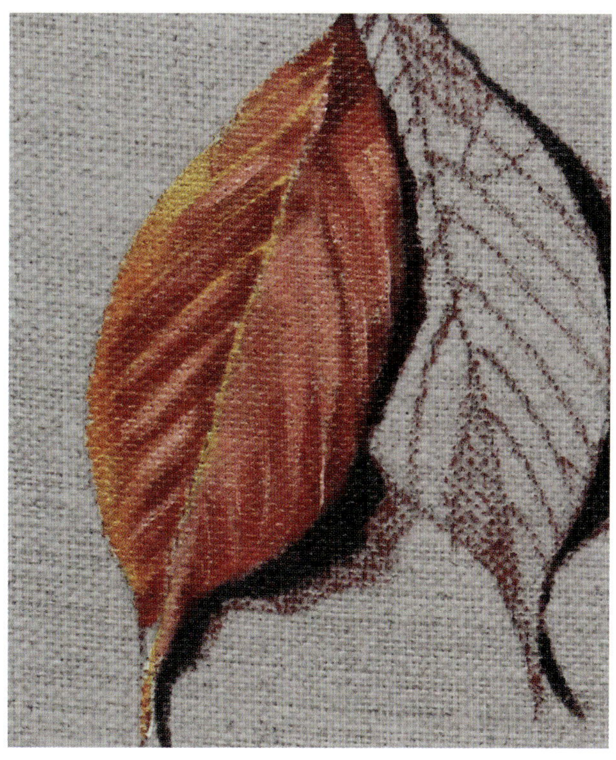

TIP

Try holding the painting up next to the leaves and squinting at them both in turn — I find this is a really useful way of checking the accuracy of my colours!

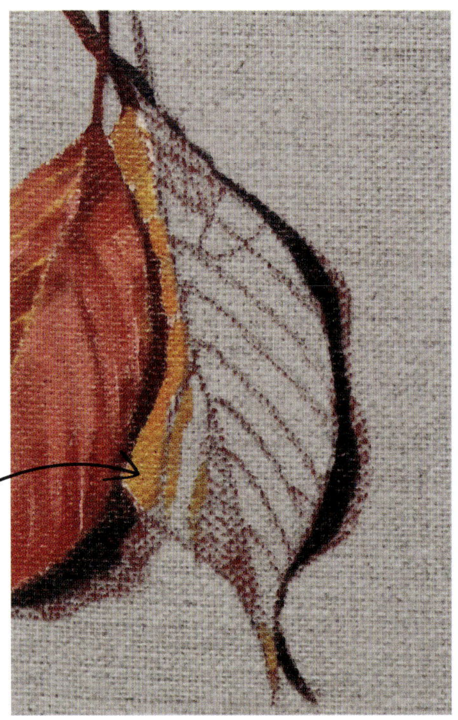

This yellow needs to be brighter than the yellow you mixed for step 7, so add more Cadmium Yellow.

10. MID-TONE ON YELLOW LEAF

Now turn your attention to the second leaf. Begin by blocking in the yellow mid-tones with the Size 0 round brush, using a mix of Cadmium Yellow, Yellow Ochre and a tiny amount of Cadmium Red.

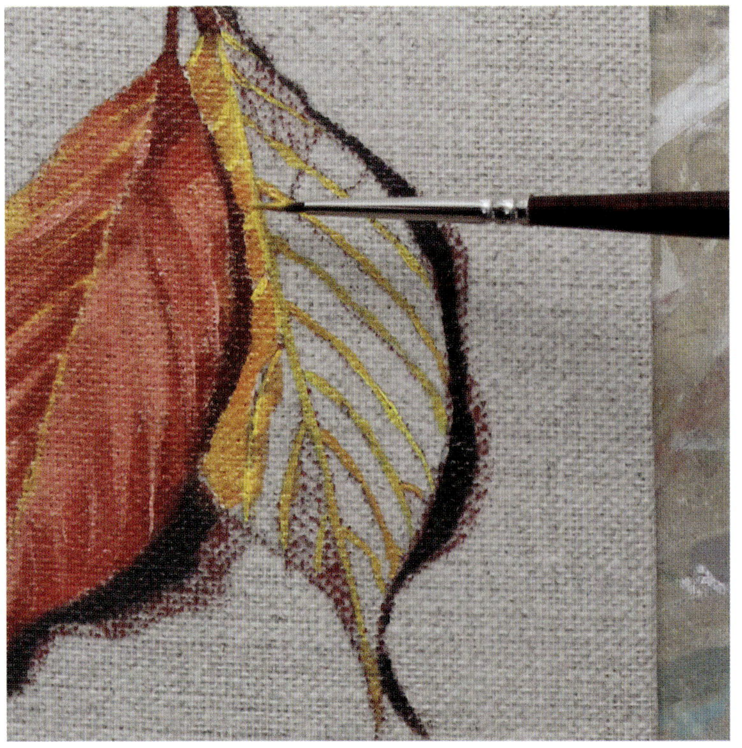

11. YELLOW VEINS

Add the yellow veins with the fine Size 2/0 brush, using a mix of Cadmium Yellow and Yellow Ochre. I thinned my paint mix with a tiny bit of diluent for this step – this really helps the flow when painting intricate details.

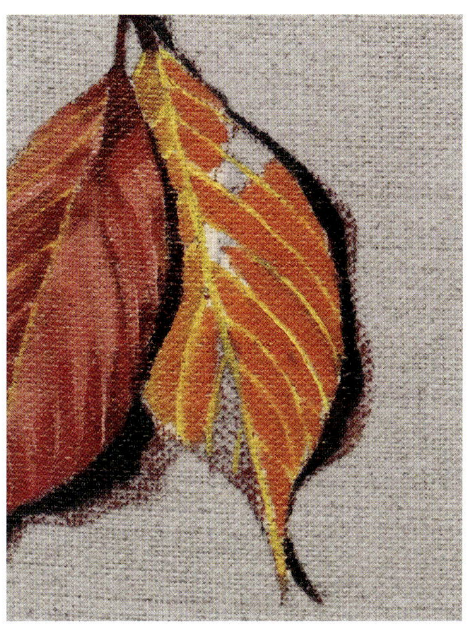

12. BLOCK IN YELLOW LEAF

You can now begin to block in the rest of the yellow leaf. You need to create a slightly deeper version of the colour mix from step 7, using Cadmium Yellow, Yellow Ochre and a tiny amount of Cadmium Red. If you have some mix left over from step 7, you can use this and just add a little more Cadmium Red.

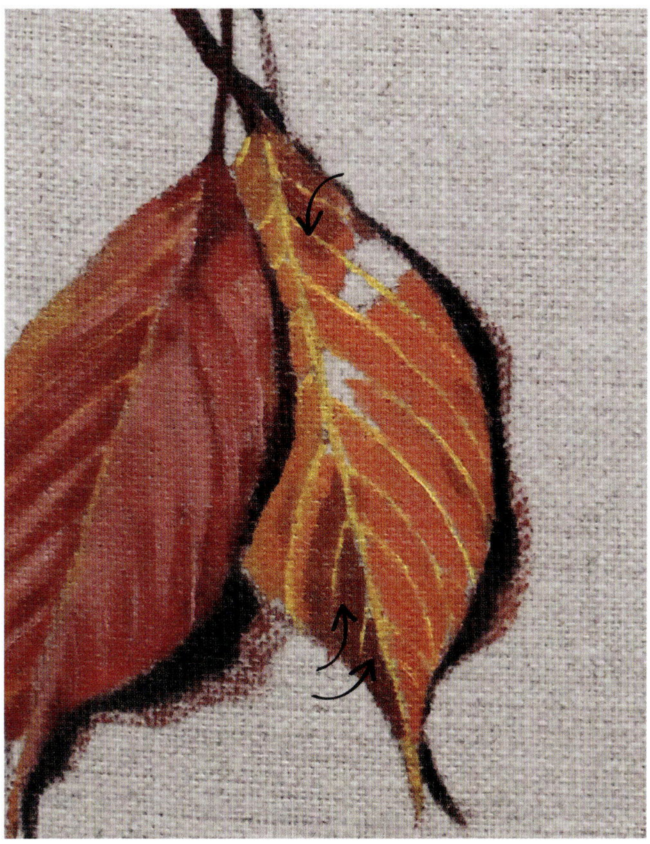

13. SHADOWS

There are a couple of quite dark shadows on my yellow leaf, so I mixed some Burnt Umber with Cadmium Red and painted these in using a Size 0 round brush.

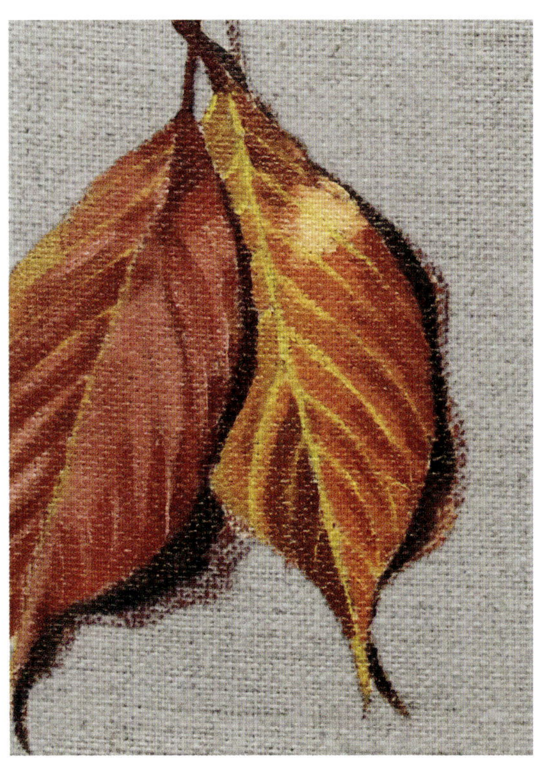

14. DARKEN EDGES

To build the sense of depth, I needed to darken the right-hand side of my yellow leaf, where it curves away from the light. Using my palette knife, I took a little of the dark mix from step 13 and added in a little more Cadmium Red to create a deep red colour. Use this mix to paint the outer edge with the Size 0 round brush. Now paint in any remaining blank areas using existing mixes from your palette. Wipe your brush and block in the highlight with a mix of Cadmium Red, Yellow Ochre and a little Titanium White.

15. HIGHLIGHTS

For the little highlights on the red leaf, lighten the mix from step 8 with a tiny bit of Titanium White and then dab the paint on using a Size 0 round brush. For the highlight on the yellow leaf, use Yellow Ochre and Titanium White and dab on a couple of brighter spots. Use the fine brush to carefully paint the little highlights on both stalks with any remaining paint mix from the red leaf highlights.

Using the mixes already on your palette, paint the tiny little spikes all around the edges of the leaves with the fine Size 2/0 brush.

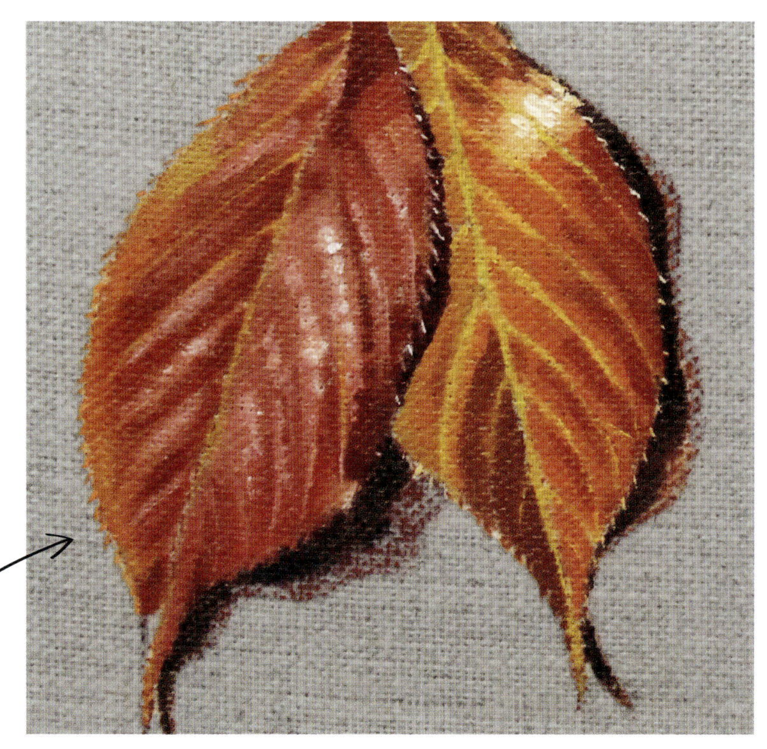

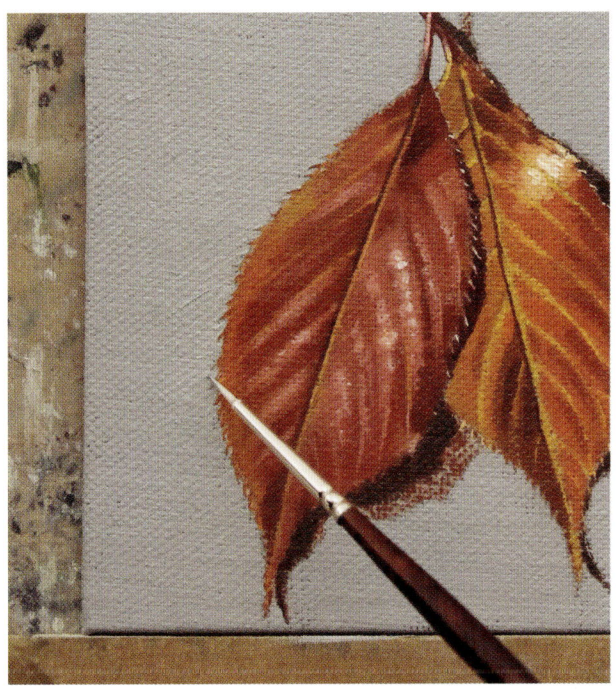

16. BACKGROUND

Next, using your palette knife, mix up Burnt Umber, Ivory Black and Titanium White to create the neutral grey background colour. Block in the larger areas using a filbert brush, but switch to a fine Size 2/0 brush for painting the more fiddly areas around the serrated leaf edges and in between the stalks.

17. FINAL DETAILS

Mix a little Kings Blue Deep and Burnt Umber for the cast shadow penumbra. Soften the outer edges by blending them with a dry brush. You can now also paint the rest of the stalks' shadows using this same mix of paint.

Using a clean, dry brush, gently blend the leaves a little, softening the highlights and the veins (and always remembering to wipe the brush on some paper towel after each little stroke, to avoid smudging your painting). I then added a few last little details, such as the tiny highlights on the spikes and some little imperfections on the yellow leaf, using only the colours I had remaining on my palette.

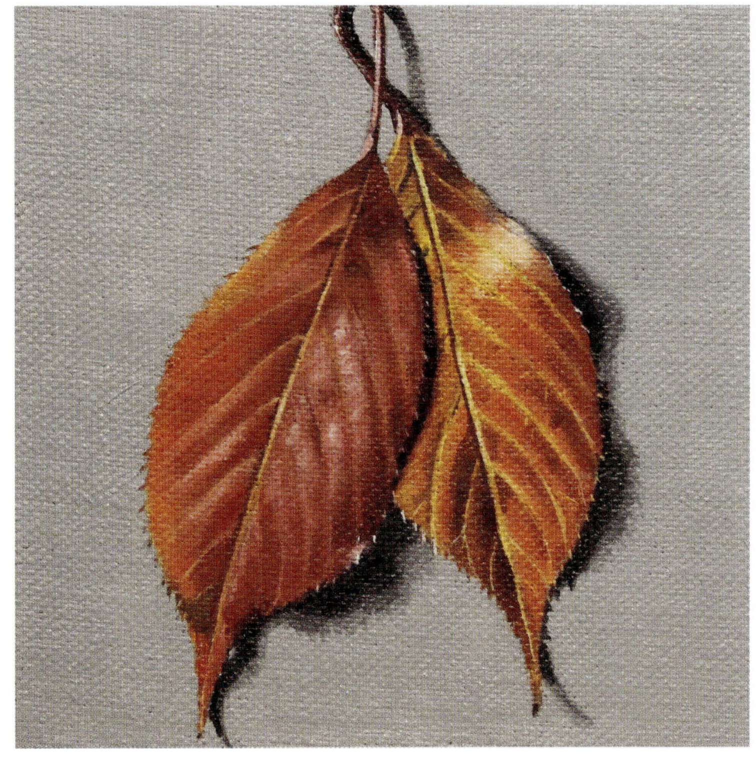

GREEN PEAR

For this project I have chosen a green Migo pear – green being one of my favourite colours. The pear makes a great still-life subject with its rich colour and curvy shape, and it has come to symbolize many things in art, including the female form and fruitfulness. To capture the pear, you will need to really look at the colours so that you can mix an accurate range of green tones.

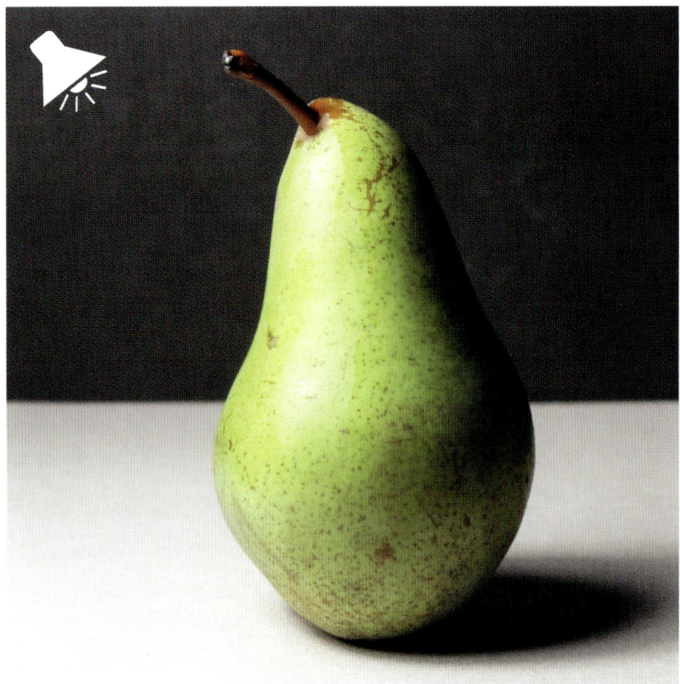

PAINT COLOURS

- ■ Raw Umber
- ■ Ivory Black
- ■ Cadmium Red
- ☐ Titanium White
- ■ Kings Blue Deep
- ■ Permanent Green Light
- ■ Cadmium Yellow
- ■ Yellow Ochre

TOOLS AND MATERIALS

- ☐ Linen board (10 x 10cm/ 4 x 4in.), primed with transparent gesso (see page 12)
- ☐ Graphite or pastel pencil
- ☐ Putty eraser
- ☐ Ruler
- ☐ Fixative spray
- ☐ Transparent primer
- ☐ Primed white card strips, for colour matching (optional)
- ☐ Small palette knife, for mixing
- ☐ Rag or paper towel
- ☐ Size 1 round brush
- ☐ Size ³⁄₁₆ flat brush
- ☐ Size 0 filbert brush
- ☐ Size 0 round brush
- ☐ Soft brush, for blending and softening

SET-UP

I placed my pear on a light, neutral surface, which allows for a strong cast shadow to anchor it in place. The darker background colour helps the pear to really stand out and my light (which is on the left as usual) creates interesting highlights and reflected light on the smooth surface.

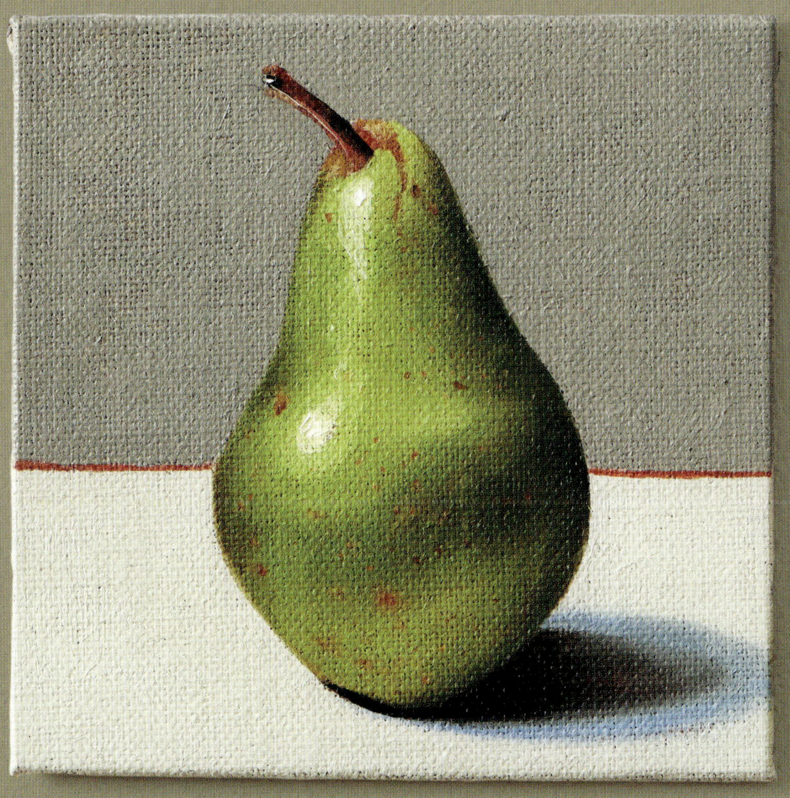

Strong colours stand
out best against neutral
backgrounds, or choose
contrasting colours for
a dramatic effect.

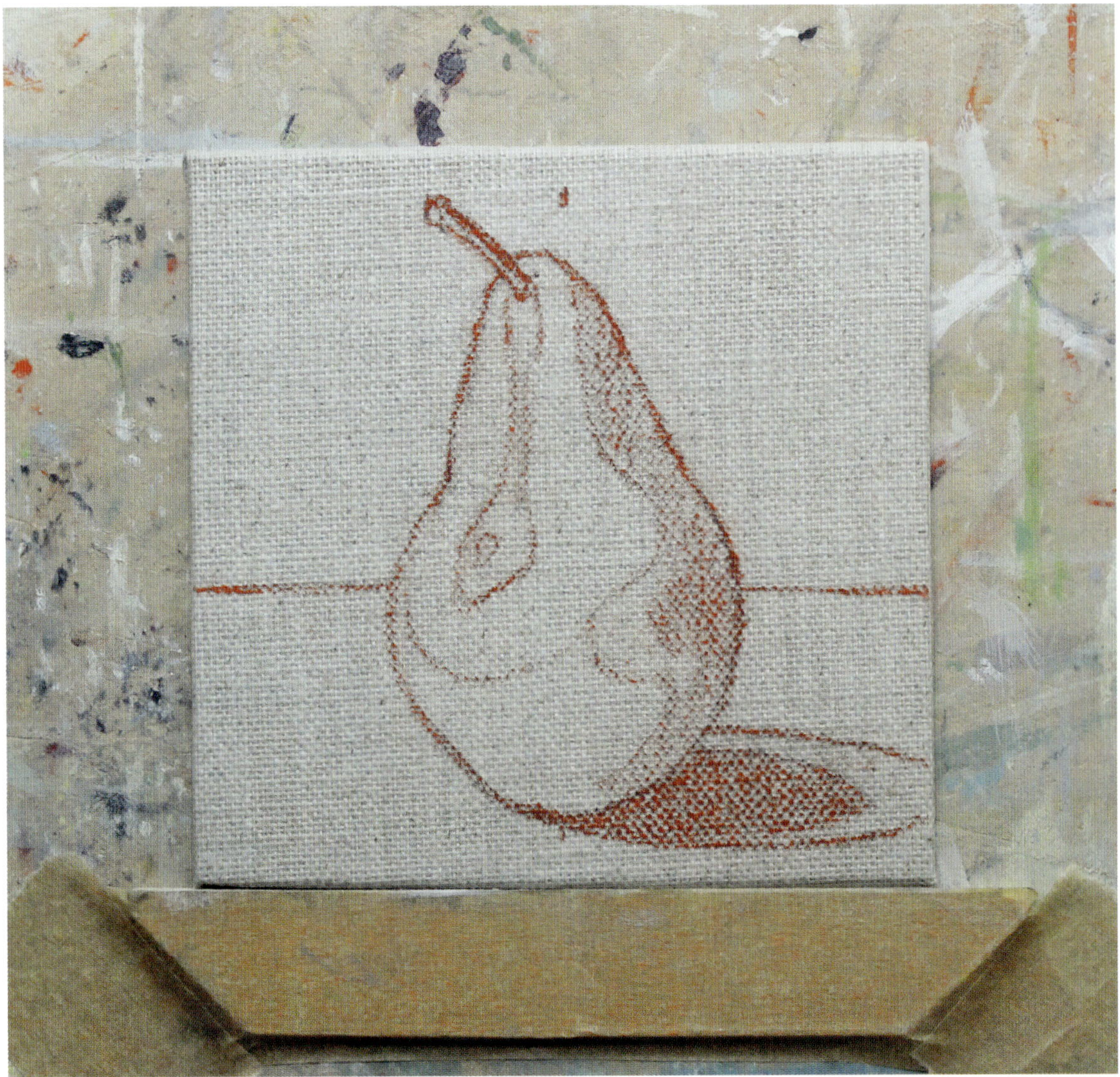

1. UNDERDRAWING

Draw the outline of the pear centred on the canvas, using a pastel or graphite pencil. Mark the shadows, highlights and reflected light, using abstract shapes and shading to establish the values. Add the cast shadow and its penumbra. Fix your drawing and, if you wish, apply a coat of transparent primer. Allow to dry.

TIP

Remember to squint at your pear as this reduces the amount of distracting detail that you see. You'll be able to see the pear's values more easily, too.

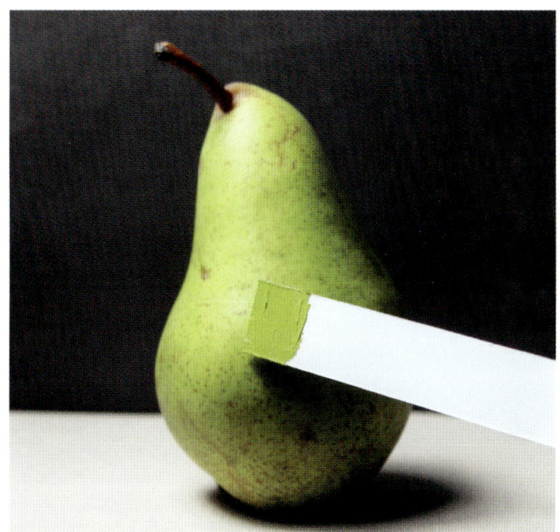

2. LOCAL COLOUR

I decided to work out the local colour of my pear first and began by mixing together Permanent Green Light, Cadmium Yellow and Yellow Ochre. Compare your mix against the pear, either using your palette knife or a strip of prepared paper.

3. A STRING OF PEAR COLOURS

Using the local colour as a gauge, you can begin to mix a range of values to create a few more colours for the pear. My string of paint mixes ranges from light to dark (1 being the lightest, 6 the darkest and 3 being my local colour).

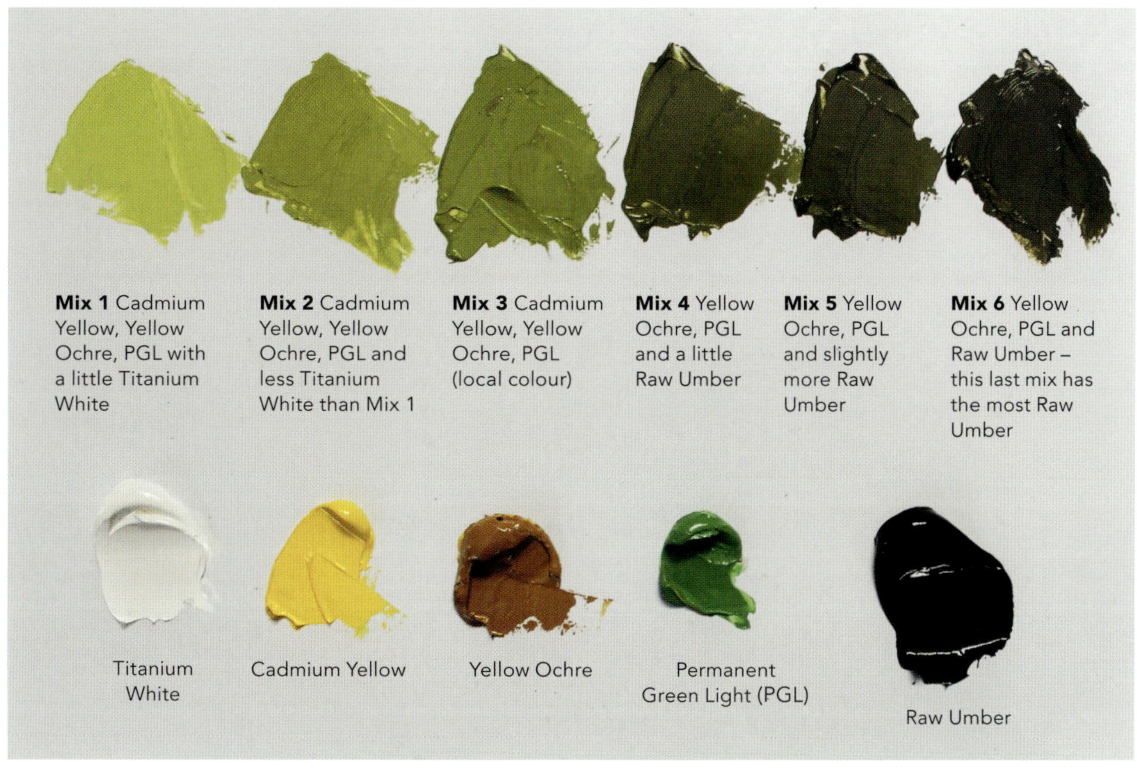

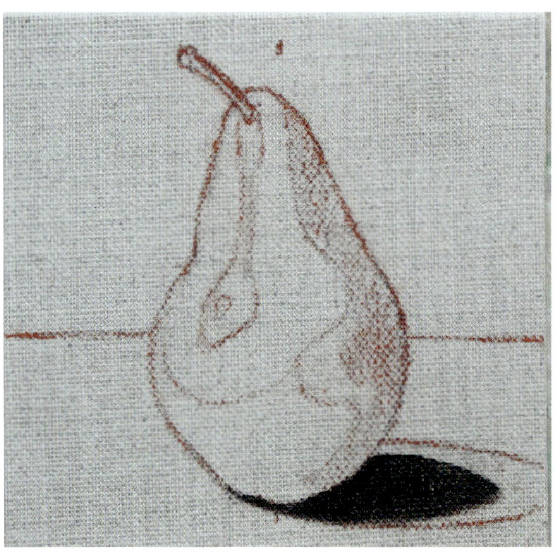

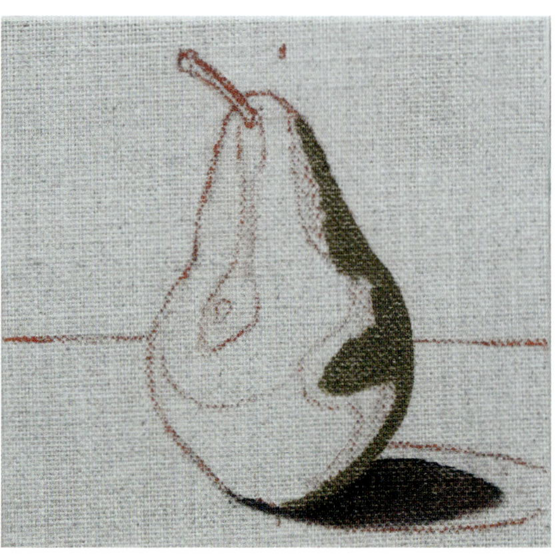

4. CAST SHADOW

Begin by roughly blocking in the cast shadow using a slightly diluted Raw Umber and Ivory Black mix with a Size 1 round brush. Leave out the penumbra for now – we will return to this once the foreground has been painted.

5. DARKEST PARTS OF PEAR

Using the darkest Mix 6 and the round brush, start to paint the darkest parts of the pear on the side that is furthest away from the light source.

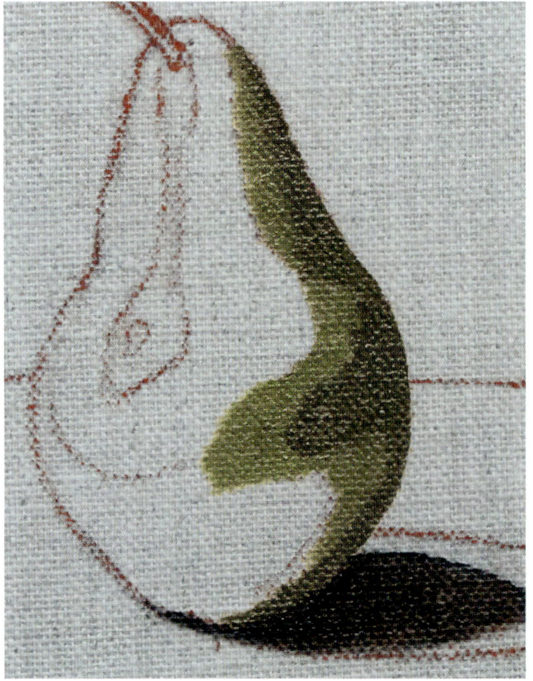

6. BUILD SHADOWY SHAPES

Wipe the brush and roughly block in more of the abstract shadowy shapes, this time using the lighter Mix 5 and Mix 4.

TIP

Don't worry too much if the colours aren't exact, just focus on blocking in the values as accurately as possible.

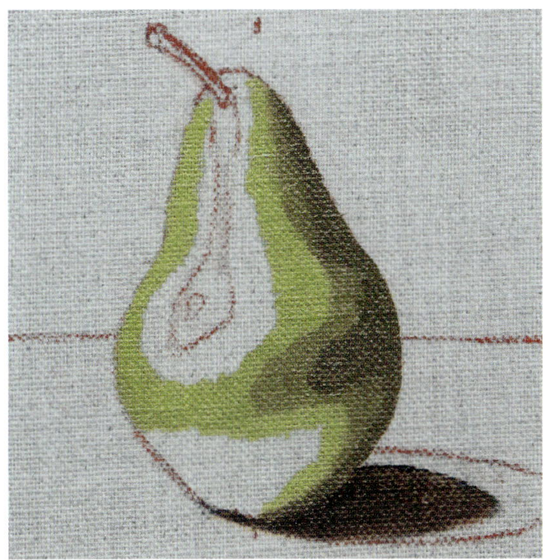

7. ADD LOCAL COLOUR

Now turn your attention to the parts of the pear that are no longer in shadow. Paint these in the local colour, Mix 3, with a clean round brush. This colour is found on the facing plane of the pear, uniting both sides.

TIP

Using your phone or a digital camera, try taking a photo of your painting and then switching the photo from colour to black and white. This is a good way to check if your values are on track!

8. LIGHTEST PLANE

Now paint the light-facing plane of the pear, using Mix 2, but leave the highlight that runs down the centre for later.

Use the same mix to block in the area of reflected light on the underside of the pear.

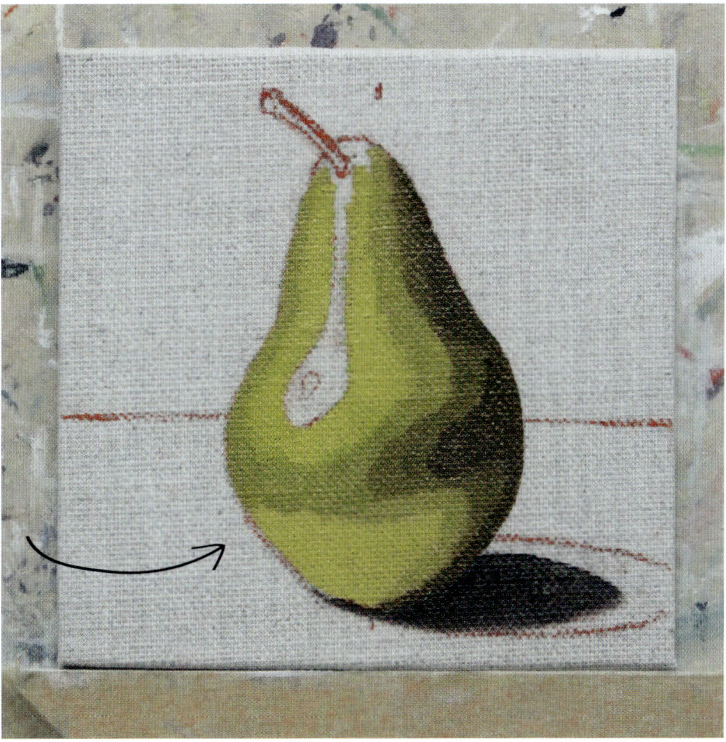

9. BLEND

Taking a dry, soft brush, very gently blend the inner edges, where each block of colour meets the next. Remember to wipe your brush after each stroke, to avoid muddying the painting.

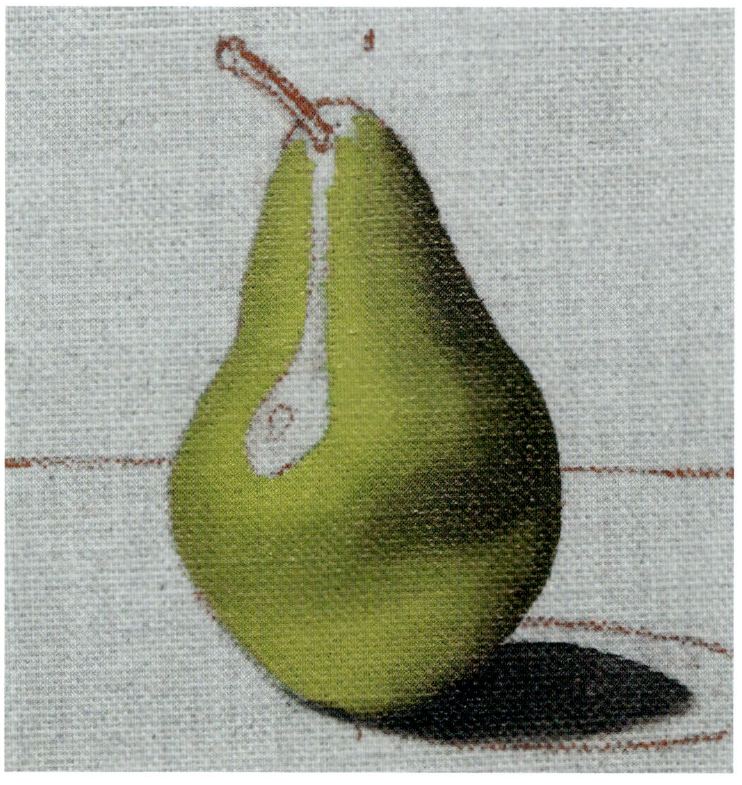

10. HIGHLIGHT

Now it's time to turn your attention to the highlight. Using a Size 1 round brush, block in the lightest part of the pear – save the sparkly bit of the highlight until later.

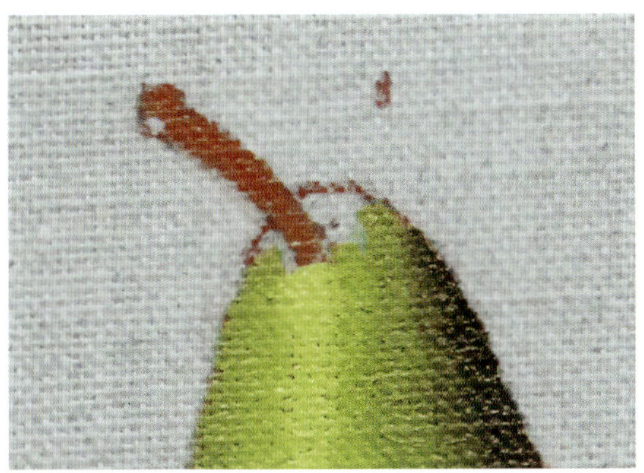

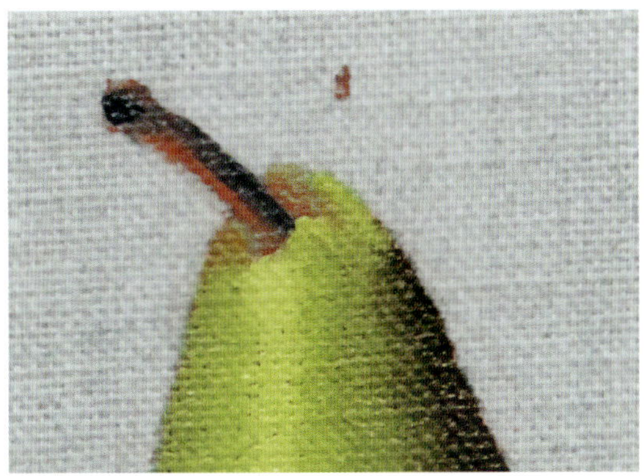

11. STALK

Mix Cadmium Red, Raw Umber and a little Yellow Ochre and block in the pear's stalk using the round brush.

12. STALK'S SHADOW AND DETAILS

To deepen the shadowy part of the stalk, mix a little Raw Umber with Ivory Black, applying the paint on the right edge. Paint the very tip of the stalk, which is very dark, with a tiny blob of Ivory Black. At this point I also painted the very top of the pear, where the stalk comes out, with a small amount of Yellow Ochre.

13. SPARKLY HIGHLIGHTS

Use pure Titanium White for the two little sparkly bits of the highlight – only a very small amount of paint is needed for these brightest areas. I also spotted a tiny little highlight on the end of the stalk.

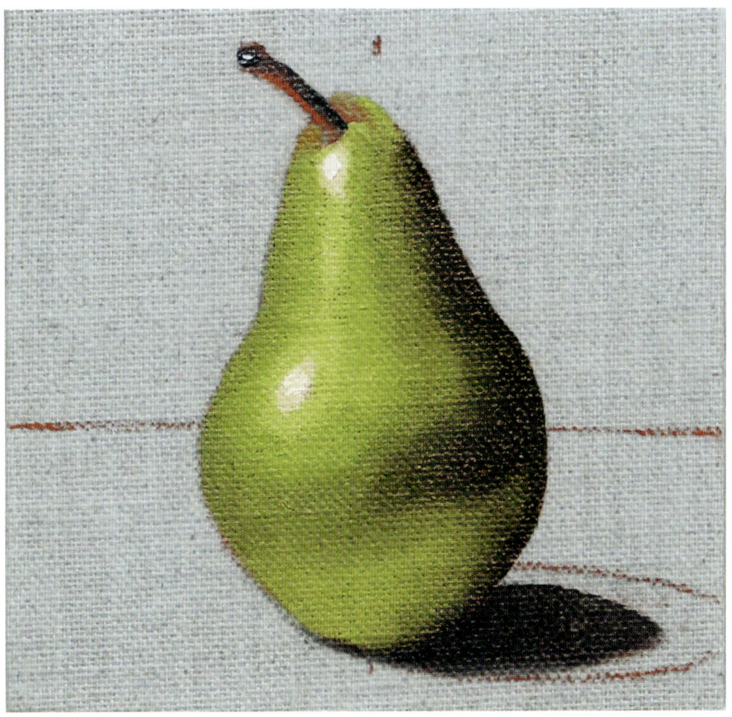

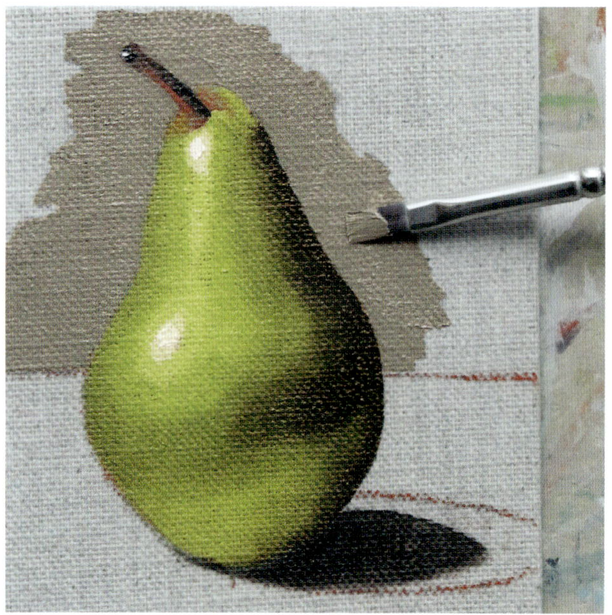

14. BACKGROUND

Mix together Raw Umber, Kings Blue Deep and a little Titanium White for the grey background colour. Apply the mix with a Size ³⁄₁₆ flat brush, which is good for cutting in around the edges of the pear.

15. FOREGROUND

For the foreground, mix Raw Umber, Kings Blue Deep and Yellow Ochre (you can lighten this mix with a little Titanium White, if necessary) and paint it on using the flat brush.

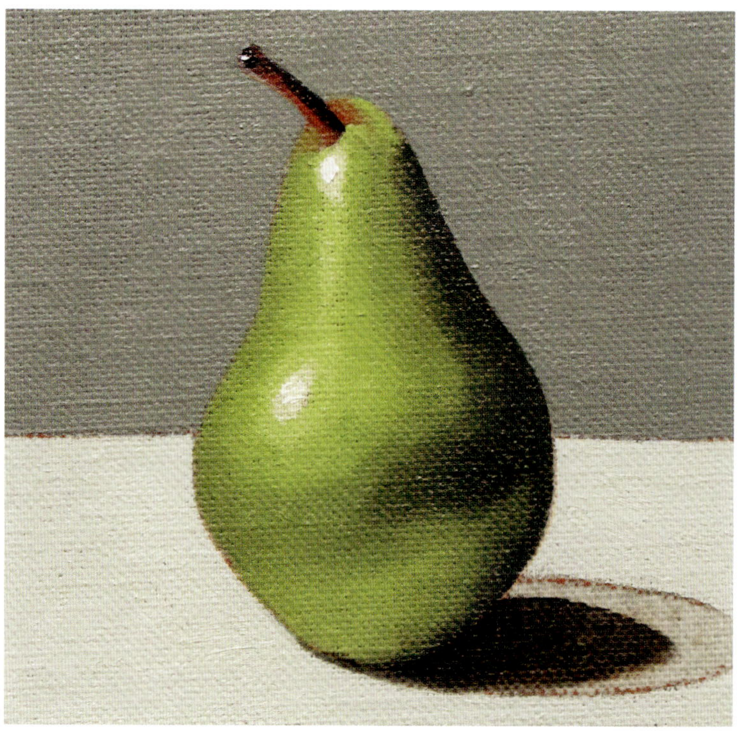

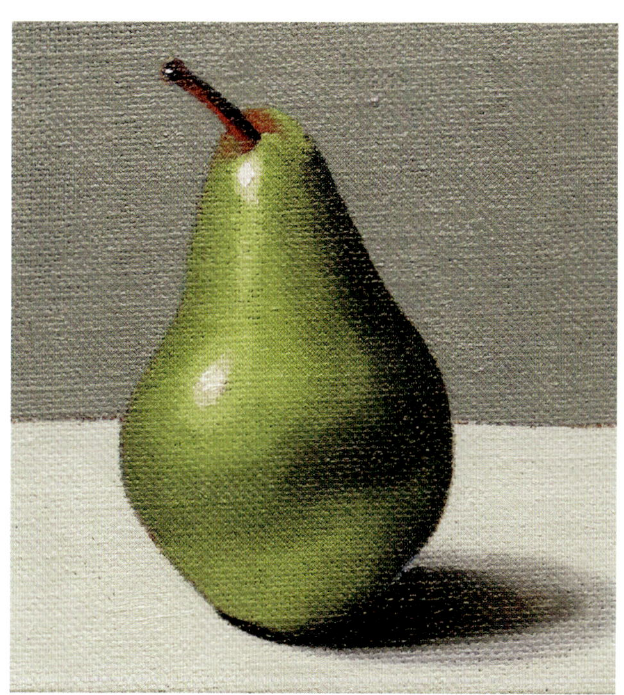

16. CAST SHADOW

Using a Size 0 filbert brush, paint the penumbra of the pear's cast shadow with some Kings Blue Deep. Blend the outer edges of the penumbra slightly with the foreground colour and then, wiping your brush first, soften the penumbra's inner edge, where it meets the main cast shadow. Switch to a fine Size 0 round brush and carefully paint the occlusion shadow with some Ivory Black.

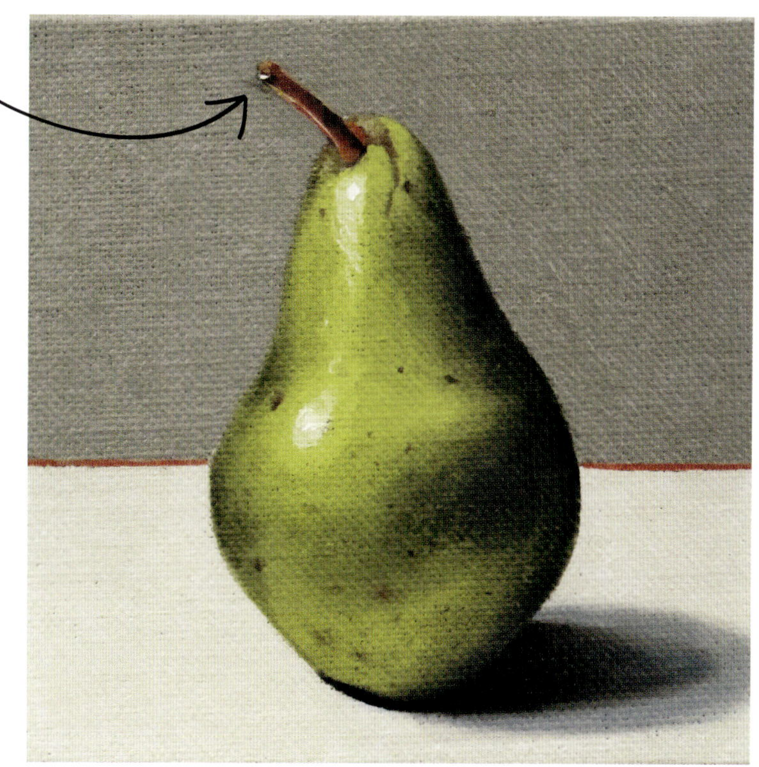

17. FINE DETAILS

I decided to add a few little details to my pear; for example, some tiny brown specks and imperfections, which I painted using the fine round brush and some Yellow Ochre and Raw Umber.

Glossary

Alla prima means 'at first attempt' in Italian and is a direct method of painting where an artist completes a painting in one session or sitting. Paint is often applied 'wet-into-wet', which means that wet paint is painted on top of wet paint, without having to wait for the layer beneath to dry first. See page 30 for more information.

Cast shadow is created as a result of an object obstructing the light and is made of several other depths of shadow. See *Penumbra* and *Occlusion Shadow*.

Core shadow is the darkest shadow that can be seen on an object, benefitting from neither direct light nor reflected light.

Curing is the process that paint goes through as it oxidizes and hardens completely (as opposed to being 'touch dry' when the layers beneath haven't dried out fully).

Diluent is a medium used for thinning down oil paint or for cleaning brushes.

Earth pigments are shades of brown that exist naturally in the earth and are considered the oldest pigments, going back to prehistoric times. They include umbers, siennas and ochres.

Fat over lean is the process of building up layers in an oil painting. With each layer that is applied, the oil content of the paint should increase, or become 'fatter'. See page 26 for more information.

Fixative spray is a colourless spray used to 'fix' drawings in graphite, pastel or charcoal in order to stop them from smudging. Use this spray to fix underdrawings so that when you start painting, the drawing doesn't smudge.

Gesso (pronounced 'jesso') is used to prime surfaces (e.g. canvas or wood), creating a stable ground to paint on and acting as a seal between your paint and the surface beneath. Applying gesso will help prevent the porous surface from absorbing the oil in the paints, which can result in your painting appearing duller.

Glazing is a technique where a thin layer of paint (made transparent by mixing it with a medium) is painted over the top of an existing layer of dry paint. See page 28 for more information.

Greyscale refers to the sequence of tones between white and black. Visualizing your subject in black and white helps to assess the values of all your colours and ensures that you have strong contrasts from highlights to shadows. See page 38 for more information.

Grisaille (see *Underpainting*).

Highlight is the lightest and brightest value, where the light source hits the object directly.

Impasto is a way of 'sculpting' with paint – by applying thick paint using anything from a brush, a palette knife, your fingers or even by squeezing paint directly onto the canvas from the tube – you can bring texture and dimension to your painting. See page 31 for more information.

Local colour is an object's overall colour as you actually see it (and not what you think the object's colour is). See page 51 for more information.

Medium can refer to a particular type of art (e.g. painting, sculpture or printmaking). In oil painting, the word medium usually refers to a substance that is mixed into oil paints to manipulate them (e.g. to make paint thinner, to make it dry faster or to make the paint stay wet for longer).

Mid-tone is in the middle of the tonal spectrum. See pages 38–39 for how to determine your mid-tones.

Occlusion shadow is the darkest shadow in your painting, usually to be found within the *Cast Shadow*.

Palette is either the range of paints you have chosen or a surface on which to mix paints.

Penumbra is the outer edge of a *Cast Shadow*.

Pigment is the pure colour usually mixed with linseed oil to create oil paint.

Priming is to make your surface/substrate ready for painting (with acrylic gesso or another type of primer). See page 12 for more information.

Reflected light on an object is caused by light bouncing back from the surface upon which it rests.

Saturation (also referred to as chroma) describes a colour's intensity and vibrancy.

Shadow box – using a shadow box for your still-life set-up is the best way to ensure consistency of light and shadow while you work on your painting. See page 48 for more information.

Index

Tone (also referred to as *Value*) describes how light or dark a colour is.

Tonking can be used to remove excess paint from the surface of the painting. See page 33 for more information.

Trompe l'oeil means 'deceives the eye' in French, and in painting, it means creating the illusion that the subject of the painting is 'three-dimensional' and real.

Underpainting can be done as a first step in painting and can help determine the values of your subject. Underpainting is usually done in earthy colours, such as Raw Umber. See pages 24–25 for more information. Also known as *Grisaille*.

Varnishing is used to 'seal' an oil painting and will protect it from dust. It should be done after the paint is fully cured (unless you use an exhibition varnish or retouching varnish, which can be applied to paintings that are 'touch dry').

Viewfinder is a device that can be used to help crop your view and check the composition of your set-up.

Wet-into-wet (see *Alla Prima*).

Acknowledgements

I owe a massive thank you to the fantastic team at Quarto – to Anna, Kate, Gemma, Rachel, Katie and Nicki – for their guidance, enthusiasm and vision.

I would like to thank both my parents, Martine and John, for introducing me to painting, for their constant encouragement over the years and for always believing in me.

Thank you also to my little sister, Emilie, and to my dear friends for always listening and always knowing what to say!

Finally, I thank my lovely husband, Rob, for his honest and valuable feedback, for his patience throughout the time it took me to write this book and for supporting me in my dream to be an artist.

RECOMMENDED READING

Color Theory by Patti Mollica was a huge help in writing the 'Understanding Colour' chapter, and I highly recommend this book if you want to further explore colour in painting.

The Complete Oil Painter by Brian Gorst is another great reference book for anyone starting out in oil painting.

The Encyclopedia of Oil Painting Techniques by Jeremy Galton is a brilliant book for beginners in oil painting and was very helpful for writing some of the techniques.

The Secret Lives of Colour by Kassia St Clair is a fascinating read and opened my eyes to everything about colour.